THE ETHICAL CHALLENGES
OF THE SOLDIER

Original title: *L'éthique du soldat français – La conviction d'humanité,* 2e édition, Economica, 2010

Translation: Air Commodore John Thomas FCIL
Copy editing: Michael Westlake

The *Stratégies & Doctrines* Series
General Vincent Desportes, Editor

General Benoit ROYAL

THE ETHICAL CHALLENGES OF THE SOLDIER

The French Experience

Preface by **General Jean-Louis GEORGELIN**

✛ ECONOMICA
49, rue Héricart, 75015 Paris

PREFACE

BY GENERAL JEAN LOUIS GEORGELIN

Former chief of staff of the French armed forces
(October 2006 – February 2010) and Grand Chancelier
of the French Legion of Honour.

What is war today? What is the role of the armed forces of western countries? What form should military intervention take in the contemporary world? Each of these questions represents a challenge for our soldiers, sailors and airmen.

The decline in wars between nation states, the growth of globalization along with the planetary consciousness this brings, the remarkable advances produced by modern technologies, all these once again give rise to the question of the relationship between modern democratic societies and the military profession.

In our old European democracies, possibly more so than in the United States, war plays little part in people's thinking. Not that our citizens are unaware that the world is uncertain, unstable and dangerous. But the idea is widely entertained that we have entered a new era in which war, as we have known it in previous centuries, is remote, and this has already led to an appreciable reduction in many countries' armed forces.

Yet as military men, we know, and expect, that wars will continue to occur as long as mankind exists. That nations will always be taken by surprise by events they have not been able to predict, that we must have men and women – soldiers – ready to intervene and put their lives at risk when everything falls to pieces. When there is uncertainty, doubt, questioning, we need to return to basic principles, in other words, to what comes first.

The members of the armed forces are the only people, in the name of the state from which they draw their legitimacy, entitled to commit the extraordinary act of killing and risk their lives in the higher interests of their country. It is therefore indispensable, well before doctrines, organizations, and weapon systems, however sophisticated, that they are able to confidently rely on their own, unambiguous ethics.

It is very much to General Royal's credit that he has courageously and unflinchingly tackled the arduous task of defining, clarifying and explaining what the ethics of today's soldier should be. Too few officers, regrettably, confront this fundamental question with the same determination that they put into the tactical, technical and physical training of their units.

This is a book that comes just at the right moment to help in this basic task. General Royal's sound, well-argued and timely thinking will encourage them to investigate and think further about this essential part of military action.

The soldier's ethics transcends all nations. While there are different ways of being a soldier, shaped by national temperaments and the military histories, there are firstly military ethical principles that are common to all. It is these that forge the moral strength and martial virtues without which we could not possibly succeed.

CHAPTER 1

IN THE NAME OF THEIR CONVICTIONS

"Conviction is human will attaining its greatest power."

Honoré de Balzac

EYEWITNESS ACCOUNT BY AN INFANTRY LIEUTENANT [1]

Chad – Pacification campaign – 1970s

Choice

I was in command of an isolated outpost in central Chad, 150 km by track from our captain's headquarters (HQ). Apart from my platoon, composed of 46 battle-hardened and disciplined French soldiers on operations for over a year, the company also contained a platoon from the Chadian army commanded by French non-commissioned officers, and a section of the Nomad Guard tasked solely with protecting the local sub-prefecture.

In recent weeks, the situation had changed considerably, thanks to our military involvement finally getting results. The main rebel gangs paralysing the country and terrorising the population throughout southern Chad had largely disappeared. There were signs that the last rebels were being won over; Major Galopin, a former member of the meharist camel corps, who spoke fluent Arabic, was supervising the early negotiations. I met him regularly. A severe looking man of taciturn character, he refused to live in the French outpost. He was doing remarkable pacification work and his charisma made a deep impression on me.

---

1. Account obtained from Lieutenant General M. Stouff.

Chad's main roads and tracks had once again been made safe, the free clinics were opening their doors. This beautiful country was starting to come alive again.

But some violent armed gangs did still survive. Organised into disparate groups of a few dozen badly equipped men, they had lost all contact with FROLINAT (the National Liberation Front of Chad), whose HQ was based in Tripoli, Libya. We were therefore continuing pacification operations in our sector.

On that particular day, my platoon had tracked down a band of rebels estimated at about thirty strong. We were well trained in this sort of operation and managed quite quickly to run them to ground. The Chadian rebels had taken refuge in a large thicket of thorn bushes. We and they were practically eyeball to eyeball, weapons at the ready. Neither side made a move.

There was no doubt about our superiority. The tactical situation, our firepower, and my men's training and determination ensured an inevitable outcome.

My men knew all that. With exemplary fire discipline they awaited my order They were hoping – I had no doubt – for a brilliant military exploit. I hesitated.

The easy solution would have been to have launched the attack. I realised how much easier it is for a commander to say "Fire" than "Hold your fire".

The rebels were about two hundred metres away. Time seemed to stand still. We watched them. No doubt they were watching us.

Something struck me: the rebels had not tried to flee, as they usually did.

I took my time. I wanted to think things over.

I thought about the spirit of my mission. Why were we here?

I thought about what motivated my vocation as a soldier.

Finally, in all conscience, I made my decision.

I didn't really know where all this would lead, but I was very determined. I called my Chadian interpreter and asked him to follow me. Hardly believing his eyes, he saw me hand over my machine pistol to my radio operator and order him to stay put. Then, unarmed, I stood up and started walking slowly toward the rebels. My interpreter followed me, utterly terrified.

I covered the space separating me from the rebels. Nothing seemed to be moving. When within hailing distance, I called out and asked to speak to their leader. A tall Chadian emerged from the thicket and walked over to me. He had a decisive air about him. He too was not carrying a weapon.

We exchanged a few words and began negotiating

Following our discussion, without a single shot being, the rebel band finished by laying down all of its weapons. The mission had been concluded without killing, without violence, without fuss... Even better, this particular rebel band would rally to our cause. Some time later, it was even converted into a Nomad Guard and incorporated into the regular army, and would serve its new leaders with great faithfulness.

This episode has of course passed unnoticed. It has not been recognised as a successful military exploit. It is nevertheless deeply ingrained in my memory and is, in all modesty, a recollection of which I am particularly proud.

What reasoning enabled this young officer to make such a courageous choice, when everything was pushing him open fire and when his military superiority guaranteed easy victory?

Did this lieutenant decide that the objective would be more easily attained by negotiation than through combat? Did he instead follow his personal convictions, saving the lives of an adversary for whom he felt no hatred? Or did he seek to give the impression of a merciful military leader, in order to strengthen France's positive image in this war-torn country?

The explanation of his decision is probably to be found in all these questions, which are by no means mutually exclusive. In any event, the decision was based on profound convictions, operational as well as ethical, forged in the course his training, his education and his personal experience.

EYEWITNESS ACCOUNT BY A PILOT [1]

May 1999. Adriatic. Aircraft carrier Foch.

Again, choice.

It's my tenth bombing mission as part of operation Allied Force over Kosovo.

Today, it's a matter of destroying a partially dug-in fuel depot in Serbia, not far from the Kosovo border. I got up at four in the morning to run through the details of the mission with my colleagues. As laser target designator, it's my job to completely familiarise myself with the photo of the target, so I can faultlessly direc, my crewman's laser-guided bomb to

---

1. Recollections of (Navy) Captain P. Vandier.

the target we were given during the night. On this photo, transmitted by satellite a few hours earlier, white fuel tanks clearly stand out on a small hill, not far from a distinctive crossroads.

Catapult launch. The formation joins up. In-flight refuelling. We are now a few minutes from 'time on target'. The tension rises. We have been over Serbia for ten minutes. There is still a significant risk of active ground-to-air defence Over the radio, we hear Serb songs transmitted by the ground-based jamming stations.

15 nautical miles. I open the protective flap of my laser designator pod and prepare to locate the target. The inertial navigation system has been well re-stabilised, and the target is certain to be on the 'TV', the pod's display screen.

12 nautical miles. I begin picking out reference points. The small hill and the crossroads. I can't see the fuel tanks yet, but given the distance, that's not surprising. Stress becomes concentration. The target is 'there'. I'm going to locate it.

7 nautical miles. The references still match up with the planning process. I tell my crewman by radio that he can release his bombs. Moments later, he radios back "Bombs away". Two 250kg laser-guided bombs are now in flight, heading towards the target that my laser beam will soon designate for them.

6 nautical miles. The references are still correct but I still can't make out the fuel tanks. It's very strange, because visibility is good and the white of the tanks must necessarily make them stand out against the background vegetation. The bombs are still in flight. Just 20 seconds left before impact.

5 nautical miles. Still no fuel tanks. Determined to complete my mission, I guide the laser emission onto the point corresponding to the one on the photo, though I still haven't managed to see the tanks. Doubt sets in. I have 15 seconds left. I ought to be able to see them. If I can't, maybe it's because I've made a mistake. Without trying to analyse further what may have caused this error, I pick out an open space in my pod, far from any dwelling, in a large ploughed field. I point the laser beam and guide the two bombs until impact and explosion.

Back on board the aircraft carrier, following an in-depth debriefing, the analysis clearly shows that the photos sent to us had been retouched to make the fuel tanks stand out more clearly, when in actual fact they were buried and therefore could not be spotted visually. In that situation of doubt, and unable to recognise my assigned target, I preferred to guide the bombs into an empty space rather than to 'fire blind' at a target that I could not positively identify.

The participant in this mission, (Navy) Captain Pierre Vandier, describes the state of mind in which the pilots of the aircraft carrier Foch had been prepared.

Since the start of French involvement in this operation, the head of state and senior military personnel had all insisted on their role in approving targets handled by France. It was not a question of 'meeting a quota' but of producing measured effects, compatible with France's objectives, particularly in regard to 'collateral damage'. At the time this mission was undertaken, this idea had not yet been fully assimilated among the group of pilots in the flotilla. In particular, no procedure had been established for dealing with a situation such as the one encountered above – in other words, last-minute doubt as to the nature of the target.

Following this event, new, more precise, orders were drawn up by the chain of command in association with the fighter pilots, in order to better specify possible 'exit gates' during mission execution. The notions of personal conviction, target validity and the responsibility of the formation commander have thus been expanded and recognised as key elements in combat engagement.

EYEWITNESS ACCOUNT BY A WARSHIP CAPTAIN [1]

Summer 2006. Lebanese territorial waters.

And once again, choice…

I have the impression that I enrolled in the Naval Academy 25 years ago, just to experience the 30 days of action in command of my frigate, the Jean Bart, off Lebanon in summer 2006. It will remain my greatest operational experience as a naval officer.

As with most sailors, all those years spent in the Navy had prepared me rather well to confront extreme situations. In fact, a warship is the amalgam of a factory, an ammunition dump and a barracks, in a confined and sometimes oppressive space, frequently sailing far from port, in an often hostile environment that one never controls. But operation Baliste was something else altogether.

The task was to evacuate from Lebanon French citizens trapped by the war between Hezbollah and Israel. Technically, the operation was not too complicated: put into the port of Beirut, or approach as close as possible to the ports of Saida, Tyre or Naqoura, in order to embark

---

1. Account given by Commodore P. Ausseur.

several hundred refugees as quickly as possible, and then to disembark them at Larnaka after a few hours at sea.

During these embarkation periods, we were extremely vulnerable. There was in practice a serious risk of Israeli bombardment or attack from Hezbollah's light anti-tank missiles, with the aim of involving France in the conflict. Our first evacuation missions were undertaken successfully. Initially, we had three ships: two frigates (the Jean Bart and the Jean de Vienne) and the enormous Sirocco, an amphibious assault ship [1] capable of accommodating several hundred refugees. The bombardments continued. They were impressive and we observed them both at Beirut from the port adjoining the southern quarter and at Naqoura directly on the front line.

My frigate's initial mission changed abruptly when Admiral Magne, commander of the French naval air group, contacted me. He told me that a new threat had arisen. Hezbollah had equipped themselves with type C802 anti-ship missiles, mounted on trucks. Chinese copies of modern western missiles, they had been delivered by Iran, via Syria. Equipped with a 'seeker head' they had been fired blind from the shore, in the hope of hitting one of the Israeli warships enforcing the embargo against Lebanon. Hezbollah had fired these missiles twice, scoring a direct hit on an Israeli patrol boat but also sinking a fishing boat that had nothing to do with the war. These missiles were of the 'fire and forget' type; once launched, it is impossible to guide them. They seek out the biggest target, whatever its nature or nationality. Therefore any of the warships might be hit, especially the large troop transport vessels being used as refugee shelters. It is easy to imagine the terrible consequences if a ship packed with civilian families had been struck by one of these missiles.

Because of this new threat, all the western military vessels rapidly moved to about 50 kilometres off the Lebanese coast. Though they were now safe from missile attack, they were also of little use. Apart from Israeli vessels, the only ships still venturing into the danger zone were the French contingent. Our orders were clear: we had to ensure the resupply and evacuation of the civil population, NGO personnel and UN forces. Admiral Magne had assigned my ship, the air defence frigate Jean Bart, to act as 'bodyguard' for the massive LSD. But how were we to do that, given the Hezbollah missile threat?

After a rapid technical study of these missiles and the capabilities of my ship, it quickly became clear that the only way to ensure the protection

---

1. In French a TCD – Transport de Chalands de Débarquement. The English abbreviation LSD (Landing Ship Dock) is used subsequently.

of the LSD was to get close to her and to offer ourselves as the priority 'target'. We would compensate for our small size by activating our powerful electronic systems, thereby appearing as a large target to any incoming missile. Once the missile had locked on to us rather than the LSD, it was up to us to destroy it – by gunfire or missile – before it hit us. The risk was considerable, because we would have only about ten seconds to react. I could see no alternative. Deep down I had already made my decision. But first I had to be certain about the technical feasibility of my plan and to be sure there really were no other options. Most important of all, I would have to confirm the support of my men – my immediate deputies first, then the whole crew. It was essential that every one of the Jean Bart's 250 sailors knew what was at stake, what the risks were, and what I expected of him.

I assembled my first lieutenant, my operations officer and the missile defence experts. We all came to the same conclusion: our frigate would have to become a 'missile trap' and run the risk of being sacrificed in order to safeguard the LSD. I could see from the seriousness of their expressions that everyone had clearly understood what that decision meant.

We therefore calibrated our electronic warfare systems so that they would transmit at full power as soon as a missile had been detected, to attract it towards us. Once this had happened, there would be no turning back. As one, the crew then prepared itself for the new escort mission, which would begin the next day. At that moment, I comprehended and felt the weight of the irreversibility of my decision and the risks which stemmed from it. In all conscience, I alone accepted full responsibility, as all commanders must be able to.

That was how we came to be at action stations 5 a.m. the following morning. The entire ship's company had been clearly briefed about our new situation and our new role as bait. I did, however, want to explain it once again to the whole crew through the ship's loudspeaker system. My men reacted calmly, going through emergency procedures in the event of missile impact: fire fighting, evacuating the wounded, etc.

At that moment I experienced a huge feeling of pride.

We completed our first mission of the day without mishap and further missions followed. On one occasion only, shortly after our departure from the port of Saïda with the LSD Mistral, which had arrived in support of the Sirocco, Hezbollah fired a C802 missile in our direction. But it passed well astern without worrying us.

> *My crew carried out this dangerous front-line mission soberly,
> with professionalism and great composure. They took great – and in
> my view very legitimate – pride in having done so.*

These eye-witness accounts illustrate how three military commanders
have taken decisions, real choices of conscience, in the different domains
– land, air and sea – in which conflicts unfold. Whatever the circumstances, whatever the environment, the questions are often similar, and they
concern exactly the same aspect of the profession of combatant.

Confronted by an adversary, the alternatives facing these officers were
what all military leaders in battle must decide: whether or not to deploy
lethal force; whether or not to commit their men to risking their lives; and
choosing the right level of force to complete the mission. These three
inseparable facets of the use of armed force are at the heart of the nature
of the military profession; and the exercise of this responsibility is its very
essence.

Some men freely choose to follow dangerous professions or to pursue
risky passions. The profession of soldier is one such, but not the only one.
The level of mortal risk which the individual decides to accept in such
cases is the result of a very personal commitment which has its roots in the
depths of his conscience and which implicates only himself. On the other
hand, the power to inflict death has moral consequences well in excess
simply of the possibility of suffering it oneself. It is in here that one of the
primary specificities of the military profession is to be found: to accept
the responsibility for killing and to risk being wounded or killed oneself.
But this responsibility acquires an additional dimension once it no longer
concerns only one's own person, but all those in the unit one commands.
A further decision-making burden lies within this dimension, for **the military commander bears alone responsibility for the act of collective
death,** whether of suffering it or inflicting it.

This responsibility is inherent in war and conflict. The success of the
mission may lead to sacrificing lives on both sides and exercising such
responsibility presents painful dilemmas. What level of risk to take? What
level of force to apply? When does the use of force cease to be an acceptable norm and become unacceptable violence? Finally, do the ends justify the use of any means to complete a mission, which must in every case
be central to the commander's concerns?

This short extract from an account by Hélie de Saint-Marc [1], among
the most eloquent I know, offers something of an answer.

---

1. Hélie de Saint-Marc *Les Champs de Braise*. [The Field of Embers]. Perrin, 2002.

The fighting I experienced from 1950 to 1953 was of a bitterness and violence which I never again came across in my military career. I understood then the conclusion reached by Winston Churchill. 'When I was young, war seemed to me to be cruel and amusing. Now, it still seems as cruel, but I know it is abominable.' Sometimes we felt it was a nightmare and that we were going to wake up. Those who claim to love war must never have encountered the carnage of the battlefield, corpses scattered everywhere, disembowelled women. War is an absolute evil. There is no joyful war, or sad war, beautiful war or dirty war. War is blood, suffering, burnt faces, eyes wide with fever, rain, mud, excrement, filth, rats running over bodies, monstrous wounds, women and children turned into carrion. War humiliates, dishonours, degrades. It's all the world's horror concentrated in a paroxysm of squalor, blood, tears, sweat and urine.

But mankind moves forward through successive crises. There are times when it becomes necessary to abolish war by war, when violence must be met by violence. Sacrificing one's life for one's country or for someone else, is a choice as irrational as giving life. It has the same weight and the same loftiness. [...]

When war seems to you inevitable, you must find within yourself an ideal which counterbalances what might be degrading in being in the employ of death. This ideal had taken hold in the elite units. During an attack, the power of a company commander was impressive. The lives of a hundred or so men depended on my judgement. I would say "Go" and the legionnaire would do so without a murmur, without hesitation. This crushing responsibility meant one avoided worrying only about oneself – an unpardonable crime, if not in life, at least in war. On operations, no-one could come through on their own. We placed our destiny in the hands of others, our comrades, our superiors, our legionnaires. We were experiencing absolute trust, up to the point of death itself.

Many of those in the armed forces have already lived through these dilemmas: when they are deployed on a mission in a theatre of war or to the heart of a serious crisis, they break through into a different world which no longer has anything to do with the realities of daily life. Questions on the responsibility of the use of force are quite often transformed into real questions of conscience, the answers to which are not to be found in tactics manuals or regulations. Certain conflict situations can confront those in the military with terrible questions that seem to have absolutely no solution.

These few first-hand experiences, as expressed in some recent accounts, show the difficulty, the harshness and the complexity of such situations.

What attitude should one take when those with whom you have just been having a discussion and whose hands you have shaken, mount an ambush against your own soldiers a few moments later, and want to make you believe that it was the other belligerents who were responsible?

What do you do when the adversary cannot be identified, either by a uniform or by any other external distinguishing features, apart from the fact of openly carrying a weapon, and can therefore melt into the local population and launch a surprise attack at any time?

How do you react when the adversary uses women and children as human shields and uses your own convictions to attack you and kill you?

What attitude should one take when for the third time one arrests a criminal terrorising the population, someone who respects neither faith nor law and who has already twice been freed without being inconvenienced?

How should one react when faced with a female sniper who explains to you that she uses her thermal imaging sight to pick out pregnant women on the other riverbank and thus kill two people with the same bullet?

What attitude do you adopt when the enemy deliberately uses civilians, even young children, to transport ammunition that will be used to injure and kill your own men?

These questions, each more unexpected and difficult than last, call for immediate, even instinctive, reactions. At the instant they appear out of the blue, it is too late to look for answers in moral treatises, international rules or agreements, even if such answers could be found there.

There is only time to choose, to decide, and to give orders as quickly as possible.

This urgency, this time pressure when faced with the dilemma of a choice that might go as far as putting life on the line, demands that those in authority prepare themselves during peacetime. Faced with such eventualities, people need something very strong and clear to hold on to, recognised as reference points by everyone. *They need meaning* – as General B. Cuche, then Chief of Staff of the [French] army, pointed out at a joint civilian and military symposium. [1]

---

1. First symposium organised by *Inflexion* magazine, *Civils et militaires: pouvoir dire* [Civilians and the Military – Being Able to Speak Out] published by La Documentation Française, 10 December 2007 at the Institut de France.

[...] Warlike action deprived of meaning can lead to excesses, to the skewing of the use of force and ultimately to the discrediting of those embodying the democracy they represent.

That is why, in order to avoid these improbable, but still possible, deviations, it is necessary to encourage debate and to combat the temptation to equivocate.

At a time when our forces are engaged in ever more difficult operations amidst civilian populations, at a time when questions of security and defence are central to what is at stake in society, the battle of ideas, this 'ability to speak out' among ourselves, fulfils a truly structural regulating function.

This in particular is what we are concerned with in these ethical reflections based on first-hand testimonies: to encourage debate, to advance teaching skills, and, if possible, to elaborate doctrines.

But what in fact is ethics?

Aristotle was one of the first to offer an account of ethics. He referred to it as an awareness "relating to the way one behaves". Nearer to our own time, the philosopher Roger Pol-Droit, a member of the French National Consultative Committee for the Ethics of Life Sciences, gives the following definition [1]: "Ethics is firstly everything that has been thought in relation to such questions as: What should I do? How should I act?" Then he adds, "The most important question is not necessarily knowing what decision we are going to take. The essential thing is to decide which solution to choose from among the two, four, five or ten possibilities that present themselves."

Ethical reflection is of course not confined to the military domain, as is clear from the many working groups of the National Life Sciences and Health Ethics Committee, working in such varied fields as medicine, biology, nanoscience, hospital data, physical and mental handicaps, euthanasia, and so forth.

Although thinking about military commitment is appropriate for the armed forces, Professor Grimfeld, chairman of the above-mentioned committee, points out the profound relevance of this issue for civil society, and argues that the military could be the yardstick against which the various studies and reflections undertaken in the committee could be measured. "Military ethics is the tip of the pyramid. I would even say that it is a tip made of tungsten which, ahead of all the rest, traces out the

---

1. Roger Pol-Droit. *L'éthique expliquée à tout le monde.* [Ethics explained to everyone]. Éditions du Seuil, 2009.

possible pathways in fields touching on life and death, which can subsequently be codified and adapted to other realities." [1]

This clarification for civil society enables the gravity of situations encountered to be understood and the difficulty of the alternatives they generate to be estimated. It can also be a way of situating the debate at the heart of society and of soliciting the help of wider populations, without whom no sustainable progress is possible, whether at the national or international level.

For the military world, the objective is to draw certain lessons and help educate people. In conflict situations that are humanly and morally unacceptable, often at the limit of what is bearable, only sound and well-grounded ethical principles will allow leaders to find appropriate responses in the field.

*

*   *

Before embarking on an analysis of recent experiences and presenting the main principles which could guide the actions of the contemporary soldier in battle, it is appropriate to engage in some brief theoretical reflection on the topic. Doing so will allow the selected testimonies to be placed in the context of the philosophical history of military ethics. The aim is aslo to demonstrate that the soldier, the lead actor in combat, having been unintcrested in the subject for so long, today can and must become one of its promulgators.

While awaiting putative worldwide peace, attempts to provide a moral framework for war have helped create a substantial body of international law

Since time immemorial, war and peace have marked out the rhythm of the lives of human communities. This is an undeniable fact: even if it is agreed that the remaining tribes of pygmies dwelling in Africa's rainforest are fundamentally peaceful, Rousseau's myth of the noble savage does not stand up well to ethnological and historical analysis. For almost all of human history and almost everywhere in the world, men have waged war for the most varied of reasons: wars of destruction, wars of diversion, wars for resources, wars for women, wars of religion or ideology, wars of national or ethnic identity... One could continue.

A fundamental question therefore arises, to which no definitive response has yet been given. Is war an unavoidable, even necessary, social

---

1. Interview with the author on the occasion of the publication of the first edition of this work.

process in the life of human societies, or should it be seen as resulting from complex, yet avoidable or even curable, pathological behaviour?

This is precisely the question raised by General Jean Cot in his book: *Parier pour la paix* [1] *(*first published in 2000 as '*La paix du monde, une utopie réaliste*' [A World at Peace, a Realistic Utopia]). In an eloquent historical synthesis, drawing on the writings of many philosophers, thinkers and theorists, he shows how the two hypotheses have clashed and continue to provoke debate. In fact, almost all the great traditions, religions and philosophical schools, whether Chinese thought in the fifth and sixth centuries BC, Christianity, Islam or contemporary liberalism, have explored the moral and political questions surrounding war.

The first hypothesis is defended by the theorists of war, notably Machiavelli, Hobbes, Nietzsche and, of course, Clausewitz. They all agree on what they consider to be an indisputable fact: mankind is wicked and war is consubstantial with politics. All nation states arise through violence and deceit and only endure because of them. Peace is therefore only viewed only as a temporary cessation of combat. War is praiseworthy because it sustains and revitalizes the energies of the leaders who give the orders as well as of those who carry them out. In this view the enemy is also respected and held in high esteem, because the enemy is essential for sustaining this eternal state of war.

The hope for peace, even though fragile, at the heart of the second hypothesis has also been upheld by many thinkers throughout history. General Cot mentions several, including Plato, Erasmus, Montesquieu, Kant and, nearer our own time, the French philosopher Alain and two popes [2] who left their mark on the twentieth century. In contrast to the champions of war, they defend the idea that it is the passions of men, not their interests, that govern the world: "Interests always compromise, passions never." [3] For these advocates of peace, war is not inevitable. People have the wherewithal to limit it, and even to regulate its occurrence: "We must act as if this thing [peace] existed, which perhaps it does not, by working for its foundation". [4]

There are two streams of thought, therefore: one maintaining that war is inevitable, even necessary, the other erecting lasting peace as the ultimate, rational aim of human efforts. Between the two, no communication or dialogue is possible. They are situated within logics foreign to each

---

1. Editions Charles Leoplold Mayer, Paris, 2006.
2. Two contemporary encyclicals address the question of peace; *Pacem in Terris* by John XXIII and *Sollicitudo Rei Socialis* by John-Paul II.
3. Alain, *Mars ou la guerre jugée* [Mars or War Judged], Gallimard collection 'Folio-Essais' 1995.
4. Kant, *Métaphysique des mœurs. Doctrine du droit* [Metaphysics of Morals. Doctrine of Right], Flammarion, coll. GF, 1994, Conclusion.

other. Yet the following observation might offer a way of bridging the gap: human consciousness is at the centre of a struggle in which, on one side, there is an aggressiveness inherited from our animal nature and, on the other, sociability and a desire for harmony stemming from our ability to think and from our humanity. For one side, this internal struggle is inherent in the human condition and destines us to place war at the core of our social relationships. For the other, humankind plays out its grandeur and destiny in winning this struggle and resisting violence.

It might appear presumptuous to want to reach a conclusion on a debate that is still unresolved, but I am driven to the conclusion that the hardly glorious litany of conflicts and wars which have succeeded one another over the centuries and continue to this day, tends to prove that the exercise of coercion remains the preferred means of managing human conflicts.

The American political commentator Kenneth Waltz makes the bitter observation in *Man, the State and War*, published in 1959, that even if all men were angels or saints, even if they had successfully undergone psychoanalysis or a lobotomy, and even if all states were democratic and peaceful, war would always be possible as a result of their diversity and the absence of a higher authority imposing itself on them to settle their conflicts or punish their transgressions.

Though no beacon of hope, this realistic and widely held view has not prevented thinking people from realising the terrible consequences that war has inflicted on humanity. They have sought to understand, and to draw lessons from, this recourse to violence. They have concluded that if the human race is inevitably constrained to make war, it is nonetheless not obliged to do so regardless of when, where and how.

The Catholic Church addressed this subject very early on. Its dogma was not initially one of non-violence, as one might have thought, but that of the just war *(jus in bello)*. It instituted the "Peace of God" which forbade violence against women, against peasants and against all those taking refuge on church land. The "Truce of God" forbade acts of war every weekend and during Lent and Easter – about two thirds of the year, therefore. Then a *criterion of discrimination* was established at the Council of Charroux in 989 in which it was no longer permissible to intentionally target civilian populations. Finally the *principle of proportionality* was drawn up by Vitoria, a Dominican from Salamanca, author of *Jus belli* around 1540; it referred to not causing damage disproportionate to the subject of the dispute, either to combatants or to third parties.

The Judeo-Christian reading of war, at the root of this approach, was explicitly synthesized and codified between the sixteenth and eighteenth centuries by numerous authors and philosophers, of whom Hugo Grotius is one of the most famous. His *De Jure Belli ac Pacis* published in 1625, considered the first real treatise on the law of war and peace, formalised what is considered today to be the first stage of the "ethics of war". In fact, Grotius did not believe that the problem was the existence of war itself, thus breaking with the original debate, but he thought it unacceptable for it to be conducted independently of any rules or law. He therefore tried, with others, to define these principles.

The first ethic of war is thus constituted by *jus ad bellum* – the justness of going to war – that is to say, the set of principles which regulate recourse to war and which examine the legitimacy of military intervention, and of *jus in bello* – right conduct in war – which covers the principles framing the techniques and the conduct of the belligerents during a war.

Within this tradition, the principles which govern the justness of going to war (jus ad bellum) are six in number:
1. The cause of the state which declares war must be just.
2. The war must be declared by a legitimate sovereign authority.
3. The authority which declares war must do so with just intentions.
4. War should only be declared as a last resort.
5. War may only be declared if there is a reasonable chance of success.
6. The cost of war must be proportionate to its benefits.

The principles of just conduct within war (jus in bello) are three in number:
1. The belligerents have a duty to differentiate between combatants and non-combatants and not to kill the latter intentionally.
2. The belligerents have a duty not to use excessive force.
3. The ills consequent to any act of war must be proportionate to its benefits.

The rules making up this code of ethics were the first points of reference for an international law of philosophical and moral origin. According to the strictest interpretation, any war which contravenes these two sets of principles is deemed to be an unjust war.

Later, other thinkers sought to complete this approach with a further set of principles, *jus post bellum* – right conduct after war. By contrast, the theory of total war applied by many strategists entails an imposed peace, the extreme severity of which – leaving aside the longer term consequences of overly harsh terms of surrender – is justified more by a wish to inflict punishment over and beyond defeat itself than by a concern to establish a just and lasting peace.

The example of the armistice at the end of the First World War makes this all too clear. For Germany, the defeat of 1918, the humiliating Treaty of Versailles, the occupation of the Ruhr and the terrible social crisis which followed, in large part explain the rise to power of Hitler, driven by an implacable desire for vengeance.

As a result, within the following broad guidelines, further principles have been developed to govern peace treaties, the possible payment of reparations, and the bringing to justice of war criminals.

1. A belligerent state must bring the war to an end if it has achieved its war aims and if the aggressor state is ready to surrender.
2. Armistices and peace treaties must be concluded by sovereign and legitimate authorities.
3. The terms of armistices and peace treaties must be proportionate to the wrongs committed by the aggressor state which justified recourse to war in the first place, as well as to the wrongs committed by the belligerents during the war.
4. Only those individuals directly responsible for the wrongs which justified recourse to war in the first place and for crimes committed during the war may be brought to justice.

The categories *justness of going to war, just conduct during war* and *just conduct after war* are intended to be independent of each other. So a state whose recourse to war is unjust – for example, because it invades a neighbouring country with the sole aim of appropriating its natural resources – might nevertheless conduct the war in a just way if it respects the principle of differentiation between combatants and non-combatants. Once the aggressor nation is defeated, it is legitimate to judge its leadership for having committed the crime of a war of aggression, but not for having caused the deaths of the combatants of the country which it unjustly invaded.

The limitations of the separation of the categories are immediately apparent and it is reasonable to ask how well founded the distinction is. For if invading a country is unjust, then killing the combatants of that country during a war of aggression must surely be unjust too, and therefore amount to murder. From this standpoint, *jus ad bellum* and *jus in bello* are interdependent. Moreover, in practice, the criteria of just cause and proportionality and of the means employed are extremely difficult to evaluate.

Without further demonstrating the limitations of the theoretical interpretation of this first approach to the just war, however laudable it may be, it is clear that no war over the centuries has ever fulfilled these criteria – not even, in that it departed from a number of these principles, the war fought by the Allies against Nazi Germany, which many people regard as the epitome of the just war.

Conscious of the difficulty of adapting ancient principles to recent conflicts, other thinkers, nearer our time, have tried to rethink them and to adapt them to current realities and changing attitudes. Michael Walzer, professor emeritus of social sciences at the Institute of Advanced Studies at Princeton, is one such. In his well-regarded book, *Just and Unjust Wars* [1], he committed himself to the reformulation of the classical criteria of a just war. In this work, he elaborates a typology of the different forms of modern warfare, distinguishing those which can be morally justified from those which cannot.

Thus sieges and blockades, guerrilla warfare, foreign interventions, the nuclear threat and terrorism are successively analysed against the yardstick of the means used to conduct them. Recalling that the defence, by force if necessary, of someone who is attacked is morally justified – because it is a way for human beings to defend their fundamental rights – Walzer insists above all on the responsibility in wartime of leaders, both military chiefs and political decision-makers. For it is they who are responsible not only for tangible decisions about the war and the way it is conducted, but also, to some extent, for the general atmosphere in which combat takes place. In democratic regimes, in their capacity as representatives of the people, they are all the more called upon not to betray the trust which has been placed in them. They must also bear the moral burden of their responsibilities and of the choices they make or do not make. In his argument, Walzer adds the moral responsibility borne by all citizens collectively. He maintains that belonging to a people creates solidarity, or even a collective guilt in respect of any evil that may be enacted.

In this way, Walzer no longer seeks only to classify and convince, but to confront the actors in a war with their responsibilities.

In fact, nowadays it is preferable no longer to speak of just war, but rather of justified war. A war characterized as *just* is freighted with moral claims and tends to obscure the necessary proportionality linked to the use of force. It thus lends itself to all sorts of excesses by virtue of the absolute character of its aims. The morality of the *just* war rejects compromise and encourages excess. Force exerted for purposes of good is much more difficult to moderate than force exerted for purposes of law. As General Desportes points out [2]:

---

1. *Just and Unjust Wars*. Basic Books 1977. Born in New York in 1935, Walzer is professor emeritus of social sciences at the Institute of Advanced Studies, Princeton, and co-editor of the review *Dissent*.
2. Desportes Vincent, *La Guerre Probable*, Economica, Paris, 2007. [English title: *Tomorrow's War*, Brookings Insitute Press].

If the first Gulf War was legitimate and limited, an instrument of politics, the second styled itself as a just war, an instrument of morality; it is on the way to becoming a total war, with no possible compromise between the parties, with no visible way out, the dramatic consequences of which are spreading throughout the world.(...) In this vision, the adversary who it is decreed should face justice, fit to be treated in accordance with his offence, falls under the jurisdiction of the righter of wrongs. The behaviour of the American guards at the Iraqi Abu Ghraib prison in 2004 probably illustrates certain excesses of this proclaimed inequality". (See the analysis of these events in Appendix 2.)

In the final analysis, Walzer very much comes down on the side of restraint and bases his analysis of the just – or justified – war on rules, yet to be established, to prevent the excessive use of force. He returns to the idea of limitation, both in the ends and in the means: "Just wars are limited wars, conducted according to a body of rules designed to eliminate, as far as possible, the use of violence and force against non-combatant populations." War cannot be an objective and it remains an evil; but in the absence of a shared search for the resolution of conflicts by non-violent means, it continues to be an inescapable prospect. But at least, "the restraint of war is the beginning of peace." His thinking is thus aligns itself with that of the originators of modern humanitarian law and the law of armed conflict.

From this brief overview of thinkers who have tried to create a classification of war, or even an attempt to explain it in a moral sense, we can make the two following observations. Firstly, it is not sufficient to try and convince or classify, because there will always be opportunities for waging war and there will always be men who decide to do so. Secondly, with the proviso that it is accepted and respected, *right conduct in war (jus in bello)* seems to be the only way of attenuating the consequences of war.

The construction of an international judicial system that finally imposed limits on warfare and could exact punishment, but was insufficiently binding

It was in 1864 that Henri Dunant became aware that the horrors of war were unworthy of the human race. A Swiss citizen and a compassionate man, he was a powerless spectator at the battle of Solferino, a veritable massacre, in the course of which more than forty thousand victims were abandoned without treatment on the field of combat. Dunant subsequently created the Red Cross and drew up the first Geneva Convention, which marked the beginning of international humanitarian law. This Convention imposes the obligation to respect and treat wounded or sick military personnel, without any discrimination whatsoever. It was particularly concerned to translate the fraternal charity of the Christian tradition into a secular humanism acceptable to all. The initiative was assented to by the leading European nations. Although outwardly restricted in scope, because it applied only to the particular situation of armed conflict, it would become the starting point for new initiatives aimed at transforming warfare into a kind of ritual – cruel though that might be – by making it subject to limits and rules. Relying on voluntary cooperation by nations, the rules of humanitarian law and the law of war were elaborated, imposing strict limits on how conflicts should be conducted. For Kant, this formalised law within warfare can be summarised as: "Conducting war following principles according to which it always remains possible to exit that state of nature". [1]

The historic dynamic initiated by Henri Dunant in the 19th century was legitimised in a timely way over the following decades. In actual fact, the 20th century would turn out to be not only a century of conflicts, but also a century riddled with crimes against civilian populations perpetuated on a massive scale; the massacre of the Armenians, the horrors of the Holocaust, the killing fields of Cambodia, ethnic cleansing in the former Yugoslavia and the Rwanda genocide were some of the worst examples. In response to these barbarities, a system of international criminal law has progressively supplemented the Conventions.

The creation of the Nuremberg and Tokyo tribunals at the end of the Second World War was the first expression of this demand for justice, even though their exceptional character has limited their scope beyond the context and the circumstances in which they were instituted. Benjamin Ferencz, a former prosecutor at the Nuremberg tribunal, considered that "There can be no peace without justice, no justice without law and no meaningful law without a Court to decide what is just and lawful under any given circumstance". Indeed, since war has been and remains the source of the worst atrocities, a lasting peace can only be concluded and consolidated if the perpetrators of such crimes – from government leaders down to those who was simply following orders – are liable to be accountable before a court of law. Such trials have a dual purpose: to punish, by way of example, particularly abhorrent crimes, and to act as a deterrent of, designed to prevent their recurrence.

Thanks to the work of these tribunals, notably around the definition of "crimes against humanity", a legal basis has been progressively incorporated into international conventions as well as into many internal legal frameworks of individual nation states. The first such agreements were

---

1. Kant, *Doctrine du droit*, [Doctrine of Law] Vrin, 1988, p. 230.

the Universal Declaration of Human Rights and the Convention on the Prevention and Punishment of the Crime of Genocide, both adopted in 1948. The four Geneva Conventions aiming to establish a framework protecting the rights of non-combatants were adopted the following year.

Although the Cold War and the reticence of some states slowed down the process after the Second World War, two new events contributed to the resurgence of the idea of international criminal law: the crimes committed in the former Yugoslavia and the Rwanda genocide. These conflicts led to the setting up of two new international criminal tribunals competent to judge the crimes committed during them. The two events, and the way they resonated with public opinion thanks to the media and the work of NGOs, contributed to the idea of creating a new court, which would be permanent and independent of nation states. Thus the Rome Conference of 15 June to 17 July 1998 gave birth to a new authority, the International Criminal Court (ICC) [1], to prosecute the perpetrators of the most serious international crimes.

But even with the prospect of a fully functioning ICC, the national legislatures of each state also have a role to play. The notion of universal competence, introduced in 1949, allows the signatory states to international conventions to prosecute all persons within their territory and who are believed to have committed serious crimes, whatever their nationality or the place where they committed the crime. In recent years, this notion has resulted in considerable expansion of court activity at the international level.

Though the origin of humanitarian rules is lost in the mists of history, and while these are expressed sometimes as customs or the truce of God, sometimes through philosophical thinking around the idea of the just war, their true codification in the form of conventions began in 1864, at the instigation of Henri Dunant. Only then can it be considered that mankind, finally aware of its potential for cruelty, asserted its humanity in the eyes of the world by creating an untarnished standard of dignity. General Cot expresses this as follows:

> *Law in warfare carries with it the hope of preserving whatever there can be of universal morality within a state of affairs, which by its very nature is outside the norms of morality. It wants to guarantee as much compassion as is possible within an enterprise characterised by excess and the right to impose one's will on the adversary by force, including by killing him. It has the ambition to fix the limits beyond which it is no longer a just war, but a debauchery of abominations and atrocities, of cruelty and ferocity.*

---

1. The Statute of Rome of the ICC currently has 139 signatory States and 105 ratifications.

For all that, the functioning of specific ICC tribunals still faces numerous obstacles. The exercise of universal competence by national jurisdic-
tions is denounced by some states on the grounds that it constitutes a violation of the principle of sovereignty. One such, the Democratic Republic
of Congo, even won its case [1] on this point in late 2000. In the final analysis, the competence of the existing criminal tribunals is still limited,
because they deal only with extreme cases, for passing judgement on the
the worst crimes: genocide, crimes against humanity, and other very
"serious crimes of concern to the international community" (as expressed
in the statute of the International Criminal Court). These tribunals constitute an insufficient deterrent and are only partially effective.

In short, nothing much has changed; we cannot expect more from *law
within war* than it is capable of offering. It provides a framework, regula-
tes, limits and – in extreme cases – passes judgement on violent acts, but
it does not establish precise rules of behaviour on how to manage confrontations. Furthermore, many Middle Eastern and Asian countries remain
uninvolved in the process, thereby undermining the notion of universality
ascribed to it. As a result, the claimed existence of universal values is
open to question. Either moral judgements are unaffected by geographic
frontiers, or values and the concept of law vary according to specific cultures. In the latter case, it would be illogical to try and impose human
rights on countries which do not recognise them, since freedom is central
to the concept of law.

Do universal moral principles exist?

According to which criteria should we continue this line of thought? Is
the western vision of morality and human rights shared elsewhere? Does
the failure of certain Asian and Middle Eastern countries to subscribe to it
mean that other philosophies advocating a different vision of justice and
the good exist? Do other possibly universal values exist, upon which to
build a philosophy of action likely to be more widely recognised?

An initial answer to this question is to be found in Aristotle. This great
philosopher asked whether, over and above traditions and language, there
might be moral principle common to all human societies. In fact he devoted a whole treatise to the question, *The Nicomachean Ethics.* Though his

---

1. On 17 October 2000, the Democratic Republic of Congo instituted proceedings against Belgium
at the International Court of Justice concerning an international arrest warrant granted by Judge Damien Vandermeersch against the RDC's then foreign minister, Yerodia Abdoulaye Ndombasi. In its
decision of 14 February 2002, the ICJ finally ruled in favour of the DRC, judging that the former Con-
golese foreign minister was protected by virtue of the immunity of his post. Consequently, it asked
Belgium to withdraw the arrest warrant lodged by Judge Damien Vandermeersch.

dictum "Without friends, no-one would choose to live", he demonstrated that there is one universal value that nobody can reject: friendship.

Using the term *philia* – friendship – Aristotle analysed the various kinds of social ties: within the family, in freely formed associations and, by extension, within the city state. Only friendship – or concord –, referring to the voluntary choice to live together with happiness as the aim, can be differentiated from the involuntary ties of belonging to a community or from ties with limited aims based only on self-interest.

Nowadays, this starting point is not viewed as uniquely western; it is anthropological, that is to say, characteristic of all human societies.

On this subject, Professor Henri Hude refers to the reasons why people live in social groups, specifying three of the main ones: natural necessity – or constraint –, self-interest and duty. But no single one of them, nor even all three in combination, is capable of holding a society together in the long term. A fourth factor must be added to these three, and that is the pleasure of being with other people. And that pleasure is precisely what constitutes friendship.

Everyone, unless they are seeking death or a life of servitude, desires friendship, the very glue that holds society together. Moreover, in other cultures and civilisations outside the West, only friendship is able to block the encroachment of extreme violence. This notion undeniably has a sort of ethical power. The French republican tradition has given this friendship – this *philia* – the name of *fraternité* (fraternity), which accompanies the other two aspirations of *liberté* and *égalité* (liberty and equality). Indeed *fraternité* allows the two other values, that are sometimes in opposition to each other, to be in harmony. It is therefore a virtually universal principle exhibiting no cultural particularity.

Kant, too, in his conception of moral philosophy, argues that moral laws are universal. He is convinced that men do not invent moral laws, any more than they invent the laws of the universe; they do no more than discover them. Man, according to Kant, possesses three fundamental characteristics; he is gifted with reason, he is free, and he possesses dignity. Kant thinks that an action is morally acceptable if it can be applied universally, in other words, if it is expected that all human beings would apply it in all circumstances and without taking account of the consequences. He thus defines what he calls the categorical imperative. It is set out for the first time in 1785 in *Groundwork of the Metaphysics of Morals* in the renowned formulation: "Act always in such a way that you you treat humanity, whether in your own person or the person of another, never merely as a means to an end and in others, but always also as an end in itself."

Roger Pol-Droit, the philosopher already quoted, elaborates this notion of respect for others human beings by pointing out that the greatest philosophers of all nationalities have always emphasised this "movement of the heart" whereby people are spontaneously moved by the distress of others.

The idea of the existence of recognisable universal moral values is widely shared by contemporary philosophers. Monique Canto-Sperber refers to this in one of her final essays, *Le bien, la guerre et la terreur* [1] [Good, War and Terror]:

I remain attached to the idea of a universality of values. Not a universality defined from a starting point of abstract principles, but a universality made from what is common to the values incarnated in each culture. I am convinced that there exist stable moral values, very widely shared, the definition of which does not depend on the social or cultural environment, even if such an environment explains the diversity of their modes of expression.

Bernard Kouchner, the politician and founder of Médecins Sans Frontières, to whom I directly and specifically posed this question of the universality of humanitarian values, replied that, in his view:

I do not know if we can affirm that our western values are universal, but what I am absolutely certain of is that human suffering has an irrefutably universal dimension.

The rejection of suffering does in fact straddle epochs and cultures. No-one believes it is right that children should be killed under the eyes of their mothers and everyone feels moved by those who suffer unjustly. One simply has to observe the emotions aroused by disasters affecting humanity, whenever or wherever they occur and whether or not they are of natural origin. Human nature is always touched by the suffering of others, whatever their ethnicity, nationality or culture.

Michael Walzer fully concurs in his defence of the existence of shared moral principles in respect of war, founded on dignity, equality and life, and upheld by contemporary human rights. These aspirations remain the distant aim of just and universal action. For Walzer, whatever the culture of the peoples in conflict, "the destruction of the innocent, for whatever reason, is a kind of blasphemy against our deepest moral commitments." [2]

---

1. *Revue de Défense*, n° 121 (May-June 2007).
2. *Guerres justes et injustes,* Belin, 1999.

Roger Pol-Droit [1] goes further, pointing out that many rules vary with different epochs and civilisations, and that certain practices which provoke horror today – such as cannibalism or the death penalty, to mention just two examples – have in the past been deemed noble or courageous. He gives as an example Inuit society, in which it was considered a gesture of pity and a moral act to take one's aged grandparents far from any dwelling and to abandon them to their fate. Doing so allowed the group to survive by no longer having to feed unproductive members of society.

Despite these particular cases of place and time-dependent norms and rules, he rejects the idea that such examples justify giving up the search for the truth of ethics.

He proposes the following common denominator, which he considers to be universally applicable: "Ethics is above all concern for others. Because the existence of others, the multiple relationships between them and me, constitute the most universal point of departure for all forms of ethics."

These widely shared viewsmay be complemented with new areas of research in biology and neurology, where discoveries are likely to create another level of universality.

Indeed, the discoveries made in the life sciences in recent years should leave no-one indifferent. Theoreticians can no longer afford to lock themselves away in their ivory towers and ignore the findings of contemporary research. The work of two researchers in particular merits special mention: Antonio R. Damasio, David Dornsife Chair in Neuroscience and Professor of Psychology and Neurology, and Director of the University of Southern California College Brain and Creativity Institute; and Professor Jonathan Haig, a psychologist at the University of Virginia.

Their work indicates the existence, in every individual, of innate physiological predispositions of a moral character, characteristic of human nature itself. It shows that these predispositions have been shaped by evolution and passed down over the millennia and are shared by all humans without exception. The authors have demonstrated experimentally that in our brains there are innate zones which are involved in making moral judgements, and are conducive to our aversion to human suffering and to the development of a sense of equity, another essential component of morality. These features are viewed as a legacy of our evolution, and are often explained by the advantages they conferred for social interaction and the survival of mankind.

The existence of universal moral values can thus legitimately be argued for on the basis of the discovery of a genetic inheritance common

---

1. *L'éthique expliquée à tout le monde*, [Ethics explained to everyone], Éditions du Seuil, 2009.

to the whole human species, thereby bringing together the philosophical principles elaborated over human history and empirical observation of our evolution.

These researchers have also shown that there is nothing to prevent these natural moral propensities coexisting with the predisposition to violence. Homo sapiens, like other mammals, possesses a reptilian brain, the seat of instinctive behaviour. An inheritance from our evolution, this makes us susceptible to aggressive tendencies, which manifest themselves in the first instance towards those similar to ourselves. Incidentally, this tendency governs behaviour in combat. It is aggravated by testosterone, the male sex hormone, a fact that explains why men are generally more aggressive than women. As in the animal world [1], this also helps explain how social hierarchies are established.

This biological digression brings us back to the same observation that the first philosophers made as regards their fellow men. Mankind is torn between its aggressive instincts of primeval origin and its aspiration to live in harmony. It is not necessarily destined to make war, but is systematically inclined towards it.

It has yet to be explained how the proportion of each of these two tendencies is determined, so that each society and each individual arrives at something they recognise as their own morality. Why do some social groups continue to kill each other, whereas others manage to learn from their experience and draw up declarations of rights? Very clearly, if the answer is to be found in their different histories, educational systems and cultures, then to suppose that western nations have a monopoly on humanistic values would be to run counter to the notion of universality. Numerous historical examples prove the contrary and combine to show that the universality of values is possible.

Consider the example of Emir Abd el Kader, a Muslim and culturally "eastern", and a man who symbolized Algerian resistance against France's occupation of his country. Despite the many, often violent, confrontations with the French invaders, the two fundamentals on which his reign was built were a genuine humanity and a sense of justice, both profoundly rooted in his convictions. With neither hate nor fanaticism towards his enemy France, which he patiently observed and came to respect and admire, his treatment of prisoners illustrated his genuine and innate humanity. He even drew up a treaty – the first of its kind – defining the rules according to which captured soldiers should be treated. Many of

---

1. For example, in the animal kingdom, the duration of exposure of the retina to solar UV rays multiplies by a factor of 1 to 5 the level of testosterone in the blood, generating aggressive reactions and courtship displays. These displays often end in physical confrontations and fights, which allow the social hierarchy of the group to be established.

these, grateful and touched by his charisma, visited him during his captivity in France and called for his release.

An occurrence several years later cemented the Emir's reputation. In July 1860, when he was living in exile in Syria having been freed by France, interdenominational problems in the Mount Lebanon area threatened to spread to Damascus. Muslims and Druze had attacked Christian areas, killing over three thousand inhabitants. Using his influence with the dignitaries of the city, the Emir intervened personally to stop the massacre and, putting his own life at risk, to protect the fifteen thousand-strong Christian community in Damascus, as well as the Europeans living there. For this act of bravery he was awarded the Grand Cross of the Legion D'Honneur and other tokens of gratitude from the entire world, notably from the Pope and the Tsar of Russia.

Even though Emir Abd el Kadr was familiar with Western culture, his example proves that despite the hesitancy shown by certain major non-western states in regard to the restrictive aspects of law within war, it is possible to build a bridge between cultures based on humanitarian values.

The history of humanity, scientific progress and the evolution of political attitudes prove that an ethic with a universal resonance is therefore possible. It rests on the fundamental reference points that can be accepted and understood by all peoples, whatever their origins and their societal relationships. It affirms the universality of humanity, repudiates the causing of deliberate suffering and, as a corollary, pledges respect for the dignity and integrity of the person. In 1948 these principles were embodied in the Universal Declaration of Human Rights, which marked the ethical formulation of the rules of life common to all people.

The Bangkok Declaration, signed in 1993 by thirty-four Asian countries, including China, Iran, India and Pakistan, was the first public political expression of this. In this report [1], these countries proclaim their firm belief in the universality of human rights, while putting the emphasis on Asian values and insisting on the diversity of their interpretation in different cultural and historical contexts.

> *The Ministers and representatives of Asian States, meeting at Bangkok from 29 March to 2 April 1993(...) [stress] the universality, objectivity and non-selectivity of all human rights and the need to avoid the application of double standards in the implementation of human rights and its politicization and that no violation of human rights can be justified.*

---

1. Report of the Asian regional conference of the world conference on human rights held in Bangkok from 29 March to 2 April 1993.

They thus explicitly recognised that it is possible to bring together eastern and western moral perspectives.

The simple truth is that every individual is the repository of this common reality.

At this level of reasoning, the observation is as follows:

– on Earth, for some considerable time to come, there will always be opportunities to wage war, and there will be men ready and willing to do so;

– built on the ruins of so many wars, international *law within war,* and its corollary, humanitarian law, indicate the minimum threshold to be reached, but are insufficiently respected, primarily by some of the most powerful western nations;

– the fundamental principles inspiring this law draw on values which can at the present time be considered to have a genuinely universal dimension.

And where is the soldier in all this?

He has not remained aloof from the debate. Operational commanders of all ranks, officers who have become politicians and military philosophers have made their contribution to the ethical evolution of warfare.

But it is possible to go even further. I am not alone in profoundly believing that the men and women in the armed forces have a particular vocation to fuel the debate, because they are the main agents of combat. They have not only the right but also the duty to contribute to the development of principles of behaviour wherever such principles are as yet inexistent or weak. The soldier cannot simply be an agent of political will, to whom he *blindly* delegates the choice of waging war, whether justified or unjust, especially since the decision as to how war is conducted lies with him. The soldiers of the oldest nations, which know the suffering caused by war, can no longer leave the burden of defending the hard-won ethics of war to the lawyers, thinkers and political leaders alone.

The military commander is best placed to impose ethical principles on combat: doing so goes hand in hand with safeguarding his men and the aims and legitimacy of any given operation

As the leading actor in combat, the soldier is the first to confront death, whether it be a matter of killing or being killed. It is thus obvious that the less violent the combat, the less the soldier will put his life at risk [1]. Although he may have freely committed himself to serve his country – at

---

1. It has been estimated that during the First World War 90% of the victims were soldiers and 10% civilians. This percentage was reversed during the Second World War.

least within all volunteer armed forces – it would be incorrect to believe that a soldier expects to die in combat. Brave though they are, soldiers do not normally have suicidal tendencies. In agreeing to fight for his country, a soldier rather acknowledges the *possibility* of losing his life. The distinction is not trivial. In fact it is essential for understanding the psychology of the soldier's behaviour in combat and its consequences. The reality of all this has been explored by various eminent psychologists and military historians.

One such commentator, Lieutenant Colonel Dave Grossman, formerly Professor of Military Science at Arkansas State University, has specialized in the study of the psychology of killing. In his book *On Killing* [1] – published in 1995 and nominated for the Pulitzer prize – he explains what has already been demonstrated by biological studies in the animal world: the natural objective of aggression is not to kill, but to impose one's will. Studies of such phenomena confirm that combat to establish superiority between animals within groups of the same species do not lead to death. Death is extremely rare and often accidental. The preservation of the species prevails and the presence of inhibition brings fights to an end well before serious injury or death.

Modern man, inheritor of an infinitely more developed social tradition, is equally subject to such inhibitions: he instinctively backs off; he is not 'naturally' made for killing. La Rochefoucauld in his *Maximes* had already noted this reticence: "It is not possible to stare at the sun or at death." What could be less natural, even for a soldier, than to be willing to inflict death on someone else, or, to an even greater extent, to be killed?

Grossman explains that men who have not been prepared – or have been badly prepared – to wage war have great difficulty in killing when in combat. A significant number of soldiers faced with an adversary who, like them, are living, breathing human beings, have chosen to fire over their heads rather than kill them. Grossman recalls that Ardant du Picq [2] was one of the first to become aware of this type of behaviour, the intentional missing of the human target. In the 1860s, du Picq carried out one of the first detailed studies of the nature of combat, based on a questionnaire distributed to a number of French officers. One of the officers questioned stated with great frankness "that he had noted that a large number of soldiers were firing into the air or deliberately at very great distance",

---

1. Dave Grossman, *On Killing: The Psychological Cost of Learning to Kill in War and Society*, Little, Brown and Co, 1995 (hardback), 1996 (paperback, in 9th printing as of October 1999).

2. Charles Ardant du Picq,(1821-1870) a colonel in the French army, was a military theorist of considerable talent, author of one of the most original works of the 19th century *Studies on Combat [Etudes sur le combat]*published in 1880 by Hachette and Dumaine. After 140 years he still remains a modern and relevant military thinker, thanks to his view of the violence of warfare and the psychology of the combatant.

while another said that "a number of our soldiers were firing almost into the air, without aiming, seeking to deafen themselves with rifle shots during critical phases of combat."

The same phenomenon was also described by the British military historian Richard Holmes [1]. In *Acts of War: Behaviour of Men in Battle,* first published in 1985, he analysed, though several historical examples and among different armies, the percentage of shots fired that actually hit their target.

In South Africa, at the battle of Rorke's Drift in 1879, a small group of British soldiers found themselves completely surrounded and overwhelmed by hundreds of Zulu fighters, to the point where it was impossible for them to miss their targets when firing into the serried ranks encircling them. However, on average, 13 rounds were fired for every enemy hit, proving that many of the soldiers had not tried to kill their enemies, despite the situation.

In the Franco-German war of 1870, during the battle for the defence of Wissembourg in the north of Alsace, 48,000 rounds were fired for 404 enemy soldiers hit, a rate of 119 rounds per target struck. In similar example, General Cook's soldiers fired 25,000 rounds at the battle of Rosebud Creek in 1876 during the Black Hills War, but hit only 99 Native Americans, a total of 252 bullets fired per man hit. Inadequate markmanship and inaccurate weapons do not in themselves account for such figures.

Dave Grossman details other examples, up to and including more recent conflicts, in which he explains that the increase in the rate of combat casualties has largely been the result of artillery fire and aerial bombardments, in which the adversary is not directly targeted. He even argues that the evolution of warfare can be seen as the history of ever more efficient mechanical devices, designed to condition men to overcome their innate resistance to killing their fellow human beings. In fact, becoming a soldier involves a preparatory training phase that enables the person to overcome his innate inhibitions. He must therefore reconstruct himself to new standards, so as to be capable not only of killing, but also to be to accept death, both for himself and for his comrades in arms.

But unless precautions are taken, removing men's inhibition to kill entails risks, in that it increases the level of violence in combat. The price to be paid can be measured through psychological damage and post-traumatic stress episodes, which are accurately quantifiable. Professor Patrick Clervoy, Head of the Department of Psychology at the French armed

---

1. Richard Holmes (1946-2011), was a former British army brigadier who wrote some twenty reference works.

forces teaching hospital at Toulon [1] specialises in this type of study. He provides some revealing figures.

In the US Army between 1942 and 1945, there were 930,000 psychological hospitalisations, which represents two psychological casualties for every physical casualty, despite a 13% exemption rate for psychological reasons during the initial selection. In the first months of the Korean War, American troops were faced with a very high rate of psychological losses, in the order of 250 per 1,000. In 1973, during the Yom Kippur War, of the first 1,500 Israeli casualties evacuated, 900 were psychiatric cases. After two days, the army was obliged to improvise a forward psychiatric hospital in Upper Galilee. Again, in 1982, during the Israel-Lebanon conflict, 23 combat psychological reactions (rendering the soldier unfit for duty) were recorded for every 100 physically wounded. Finally, and more recently, amongst the American soldiers serving in Iraq the proportion presenting psychological difficulties on return from a tour of duty is estimated at 34% – evidenced by depression, addiction to alcohol or drugs, and aggressive behaviour with a high impact on social, family and conjugal life. The great majority of the soldiers subject to these psychological ailments have encountered violent death in one way or another: they have killed, they have been wounded, they have had a brush with death or have seen comrades killed.

In a book which caused a sensation in the United States, Jimmy Massey [2], a former NCO in the US Marine Corps, highlighted the behaviour of American troops in Iraq. He draws attention, in this work, to the sinister changes that have occurred since the Second World War. During that conflict, American troops exhibited a profound resistance to the killing of other human beings, even when they were being fired on. According to S. L. Marshall, only 15% of the soldiers sent to the European front ever pulled the trigger. "Fear of killing, rather than fear of being killed, was the most frequent cause of individual failure in battle." He adds: "We must free the mind of the person firing as regards the nature of his targets". He emphasizes that "pseudospeciation", the capacity to classify one's fellow humans as "different", may allow the inhibitions that seemingly deter killing to be neutralised.

Marshall explains that studies were therefore conducted in the United States in order to develop the reflex to open fire by stressing psychological conditioning, particularly the dehumanisation of the enemy. To this end, the American army emphasised desensitisation techniques, conditio-

---

1. Professor agrégé of Val-de Grace, author of *Syndrome de Lazare, Traumatisme psychique et destinée* [The Lazarus Syndrome, Psychic Trauma and Destiny], Albin Michel, Paris, 2007.
2. Jimmy Massey with Natasha Saulnier, *Cowboys from Hell*. Published in French as *Kill,Kill,Kill* by Editions du Panama, 2005.

ning and putting in place mechanisms that facilitate denial. It was also necessary to make training more realistic: soldiers would from now on fire at mobile targets that look like people, and the act of killing was deemed to be the requisite outcome for their mission. The efforts of the American army were successful: according to internal estimates, during the Vietnam War 90% of soldiers used their weapons in a more mechanistic manner. But this success actually obscured the price paid by soldiers forced to live with the feeling of having acted in contravention of the good and who were traumatised for life as a consequence.

Rachel MacNair, a specialist in the psychological effects of violence, has worked on data from the National Vietnam Veterans Readjustment Study, a programme financed by Congress. She has observed that combat trauma was significantly more frequent amongst Vietnam veterans who had killed in combat. "These data demonstrate that, in humans, killing is against their nature. Killing another human being will have traumatic consequences, except for a small minority of already psychotic subjects."

Faced with these ultimately reassuring observations on human nature, it can be concluded that that by decreasing the level of violence in combat, it is possible to reduce the level of psycho-traumatic damage. The concern to protect human resources can go hand in hand with the working out of moral convictions and a sense of history.

Another reason for adhering to principled behaviour derives from the nature of contemporary conflicts, which increasingly involve winning the support of the local population. This is the price of legitimacy. It is a question of winning the hearts of the peoples in those countries where military operations are conducted.

In his book *The Utility of Force*, General Sir Rupert Smith [1] tackles the necessity of obtaining popular approval through enacting a real "strategy of war amongst the people". He considers it to be a condition for operational success.

> *...if one is operating amongst the people, and the objective is achieve and maintain a situation of order in which political and economic measures are to take hold, then by implication one is seeking to establish some form of rule of law.*
>
> *Indeed, this may be defined as a strategic objective – which means that to then operate tactically outside the law is to attack one's own strategic objective. This is effectively what happened with incidents of abuse by US soldiers in Abu Ghraib prison in Baghdad or British soldiers in Basra in 2004 – and of course the US administered camp in*

---

1. *The Utility of Force*, Penguin Books, London, 2005.

Guantanamo Bay Cuba, in which terrorist subjects captured during the war in Afghanistan were and are detained. Moreover, such acts and policies provide evidence to one's opponent to support his strategy of provocation and the propaganda of the deed, which will only assist him in gaining support from the people and turning their minds against you.

*This leads us back to the crucial point that **the objective of all our operations amongst the people is the will of the people,** [my emphasis] and if we want a stable state and to remove our forces from maintaining a 'condition', they must be sufficiently content with the outcome that it remains intact.*

Undoubtedly the defeat or neutralisation of those advancing the opposing view by force of arms is a necessary step, but it must be done in such a way that the people at large reject them or at the least no longer support them."

Winning the will of the people consists above all in conveying to them an image of a military force beyond reproach, or at least with no intention of unworthy conduct. As well as the advantage which the armed forces gain from this, it lays the the ground for the next stage, the negotiating phase, 'the day after'. At that point, the possible accountability for any violence and atrocities committed by the forces in place will have a bearing on the political discussions and will often condition the modalities of the final agreement.

General Vincent Desportes, in his book *La Guerre Probable* [1] follows the same logic."The target of the action is no longer the adversary, but the population. The aim is to win the battle for support at the heart of the towns, while at the same time rebuilding the social contract". He continues this line of thinking by showing that if legitimacy is essential before the intervention, it is reinforced or collapses depending on the way in which the action is subsequently conducted.

"The first difficulty which the intervening power comes up against is that its legitimacy is by nature uncertain, as it can only be conferred once the action is completed, even if the legal conditions for its launch have been fulfilled ex ante [publisher's note; for example by a UN resolution]. Legitimacy ex post rests on the tangible results of the intervention [...]

---

1. *La Guerre Probable*, Economica, Paris, 2007. [English title: *Tomorrow's War*, Brookings Insitute Press].

Thus, legitimacy cannot be decreed. It is built on perceptions, and the judgements of international public opinion are not shaped by the laws of war. Once the intervention is launched, legitimacy is intimately linked to its conduct, and must exist within a dynamic perspective, that is to say, ceaselessly constructed, consolidated and preserved within the fragile boundaries of perception. Linked to the choice of ways and means, to the modalities of force and its intensity, to the rules of engagement, it is unstable, every day dependent, in the eyes of local populations and international public opinion, on events and behaviours. To some extent, the application of jus in bello *retrospectively conditions* jus in bellum.

The more fragile its legitimacy, the less margin for error the force has, and the more its freedom of action is constrained; the best reasons for going to war can be ruled out of order, after the fact, by the way in which the war is conducted."

As well as the population of the country in which the military intervene, the issue of legitimacy also concerns the people of the states supporting the military action. In both cases, the question is one of winning the battle for public opinion. That is why all servicemen and women with command responsibilities must unquestionably view themselves as potential standard-bearers of that legitimacy, in order to maintain the force's freedom of action as well as its legitimacy.

This requirement is especially important for the French armed forces, as the lower ranks benefit from considerable operational autonomy. Such freedom of action is one of their internationally recognised qualities and an acknowledged focus of excellence. In fact, this "subsidiarity principle", applied to all intermediary levels of command, has been shown to be relevant in recent engagements, by granting a degree of autonomous decision-making down as far as the combat section of around ten men. This principle gives full meaning to the expression *strategic corporal*, first used in 1999 by General Charles C. Krulak, commandant of the US Marine Corps [1]. It must be clearly understood that an error, or "gaffe", by a rookie soldier today – amplified by the media – can, in certain cases, lead to the overall strategy of the entire operation being thrown off course (or even to its failure).

Focussing on actions taken by subordinates requires perfect clarity of orders, and total understanding and ownership of the mission at every level of responsibility. This alchemy is only possible in a spirit of mutual

---

1. The expression was used in the article "The strategic corporal: leadership in the three block war", published in *Marines Magazine* in January 1999.

trust and cohesion, underpinned by a genuine sharing of human values and interpersonal skills.

More than ever, an ethic of good behaviour in combat is indispensable to the soldier, who is both the agent and victim of war. It will protect him from the consequences of his actions, both in regard to the law and to his own moral and psychological health. It will also respond to the expectations of the population, not only of his own nation from whom he draws his legitimacy, but also the people whose support and respect he must win.

Those who exercise legitimate force must therefore subject themselves to a veritable "conscience improvement programme", for that is the only way for them to acquire the means to be able to confront the most extreme situations with humanity and dignity. It is on that condition alone that the soldier can play a real part in the evolution of ethics in war.

CHAPTER 2

BUILDING CONSCIENCES

> *All of humanity's greatest achievements have been accomplished in the name of absolute principles.*
>
> Ernest Renan

P REPARING a soldier for combat does not involve completely dismantling his instincts for self-preservation and protection. Training without any limits can increase both the level of psychological damage in combat and the risks of action going awry. A commander has the responsibility of preparing his men for combat, and to injure or kill if necessary, while preserving their moral and psychological balance and controlling the level of force exerted.

The point of balance is hard to find, but that is what makes it so valuable. The military leader will find this balance if he manages, in peacetime, to provide his men with the moral and ethical benchmarks which they will hold on to in dangerous and uncertain situations. These standards, rooted in their individual conscience, will give meaning to their actions in battle.

Building up their men's conscience is a duty incumbent on military leaders. They are obliged to do so because of past mistakes, on the basis of which training courses have been constructed. They are obliged to do so in the name of those who have been able to confront terrible human tragedies without deviating from the rules. Finally, they are obliged to do so because of the humanitarian values and principles defended by France, which all have freely chosen to serve.

Without claiming to be exhaustive, the thinking of the French military on ethics is among the most exemplary. It enables the main rules of behaviour to be centred on fundamental principles composed of three ideas. Presented in this chapter in support of new accounts from the three services – Army, Air Force and Navy – they bring together certainties acquired throughout history. These certainties may be considered as "humanity's convictions".

*

*   *

1. First principle

Fight hard, kill when you must, but respect life

> *Respect for the human person, particularly for his or her life, is an absolutely fundamental requirement in our society, of which the soldier is merely the delegate.*
>
> *Exercising the profession of arms.*
> French Army.

EYEWITNESS ACCOUNT [1]

Somalia. Mogadishu. 1993

5 June.

A Pakistani unit has just been decimated. The method used is a first in contemporary military history. General Aydiid, one of Mogadishu's strongmen and the most resistant to UNOSOM[2] actions, sends women, children, adolescents and unarmed men towards the Pakistani contingent. Displaying the exuberance for which Africans are known, the crowd approaches the Pakistani contingent, surrounds it and mingles with the unit. The unit fires into the air to extricate itself.

Then suddenly, from within the crowd, armed Somalis open fire, shooting to kill. A fierce struggle ensues, lasting several hours and leading to the death of a number of Pakistani soldiers.

12 June.

The UN decides to act. During the night, American combat aircraft destroy Aydiid's weapons storage facilities, which are immediately occupied by Pakistani and Italian units and the French group. [...]

---

1. Major Bonnemaison is today a major-general and in command of the French military academy at Saint-Cyr Coëtquidan.
2. United Nations Operations in Somalia.

17 June.

The operation reaches a climax. UNOSOM intends launching a major offensive against General Aydiid's neighbourhoods. Italian and Moroccan troops will form a cordon around the Pakistanis, who will search the objective. The French, who control the main 21 October road, will operate as a rapid reaction force. Deployment is completed by 5 a.m.

At 6 o'clock, shooting breaks out in Aydiid's areas in the centre of town, residential neighbourhoods with wide roads bordered by elegant houses, usually with two storeys; the roof terraces are surrounded by high walls offering protection and cover. General Aydiid's partisans have melted away under cover of darkness, pulling back to houses and onto rooftops, from where they fire on the Pakistanis and the Moroccans, who courageously return the fire.

Then the Moroccan commander is killed and his second-in-command wounded. Their troops attacked from all sides. The French will need to intervene. It is 8.30.

Confused and contradictory intelligence reaches us. The Moroccans are over there, no, they're there! The rebels are occupying the hospital. Or maybe not. We don't really know. We can reach the combat area by the main road. No, the crowd has built a barricade. We'll have to go the other way. But time is short. My unit commander finally decides to approach the friendly positions by the route offering the best field of fire, suitable for the ERC 90 [1] Sagaie and the heavy weapons of our VAM [2] and VLRA [3].

A second echelon, with one section mounted on an armoured VAB vehicle and another on a VLRA truck, will hold the military hospital crossroads, ready to retrieve the first echelon.

The last section is held back at the military academy crossroads, from where some snipers are firing on us. We are unable to respond effectively. Dozens of families are squatting in the academy and it is out of the question to open fire in such conditions.

No matter. The French army is used to this sort of situation, calling for a cool head and restraint. Although it may look like passivity, it in fact stems from this unwritten law, this remarkable tradition of French military humanism, which requires that the saving of lives must take precedence over all else.

---

1. Engin Roues Canon 90: a light wheeled tank armed with a 90 calibre canon.
2. Véhicule de l'Avant Blindé: a lightly armoured troop transport vehicle.
3. Véhicule Léger de Reconnaissance et d'Appui: a light reconnaissance and support vehicle – in other words, a troop transport truck.

It is 09.00. Our time of doing nothing is over. The first echelon has deployed into the large open area to the north of Aydiid's neighbourhood, dominated by the tall buildings of the three hospitals held by the rebels. All our fire is now concentrated on them, allowing the Moroccans to break free after an hour. There is shooting everywhere.

You just have to imagine the surreal spectacle of this unrelenting gunfire, watched by a large crowd. People are leaning over the hospital balconies and sitting on the stadium steps, indifferent to the danger and probably unaffected by the spectre of imminent death. For the enemy, they serve as human shields and, were we inclined to fire blindly, potential martyrs in the eyes of international opinion.

But it is a source of pride for us that we have never fired without being absolutely sure that no innocent people will be injured. This restraint on our part explains the length of the firefight, almost three hours, when it would have been all too easy to fire a high explosive shell into a house, and give the devil his due.

It is still 09.00 when the second echelon arrives at the crossroads. The intention was to occupy it quietly. What was not expected was an ambush. But this is what happened, with the lead echelon being taken by surprise from the rear. We are trapped by a lethal crossfire from light weapons, machine guns and anti-tank rocket launchers. The troops scramble out of the vehicles and return fire, supported by the VAB machine guns.

Very soon we have one, then two, then three injured men. The obvious, and most audacious, solution may turn out to be the most effective. We have to take the strongest position held by the rebels: the tall buildings of the military hospital. They certainly knew what they were doing, as this position is the best available.

Captain Y's platoon mounts an assault. House by house it moves forward 150 metres, finally reaching the main building, which in turn has to be cleared room by room. At this point two rebels send a non-combatant civilian – a woman – to retrieve the rifle of a sniper killed by one of our marksmen. An act of supreme cowardice on their part? No, simply another philosophy of warfare. We were obliged to make the decision to fire... not at the woman, but at the rifle.

A little later we succeed in taking the hospital building and the assailants flee.

All in all it took us three hours – though it seemed like three minutes. We had excellent intelligence support from the helicopters, a great deal of luck, and the outstanding bravery of our men, some of whom had less than seven months' service. But it also cost us four wounded, one of whom was hit full in the head by a sniper. The rebels lost thirty men.

Intense images will remain with us. Eyes scrutinizing a building with too many dark windows; a marksman neutralising the sniper who had denied us access to a corridor for an hour; the haunting laughter of the children who think it's a game; that woman risking her life for a rifle; the unit commander's driver pushing his jeep into cover between two armoured vehicles; the marine, wounded in the foot by a bullet, who refuses to be evacuated; the sigh of a Moroccan when he saw the French arriving.

And lessons relearned, never to be forgotten. Hold the high ground; holding a crossroads confers great tactical advantage; in an urban environment danger comes from every point of the compass; a calm leader means calm troops; exercise command facing the action and if necessary lead from the front; a successful assault is only possible with good support. And so forth.

But above all, what will remain with us is the legitimate pride at having fought as men, not as beasts, albeit against people who did not much care for us, with discernment and without hatred, as every French unit would have done.

Nothing needs to be added to this account. It says it all, superbly illustrating the principle *Fight hard, kill when you must, but respect life.*

Colonel de Saqui de Sannes, the commander of this regiment, acknowledged that he was confronted with a real test of conscience in imposing restrictive rules of engagement and orders for opening fire on his men. In choosing to fight as a soldier respectful of the lives of others, he exposed his own men to greater danger. He also knew that he reduced the chances of gaining the upper hand locally over his adversary.

Faithful to the convictions within his soul and conscience, he decided to accept responsibility for the choice. In particular he took the time to explain his decision to his subordinates who, in turn, were able to relay it down to the rank and file. One of the key factors in the success of this engagement was that every man without fail held fast to that decision. From the beginning of their initial training they had been instructed to respect life in the execution of the mission, were welded together by a remarkable esprit de corps with total confidence in their leader, and finally, while accepting all the risks, were victorious in a wholly admirable manner.

On this subject, the unit commander later wrote:

An important place must be given to the development of the moral strengths that contribute to the cohesion of a unit and allow it to suffer a serious blow without falling apart.

The behaviour of the personnel in the units involved in the violent clashes of 17 June has proved that the style of leadership built on support from within the ranks is suitable for crisis situations. A sense of initiative, team spirit, the habit of manoeuvre, and confidence in one's leader and in oneself are just some of the elements that contributed to such generally good behaviour during a particularly severe baptism of fire.

Eyewitness account by a pilot [1]

Afghanistan 2006

Two Super Etendards are catapult launched from the aircraft carrier Charles de Gaulle, sailing in the Arabian Sea, on a flight that will last more than five hours. They are armed with laser guided bombs. They fly towards the north of Kandahar, more than a thousand kilometres from the launch point, with the mission of supporting the advance of an allied force along the bottom of a valley.

The environment is unique. The mountains are magnificent, ochre in colour and devoid of vegetation. Life is clustered in the valleys, verdant from the fields abutting small walled farms, crammed up next to each other. The two aircraft approach a large coalition refuelling tanker. Other allied fighters are there too, each waiting its turn 'at the pump'. This is the third time they have refuelled. Time passes inexorably, a combination of the discomfort of a cockpit intended for short duration flights and the concentration needed to monitor flight parameters. Senses are on the alert, looking out for any indicators warning of a possible critical fault.

Suddenly a radio message disturbs this relative monotony: the ground forces are under attack. They have been ambushed while going through a hamlet. The allied soldiers cannot advance and their vehicles have been subjected to RPG7 fire, which though inaccurate gives reason to suppose that the worst is yet to come. The joint terminal attack controller (JTAC) of the unit in contact on the ground is requesting air support. The sounds of combat can be clearly heard over the radio, and the significance of what is at stake becomes clear with the controller's account. The pilot is abruptly plunged into a tactical situation that was still virtual just a few minutes earlier. He has potentially become a major player.

The guidance procedure is set in motion; the target is a farm, described by the controller. The pilot identifies the target and the final run

---

1. (Navy) Captain Zimmerman.

begins. It will be the only one because the fuel gauges are indicating on minimum. With no further attack runs possible, this is the last opportunity to come to the aid of the troops on the ground. The crewman prepares to drop his laser guided bomb, the blast of which is devastating inside this type of structure. The leader illuminates the target with his laser designator pod, takes a final look at his control display... and then, to his great surprise, there appear one, then two more farms, identical to the first. Which is the right one? Unable to decide, the pilot asks for a more detailed description... Nothing to be done, impossible to resolve the uncertainty. Which of the three farms should he target? Where are the enemy gunmen dug in? At the altitude the planes are flying, over 15,000 feet, it is impossible to pick out firing at ground level. Who might be sheltering in the other farms? Civilians gone to ground waiting for the end of the battle?

Long minutes pass. Disconsolate, the pilot announces that he is unable to identify the target and resolves to turn back. He sets off back to the aircraft carrier with a terrible feeling of impotence, of disappointment and frustration, but with the conviction that, on this occasion, there were no acceptable alternatives.

The French fighter pilot, a naval officer, concluded that he was not willing to sacrifice innocent lives for the support and safety of friendly forces. His sense of personal responsibility was elevated to the level of a question of conscience, the answer to which he freely chose. As he explains, only the questions which one asks of oneself *before* going into action can allow one to find the right answers in an emergency. "Such questions are genuine marker buoys for one's decisions, just like navigation landmarks, the relevance of which will be confirmed or invalidated during the engagement. The mind is much too occupied when in action in real time to take these things into account."

This example attests to the maturity of ethical thought amongst pilots – whether navy or air force – as well as to the setting up of air support procedures that demonstrate how this area has evolved since earlier conflicts. However, behaviour of this kind is also sometimes subject to criticism internally. Indeed, there sometimes is a simplistic temptation on the part of some service personnel to maintain that it is better to risk the lives of a few civilians, including women and children, rather than expose soldiers to more danger – as in the Somalia example – or not complete one's mission in support of ground troops – as in the preceding case. This attitude prefers to give free rein to the initiative of individual combatants, while saying that responsibility for any collateral damage ultimately lies with those who provoke it in the first place, that is, the enemy.

Such thinking should be viewed as an unacceptable denial of strict standards of behaviour in combat, generating excesses and serious misconduct. Moreover, in the particular case of the Mogadishu battles, such a mindset would indicate a serious misunderstanding of custom and practice in Africa, and most particularly in Somalia. For the warrior tradition of the local ethnic groups can lead to the participation in warfare of all members of the clan, as and when it may be involved. For all that, though the loss of women and children might be accepted in tribal confrontations, it would never be tolerated if it was caused by a foreign adversary.

What happened next demonstrates this. Some days after the battles, negotiations were organised between chiefs loyal to General Aydiid and representatives of UNOSOM. During a very tense meeting, there were scathing verbal exchanges and threats of direct reprisals against UN troops. While this altercation was taking place, the Somali chief turned to the French officer present, and said: "Not you French, we won't bother you because you've shown you know how to fight as soldiers."

According to a French adage, *a good deed is never wasted.* In the ethical field, one might say: *exemplary conduct can also lead to respect.*

In a nod to history, in regard to Captain Zimmerman's account, the terrible collateral damage in Lebanon some time later became news worldwide and generated some very heated emotions. Certain high-ranking military officers made the link with this phase of the combat and drew attention to the cool heads of the air group pilots.

WHAT SHOULD WE DEDUCE FROM THIS...

... and, what should military personnel, **whose primary mission is, and will remain, combat**, ultimately make of this principle?

The above example perfectly illustrates the French military's current doctrine on the use of force, which advocates the controlled use of force during missions. It is really therefore a question of never confusing combat with violence. In practice, there is a great difference between the controlled use of weapons to oppose violence – that does not exclude firmness and determination – and the unbridled use of force which invariably leads to the same violence one is up against. The boundary between the two is unstable and difficult to determine, but it is up to the commander to find it.

The archetypal and often cited example of the Somalia clashes demonstrates the real advantage gained by the judicious use of force during combat missions amongst the population. General Sir Rupert Smith gives an account of his experience in this area.

I have found it helpful when operating amongst the people to hold in mind that the military are there to impose order. To this end there is a good principle in English common law which is that when you are faced with violent disorder and it is your duty to quell it, then you are to take the course of action with the least likelihood of causing loss of life and property. And while of course the military must fight and defeat their armed opponents to best advantage, they must do so within this guiding principle. In the worst cases of fighting and disorder the imperative for firm action will tend to result in casualties, destruction, crude judgements and rough handling; nevertheless, the controlling measure remains the law and the military should be accountable to it [1].

The principles of proportionality and reversibility are nowadays clearly incorporated into concepts of the operational use of force [2]. Reversibility should be understood as the ability, after the use of weapons at the highest intensity, to change one's approach and engage in types of activity involving a very low level of force. Examples of this would include crowd control using reduced lethality weapons or assisting the civil population. Current doctrine defines the concepts of 'minimum force', 'proportionality' and 'necessity' – the three reference points to bear in mind if one is to act justly. These principles have a symbiotic relationship with the laws of armed conflict, the law of war and domestic law, because they precisely convey France's conception of the use of armed force.

The principles are applied in the Rules of Engagement (ROE) which are nowadays an obligatory framework for all military operations outside and inside French national territory. They lay down the upper and lower boundaries, enabling the commander to respond to the greatest number of situations. Action can be taken anywhere within these two boundaries. ROE are just as much the authority to act as they are limitations. Therefore, in response to the question arising in the example above – "what do you do when faced with a hostile armed group, using women and children as a shield?" –, the answer is not as simple as "open fire" or "hold your fire". Rather it is to be found in knowing, and foreseeing, the boundaries, in one's individual conscience.

The duty of the serviceman is therefore to reply to unscrupulous combatants, murderers and thugs with an attitude just as determined as theirs, but respecting innocent life, even when this ethical code may be used against him by his adversary. It is therefore more than ever a question of

1. *The Utility of Force*, Penguin, 2005 pp379-380.
2. PIA Number 05-203, 2006 Edition. [French] Joint doctrine on the use of force during military operations outside French territory.

pitting one's will the enemy's, though not to match barbarity with barbarity. Using force is an act neither of violence nor cruelty, and it is possible to fight resolutely while at the same time respecting the principle of the preservation of human life.

The following account from Côte d'Ivoire gives another example of the intelligence and courage of a leader who was able to weigh up matters correctly, even though he had received permission from his superior to use extreme measures.

EYEWITNESS ACCOUNT [1]

Republic of Côte d'Ivoire – Spring 2005.

I have been commanding the battle group based at Bouaké for some weeks. It is a few months after the November 2004 crisis which followed the shelling of the Lycée [secondary school] Descartes at Bouaké in which nine French soldiers were killed.

Following these events, everyone in the region has good reason to be angry with the French army. The rebels accuse us of having let the Ivorian armed forces cross the buffer zone [2] to help their operation intended to reconquer the north of the country. Whereas the loyalist Ivorian forces hate us because, according to them, we caused their operation to fall by destroying their aviation after the bombing of Bouaké. Finally, the force deployed by the UN (UNOCI) feels it has been supplanted by France. My mission therefore is to lower the tension between rebels and loyalists, eliminate ill-feeling about operation Licorne [Operation Unicorn, the French armed forces' peacekeeping mission in Côte d'Ivoire] and to re-establish good relations with UNOCI.

As the weeks pass, we manage to reduce the tension, but there are numerous incidents with the Ivorian army. Several times we are just a hair's breadth from a serious skirmish, avoided only by the units' cool heads and discipline.

During the Easter festivities, the battalion is deployed into the buffer zone. Its mission is to deny both opposing parties access to the buffer zone – the rebels on the one side and the Ivorian army on the other. It is a sensitive period, and highway robbers are taking advantage of it, holding to ransom the population which has gathered in family groups in the villages. On this particular day, I am in my battle group's command post, situated in the village of Raviart, in the centre of our area of responsibility.

---

1. As recorded by the author.
2. A neutral zone acting as a buffer between the two belligerents.

Over the radio, we suddenly get an urgent call from the section commander in charge of the M'Bahiakro sector. He explains that he is confronted with a substantial number of clearly very determined Ivorian soldiers, who are attempting to enter the out-of-bounds buffer zone. I order him to stop them. A little later, he reports that despite warning shots (in the air), the Ivorians are continuing to advance and are trying to skirt around his section. This does not feel good. The Ivorians do not normally display such an aggressive attitude. What do they want? I am a little perplexed. My chief of operations suggests using the squadron's light armoured vehicles to support the section. He is right. We need to show our determination and react immediately with some heavy kit, so as to leave no opportunity for the belligerent intentions of today's adversaries to be realised. To take stock of the situation on the ground I decide to go there myself by helicopter. The chief of operations will coordinate the action from the command post. I ask him to contact UNOCI and for them to send observers to the site quickly. I have a feeling that I am going to need witnesses.

I board a Puma with my close protection squad, and after a fifteen minute flight we land 3 kilometres from the site of the incident. A light armoured vehicle (VAB) is waiting for me. I soon arrive at a point near the section. They are deployed along the road, while one of our tanks keeps its gun aimed at the Ivorian post 400 metres away, where the buffer zone starts. The situation is very tense. The Ivorian soldiers present are hyped up, visibly drunk and very aggressive. They do not want to withdraw. According to them, the buffer zone is badly demarcated and the true border is situated where we are now standing.

I send regular situation reports to the Licorne force command post (CP) in Abidjan; we are in an extremely tense situation which at any moment could escalate into an exchange of fire. Both sides have their weapons levelled at each other. The slightest loss of composure by my soldiers might degenerate into bloody killing.

Then I get a personal call directly from the general commanding the force. He orders me to stand firm, not to compromise and to take the Ivorian post by force if things get worse.

This very aggressive order takes me by surprise me and raises questions in my mind, given the context of my mission. I cannot easily see myself entering the loyalist zone – where I am not supposed to go – and fighting an improvised offensive in the middle of a settlement full of civilians. Have I expressed myself badly in my situation reports?

Whatever the answer, the CP in Abidjan does not seem to have an accurate picture of the local situation, and there is no time for further discussion with them. As of now, I consider that I'm the only person able to fully appreciate the reality of the situation and the risks involved in making a wrong decision. I am in the midst of my deployed troops and I have a foreboding as to the dangers of the situation. Very conscious of my responsibilities, after weighing up the potential risks I decide to do everything possible to avoid a dangerous escalation, despite the general's 'carte blanche'.

Meanwhile, the UN observers have turned up. I seize the opportunity offered by their arrival to begin a discussion with the Ivorian commander and lower the tension of the present standoff.

He holds forth volubly about the incorrect demarcation of the buffer zone. But I sense this is only a pretext to pick a quarrel with us. Nevertheless, I decide to play along with his game and even get in a word of my own! In a moment of sudden inspiration, I interject, "If the demarcation isn't right, let's go and discuss it at your place, in your post at M'Bahiakro. Come on, I'll buy you all a drink!"

In suggesting this, the idea was to take him back to his camp and buy some time. Today, with hindsight, I realise that offering already seriously drunk people more to drink was perhaps not the best of ideas. However, the prospect of having a drink at French expense was greeted enthusiastically by several of the soldiers flanking the Ivorian commander and immediately lowered the tension.

I get into the UN observers' vehicle and we drive to the Ivorian PC, escorted by my team of bodyguards. On our arrival there, I don't stint. I pull out a roll of banknotes and offer to buy a round for all the assembled troops. While they go and fetch the drinks, I unfold the map of the region on the table in the bar next to the Ivorian PC and start discussing the situation with Lieutenant Zadi – who is visibly more interested in sounding off over a drink or two than engaging in HQ staff-type discussions. Eventually we manage to convince him that the limit really is where we say it is, but we agree to check it anyway with the UN. I ask Lieutenant Zadi if I can return with him in his vehicle to the scene of the confrontation. Sitting next to him, I figure, there'll be less risk of a stray bullet ... He agrees and on the way there we talk things over like old friends.

I realise at this point that the game is won. Everyone will be able to go back to their zones without any blood being spilt. Lieutenant Zadi even confesses to me how much he admires the French armoured vehicles we are equipped with.

He was right. They are excellent machines. Very effective.

What lessons may be drawn from this experience in relation to the ethics of command? The officer concerned could have demonstrated his 'firmness' and cut down some of the Ivorian soldiers who had ventured into a prohibited area. He had even implicitly received the go-ahead from his higher-ranking officers. He certainly had the military capability to do so, as the balance of forces was very much in his favour. However, he considered that such a decision would fall within the ambit of gratuitous violence resulting from an excessive use of force. There was no immediate need for combat, and it would only have served to aggravate hatred toward us. Nor was it in the spirit of the mission, even faced with one of the hard men of the Ivorian regime, who unquestionably deserved to be taught a lesson.

What was needed was to find a way to negotiate and ease the tension. The idea of having a discussion with Zadi in his CP wrong-footed him. In reality, the deployment of the armoured vehicles around the section meant that overwhelming firepower was available, limiting the Zadi's belligerent ambitions. No longer having a military solution available, his only room for manoeuvre was to provoke a mistake by the French forces. The presence of the UN observers allowed an 'African style' negotiation to take place in which neither party would lose face. A few thousand CFA francs and a good measure of level-headedness on the part of all the French soldiers present undoubtedly enabled the worst to be avoided that day. Not opening fire is often more difficult than giving one's warrior instinct free rein.

Before concluding our exploration of this first principle, one final account deserves to be included. Its title was specifically chosen by the soldier recounting his experience.

EYEWITNESS ACCOUNT

The paratroopers who didn't like the easy way

September 2008. Afghanistan. Tagab valley. The 8th Marine Infantry Parachute Regiment is on operations.

On that day, 2 Company enters a suspect village and comes under fire from rebel forces. The insurgents appear to be relatively few in number. The captain thinks that it won't be long before they stop firing and take advantage of the cover provided by the vegetation to disappear. He decides to prevent them doing that. The village is small, and another section rapidly skirts around it to the south.

The village is now surrounded. So too are the insurgents, but as yet they are unaware of this. The men blocking off the south deploy themselves unobtrusively and wait. The landscape is sparsely covered with trees and a few areas of crops, separated by low mud walls and rough hedges.

Well hidden in their makeshift outpost, three of the company's paras are facing a patch of land hardly bigger than a tennis court. In front of us, on the far side of the fallow field, the view is restricted by a line of bushes. We hear the sound of gunfire from the north become less intense. The situation is calming down. The minutes pass.

Suddenly, we see an insurgent burst out of the vegetation. He is hurrying, but not running. He crosses the field at a good pace. Unknowingly, he is heading right towards us. He is holding an AK47 and is wearing a makeshift smock to carry his magazines. He is a rebel. There can be no doubt as to his identity. Our weapons are levelled; all we have to do is pull the trigger. The man is very close. He stops, turns around as if expecting someone and crouches down. He is now less than 10 metres away.

We could open fire. Yet we don't. Why? Difficult to say... One of us signals to the others not to shoot. He has another idea. He decides to give the man a chance. He calls out loudly to the motionless insurgent just in front of him, then reveals himself.

Totally surprised, the man jumps and falls, tries to get up, then trips and sinks back into a sitting position. Three assault rifles are aimed directly at him. He is clearly terrified. He remains motionless. He drops his Kalashnikov and shows his empty hands, indicating his surrender. Evidently he does not want to join Allah in paradise just yet.

In combat in Afghanistan, it is often easier to kill an insurgent rather than to take him prisoner. But this does not always happen. These soldiers chose another solution. Though it was not the easy one, it was that which their conscience dictated.

To conclude our discussion of this first ethical principle, let us give the last word to General Pierre Billotte [1].

In the ideologically driven conflicts of modern wars, victory must go to the noblest ideology. One of the most effective means of prevailing rightly lies in the greatest possible respect for moral and human values, because it goes right to the heart of the people who are temporarily hostile to you... Although it may seem harsh, a leader must not hesitate to make his troops run greater risks, rather than accept a dishonourable practice [...] A leader who did not have the moral strength to fulfil such a duty would be unworthy to command French troops.

---

1. Pierre Billotte (1906-1992) was a French general and politician. General de Gaulle's chief of staff and secretary of the Committee for National Defence in London, he landed in Normandy at the head of one of the three battle groups of the Leclerc division. Made a Companion of the Liberation, he was minister of defence in Edgar Faure's government in 1955.

*
*   *

2. Second principle

Unconditional respect for human dignity

> *Human dignity is not a peaceful legacy to be enjoyed. For each of us it is a responsibility, a question, a burden and a struggle [1].*
>
> Henri Hude

EYEWITNESS ACCOUNT [2]

Rwanda – 1995

On the day in question, we mounted an assault on a position where a group of men dug themselves in after committing a robbery and throwing hand grenades into the crowd to cover their retreat. They opened fire on us with automatic weapons. Just as in training, we pinned them down, outflank them, carried out the attack, searched them and secured our position. During the operation, we killed one man and took three prisoners. Some minutes later, as the tension eased, a man detached himself from the crowd which had gathered, and furiously attacked one of our NCOs with a machete. It was the father of the man we had killed. Though he was old, his rage and skill in wielding his machete made the attack potentially lethal.

The NCO had his hand on the butt of his Famas [French assault rifle]. All he needed to do was to raise the barrel and pull the trigger. But behind the attacker was a dense crowd of people. Rather than firing, the NCO put his weapon to one side, and parried the machete blow then overpowered the man without harming him. He thus chose to put his own life at risk rather than take innocent lives, starting with the bereaved father, maddened with grief.

It was unquestionably heroism. Though took him but a split second to act as he did, how many years had it taken to prepare for that act, that decision? During training he had practised parrying a downward

---

1. Taken from the proceedings of the 3rd Colloquium "Dignity of Man" held at the Saint-Cyr Coëtquidan Military Academy on 23 April 2004.
2. Provided by Commodore Marin Gillier.

blow hundreds of times. But his thinking had also gradually matured. A few days previously, this NCO had come and confided in me, telling me how his nights were disturbed by going over the horrors we were witnessing day after day. This man appreciated the value of life as much as he understood the destructive potential of grief.

Compassion does not prevent you becoming a hero. It can even help you to make a split-second decision that respects human dignity more than you can imagine. In such situations, truth is to be found within us, and nowhere else. You have to allow it to mature, quietly, silently.

This account illustrates one aspect of the principle of respect for dignity in combat. It describes a situation, the essence of which we need to grasp: in a cruel environment, maintaining his conscience at the right level allows the soldier to keep faith with the principles of action that he has set himself. It also allows him preserve his own humanity, and his own equilibrium. And when next he is in combat, such equilibrium will be indispensable to him.

EYEWITNESS ACCOUNT [1]

Rwanda – 1995

My company was deployed on Operation Turquoise in Rwanda.

We soon found ourselves in the position of having to establish a secure humanitarian zone and having to protect the Hutus. It was the Hutus who had been responsible for the massacres, and were now attempting to flee to Goma, where there had been a terrible cholera epidemic. We were therefore in the paradoxical situation both of seeking out the Hutu killers, the perpetrators of atrocities and horrors for the past few weeks, and of protecting and freeing the few Tutsi survivors, who had been surrounded. At the same time, we also had to protect the Hutu population, many of them mortally ill with cholera, who was surging back towards our base. All this was happening partly in liaison with the humanitarian organisations. The relationship with them was complicated and situated within a general framework that was becoming increasingly difficult to comprehend. The situation was evolving rapidly and radically. Our soldiers kept wondering about the point of our mission and we had continually to explain and try and make our actions clear.

Our zone of responsibility extended over some 300 to 400 square kilometres, an enormous area for an infantry company of 120 men to cover.

---

1. Supplied by brigadier general Lecointre, in command of the 9 French Marine Brigade.

One day, with one of my platoons, while trying to repair a village dispensary, we discovered a mass grave of babies. About thirty tiny bodies protruded from the ground. Despite the horror of the discovery, we had to bury them afresh, to avoid any risk of contagion. The day after this disagreeable duty, the population of the village seized a man, claiming that he was one of the men who massacred the children. They were preparing to exact vengeance and lynch him, but I asked for him to be handed over. The villagers refused to do so. I therefore gave the order for the platoon to intervene. My platoon then went in to take the man from the angry villagers. It was our job to protect him, even though he had been identified as an assassin of the babies they had buried the previous day.

I arrived in the area an hour later. I found that the man extracted from the crowd was tied up and exposed to the blazing tropical sun. Not only that, but every time any of my soldiers passed by, they kicked him in the ribs. The prisoner was clearly not being given any water, despite the heat. My men were waiting for him either to die of thirst, or to attempt to escape, so that they could then kill him.

I didn't know whether he really was guilty, and no-one had given us any proof. If he was guilty, it was not for us to act as judge and jury; and if he were innocent, it was our duty to protect him. Objectively, he had the right to our protection, and we were under an obligation to respect his dignity as a man, whether he was guilty or not.

I therefore had to explain to my men why they had to act as his protectors. At that point I discovered and understood how easy it is to let oneself be taken over by this feeling of revenge, by this violence that brings with it war, death and crises.

In that situation, had not the captain held fast to the real meaning of what he was doing in Rwanda, and to his primary mission, which was specifically to put an end to the spiral of violence, his men would in turn have become actors in that terrible murderous game, they would have become torturers and assassins. One act of revenge inviting another. And how would the commander have been able to contain the spiral and to prevent his men from acting as judge and jury for the remainder of their mission? If one tolerates a first transgression, how then does one subsequently draw a line in the sand?

The only possible ethical attitude is to define an absolute standard of self-discipline and to remain committed to the greater requirement for dignity, to which every man has a right. The action taken by the officer in this example is the fruit of profound thought and the manifestation of great moral strength.

WHAT CAN BE DEDUCED FROM THIS?

In the fiercest heat of combat as well as in its peripheral phases, absolutely no divergence from the highest standards is permissible in a soldier's behaviour towards those he encounters. Whether it be high intensity combat or population management operations, whether it be intelligence operations or special operations, unconditional respect for human dignity must govern all combat activities.

The obligatory starting point for the first principle of ethics in combat is respect for the international conventions to which France subscribes. The law of armed conflict and the Geneva conventions are still flouted all too often. Humanitarian law is much less well known and understood than one might imagine. Many nations, and not only the less powerful ones, tend to use their dominant position to increase their freedom of action and to achieve their aims, even when that involves violations of international agreements, or even of international law itself.

But the law does not provide us with all the answers, particularly in the context of operations over the last few decades, when winning the peace has been the primary goal. Intervention operations of the "soldier of peace" variety, and the implementation of restrictive rules of engagement, generate ambiguous situations, requiring recourse to a set of rules much broader than the law. These rules impinge upon the individual and collective conscience; they allow meaning to be ascribed where the law merely frames and delineates; and they broaden the notion of human dignity.

The philosopher Henri Hude maps out the contours of this dignity [1].

Violating people's dignity is not simply an attack on their freedom, by not treating them as equals, but it is also to wound their body, their most fundamental relationships, their social status, and, for all I know, their property. There is also the question of respect for the system of laws within which this dignity is given form [...] One very important point – a classic among philosophers – concerns the extent to which the recognition of human dignity is inseparable from the recognition of a moral law, in regard to which people are truly free [...]

To respect human dignity is above all to recognise the value of the person. And dignity lies in the fact of a just and universal recognition of the value of the person [...]

That is why dignity [...] is seen to be extended to tangible individuality, to the individual who is by nature human, to all those elements that make up his nature and to his existence in all his states.

---

1. Extracts from the proceedings of the 2002 and 2004 colloquiums "Dignity of Man" of the Saint-Cyr-Coëtquidan Military Academy.

In combat, one of the central principles of dignity is to never descend to the level of the adversary when his behaviour falls short of acceptable standards. If a soldier can only meet barbarity with barbarity, the conflict descends into mutual violence and the very idea of civilisation suffers. That is why every combatant must be capable of a sufficiently high standard of conscience to allow him to judge the scope of and the responsibility for his actions, without allowing himself to be potentially contaminated by the value system of his adversaries. The value of his own dignity depends on his ability to respect the dignity of others, despite everything, whatever the conditions of the operation may be. It is this that we call "giving meaning" to the operation.

The following account illustrates the all-important emotional stability that every combatant must be able to demonstrate in a situation with no points of reference and against an unprincipled adversary.

EYEWITNESS ACCOUNT [1]

Côte d'Ivoire – February 2003

The situation has been tense at Lumio for some days – four lynchings in the neighbourhood, and especially a torrent of refugees, though this for no obvious reason has abated. It is 10.45 when an adolescent, from the north, runs up the road towards us. He is in a state of panic, but is able to tell me that he and his three brothers were attacked by rebels while they were looking for food in a coconut plantation. He managed to escape, but he thinks his brothers have been killed.

At 13.00, there is a new arrival – one of the boy's brothers. He has a badly bruised face. He explains how he pushed aside the barrel of the rifle pointed at him just as it was fired. He shows me the burns on his hand.

Around 15.00, a group of rebels appears some 1,500 metres away, on the road that we have under surveillance. They walk down the road towards us. We see there's a naked child in the middle of the group. The rebels order the child to run in our direction, which he does. Immediately afterwards, they open fire.

At first I think they are going to kill him, but the child continues running without being hit. I then realise that they are not firing at him, but at us, and hoping we won't respond for fear of hitting the child.

I stay calm. I call for some warning bursts from our machine gun, carefully avoiding the child's line of approach.

1. Account taken from *'Le Code d'honneur en action'* Opération Licorne au 2ᵉ REP (Régiment Étranger de Parachutistes) *['The Code of Honour in Action' Operation Unicorn and the Second Parachute Regiment of the Foreign Legion]* Preface by Colonel E. Maurin, SEPP, Toulouse, 2006.

It is enough to stop the rebels and to save the child, who finally reaches us.

He is 11 years old, and has machete wounds in his chest. We treat him, give him something to eat and drink, dress him and return him to his family, happy to have kept him in one piece.

Alas, we will never again see the last of the four brothers.

As we have seen, human dignity in warfare can certainly pertain to the civilian population, as well as enemy prisoners and the enemy wounded. But there is another topic that is less frequently addressed, that of the enemy dead. Colonel Le Nen came up against this problem in Afghanistan, and gives his account.

EYEWITNESS ACCOUNT

Afghanistan – March 2009.

I am taking part in a Shura [1] at the district centre of Alasay. Together with our comrades from the Afghan National Army, we have for the last ten days been occupying the Alasay valley bottom, where we have just finished constructing two FOBs [2].

During the meeting, the maleks [3] from the upper valleys of Shpee and Skent, where the insurgents have fallen back after our offensive, ask to see me. They have come to ask for a cease-fire. They explain that the Taliban want to retrieve their dead and bury them as quickly as possible, in accordance with Islamic law. I think this over for a few minutes, then decide to agree to their request, despite the reservations of my Afghan counterpart commanding the 1st Afghan kandak [4].

In fact, despite the fierce battles of recent days and the death in action of one of our own men, I respect these Taliban, who have fought with courage and a certain panache. They have little in common with the cruel and duplicitous men who place improvised explosive devices along our routes or turn adolescents into human bombs. The insurgents in Alasay have fought and died as soldiers, and consequently have the right to a soldier's burial.

The French soldier, whatever his rank, has a duty to set standards in terms of behaviour. In the first instance, he is personally responsible for his actions. He also has a collective responsibility, in that he represents a

---

1. A meeting with local leaders.
2. Forward Operating Bases
3. A 'mayor' designated by the village elders.
4. Afghan battalion.

part of the nation in whose name he acts and whose colours he wears. He must accept full responsibility for this and, if necessary, he has to act accordingly.

France has been one of the pioneers in the defence of humanitarian values and of as the rights which derive from them. These rights inspired the United Nations charter and those of other international organisations. Awareness of human dignity has become a universal value. In France and more generally Europe it is one of the main driving forces of the behaviour of our contemporaries, who view any violation of the dignity of a human being as an attack on their own dignity.

A large part of the legitimacy of the French combatant rests on the trust accorded to him by his fellow citizens in carrying out his mission, which he undertakes in their name and in the name of France. The ability of the combatant to respect the values represented by this legitimacy will ensure its durability.

*

*   *

3. Third principle

> **Cultivate the absolute primacy of example**

> *Not to practise what one teaches is to dishonour one's word.*
>
> French tactics course, 1922
> Book II: *Moral strengths*

EYEWITNESS ACCOUNT [1]

Côte d'Ivoire – March 2003 – Zone of Instability

I am manning a post in the Diboli region. It's routine – searching vehicles, checking people, verifying papers.

On the day in question, I see a small group of people, probably a family, agitatedly talking to a corporal. I walk over to them and learn that their daughter has been taken captive while passing through a rebel position. These guys are brutes with few, if any, principles. The parents are terrified. Not an easy matter to sort out. We have no direct

---

1. Account taken from *'Le Code d'honneur en action'* Opération Licorne au 2ᵉ REP (Régiment Étranger de Parachutistes) *['The Code of Honour in Action' Operation Unicorn and the Second Parachute Regiment of the Foreign Legion]* Preface by Colonel E. Maurin, SEPP, Toulouse, 2006.

*contact with the rebels. I report to my section commander. Determined
to do something even if there is precious little hope, he writes a letter
and has it delivered by an Ivorian go-between.*

*The letter says: 'You captured a girl this afternoon. Her parents
are very worried. Free her before nightfall. That would be the act of a
soldier.'*

*Briefed on the story, the entire section is awaiting the rebels' reac-
tion. Time passes... Three hours later a vehicle approaches. A civilian
gets out with the young girl. He is holding the letter sent by our section
commander, to which a note has been added.*

*'To French commander "X". He is bringing back the girl you
spoke about. Forgive us for this mistake, something came over us.'
Signed: Post commander MPCI.*

*The family are overjoyed to have the girl back safe and sound. The
parents are very moved, and confess that they never expected to see
their daughter again. An unexpected moment of humanity in this violent environment.*

There are many aspects of the principle of behaving in an exemplary
manner. The above account illustrates the attachment of this section commander to the principles that govern his actions, and the hope that his convictions might in part be shared by an adversary who up to that point had
shown themselves to be unscrupulous. The outcome is reassuring: the initiative of the French outpost commander generated respect from a combatant who was operating within an ethical framework at the opposite
extreme of the standards being defended. With the phrase "That would be
the gesture of a soldier", he gave his adversary the opportunity to raise
himself up to the same level and express his humanity and honour. In all
men, however different they may be, there are common sources of humanity, which can meet if they are sometimes just given a chance.

WHAT CAN BE DEDUCED FROM THIS?

The sergeant in the above account applied the example-setting strategy
I advocate when using force, which is applied by implementing the two
preceding principles. It is a matter of demonstrating that, in every aspect
of the exercise of force – the preservation of what is moral, the earning of
legitimacy, operational success, and respect for the law – there is more to
be gained by being exemplary than by being violent. The reaction of
General Aydiid's Somali troops after the battles in Mogadishu strikingly
demonstrates that this principle is positively contagious, including when
faced with adversaries who seemingly lack any moral principles. Being

exemplary translates into the ability and the commitment to respect all the principles of behaviour, come what may. It attests to the degree of moral strength attained by a unit. The sometimes underestimated potential of the moral strength of a unit of men, faced by enemy who may be less scrupulous, is a major element in gaining the upper hand. Through his example, this young post commander, sure of his reasoning and his rectitude, morally dominated the will of his adversary and won the day.

This excellent example must not serve to hide the difficulty which the search for exemplary behaviour can entail, when acting within a coalition or beside an ally who does not necessarily understand things in the same way. This captain of the 27th battalion of the Alpine Infantry gives us an insight into this, and food for thought.

Eyewitness account

Afghanistan – May 2009

On 6 May, the COP [1] furthest up the Alasay valley came under frontal attack in the early hours of the morning. In a largely uncoordinated and poorly prepared manoeuvre, the insurgents attempted to inflict losses on the coalition forces, deployed in defensive positions the day before. So great was the disparity of forces, that the attackers were repulsed within thirty minutes, leaving them barely time to collect their dead. But before fleeing, they were able to fire some rockets close to positions jointly held by several of my sections and the Afghan national army. The Afghan personnel, having spotted shots being fired from a village 1,500 metres away, trained the guns of their T55 tanks on a number of houses in the village, without seeking to determine whether they were really sheltering insurgents. The second in command of the Kandak [2] told me that the next time there was an attack from that village, they would open fire on the designated houses and destroy the settlement. When I pointed out that he risked killing innocent villagers, he replied that was not something he needed to take into account. If we were fired upon from the village, he said, it was because the inhabitants were allies of the Taliban, and they would be punished as a consequence.

Faced with this rather questionable logic, I again tried to explain to him the disadvantages of acting like that. Doing so risked entering into a vicious circle, by creating more insurgents than government sympathisers. He gave the well-worn reply that we French did not understand anything about Afghans, and that in such circumstances,

---

1. Combat Observation Post.
2. Regiment of the Afghan army.

we had to use force. 'The mission of the coalition troops is to support us. Consequently, if they fire, we must fire back, and the inhabitants will respect us even more.' When I asked my interpreter what he thinks, he answers along similar lines: 'They are all Taliban in that village, you must shoot.'

Fortunately, we took no more fire from the village before that particular Kandak was relieved.

The ethical question raised by this account is whether the principle of respecting cultural differences can legitimise an action that runs counter to the moral values we wish to defend. Although certain values are recognised as universal, this example proves that it is nevertheless difficult to advocate this universality in the field, with soldiers or populations confronted each and every day with the cruelty of war. In Afghanistan, the mission of the military in the coalition is to support the Afghan national security forces in resolving their own conflict, but the desire to see our concept of morality adopted in combat seems sometimes to pass for misplaced pride, or even weakness, and can be badly perceived by our Afghan allies. French advisors, therefore, sometimes finds themselves with nothing to offer when faced with soldiers living alongside death and who may have had members of their own families murdered during Afghanistan's thirty years of war. Such advisors therefore need to demonstrate great strength of character, and an equally strong nobility of spirit, if they are to retain their ability to decide what is right.

Drawing on these harsh realities, the strategy of example advocated in this chapter leads to a respect for one's adversary, however he acts. It is not a sign of weakness, because it does not preclude reacting with all the force necessary to fulfil the mission, when the time is right to do so. Respecting your adversary and making him aware of your respect, shows that you consider him to be your equal and offers him the chance to raise his dignity – and his honour – to the level of those who are set before him as examples. It is important not to forget that in affecting the enemy, one also has an impact on the population, whose opinion of you is sometimes acquired from the enemy. As we have already made clear, mission success in stabilisation operations relies on the capability of the contingents deployed to win the support of the population. This objective becomes all the more important the longer the operation lasts. The use of force by foreign troops who impose themselves in the midst of the people must therefore be irreproachable. The success of the mission is conditioned by the image they project and by their standard of behaviour. More generally, it is now a well-established fact that the legitimacy of the entire intervention itself can be called into question, if the way the operation is conducted deviates not only from the law, but also from a certain morality, which is, by its very nature, more demanding.

Before concluding this section on exemplarity, I would like to extend the purview with a marvellous account dating the time of Dien Bien Phu [1] during the war in Indochina. It shows that despite the extreme severity of the battles that occurred, there is always a place for exemplarity, when demonstrated by exceptional men. It also shows that *positive contamination* might simply be called *recognition*.

EYEWITNESS ACCOUNT [2]

Dien Bien Phu – 31 March 1954

2 company of the 8th Choc retakes the hill Dominique II at the cost of a superhuman effort. The Viets fall back, completely routed. Sergeant Franceschi and Private 1st class Froissard from the second assault, having reached the summit, head for the mortar emplacements hoping to find some shells to fire at the fleeing enemy. On the way, they come across a wounded Viet. His AP [3] and a map case show that he is an NCO. The sergeant sees that is a cân-bô, or political commissar, the worst type of Vietminh.

Froissard does not beat about the bush.

"Do we finish him off Sergeant?"

"No! He is wounded, and we do the same for him as for anyone else who is wounded. Put a dressing on him."

"Even when we haven't enough as it is?"

"Do what I tell you, there are enough dead around us for you to find one."

The dressing is applied, the sergeant takes the map case, and especially the AP – a P08 Luger, a real prize.

The French are then ordered to fall back immediately, since the position cannot be held. The Viets are preparing a counter-attack. As they depart, Franceschi and Froissard think no more of the wounded commissar. But there is no question he has had a good look at them.

---

1. Account provided by the regimental history officer of the 8th RPIMa, to whom the author addresses his sincere thanks.
2. Account by Colonel Paul Franceschi (retd) 8th Choc [8e Bataillon de parachutistes coloniaux - The 8th battalion of colonial paratroops was known as the 8th Choc.]
3. Automatic pistol.

Mid-May 1954.

The camp dug in at Dien Bien Phu has fallen and almost the entire garrison is dragging itself along the road into captivity. The men are exhausted, and many of them ill. Any stragglers are abandoned where they fall. They are given no treatment, but simply left to die.

Sergeant Franceschi and Private 1ˢᵗ class Froissard, whose face has been injured, are still together. At the Black River, as the column of captives prepares to wade across, a jeep carrying Vietminh officers becomes stuck in the mud. A number of prisoners are sent to push the vehicle. Froissard points out to his fellow prisoner that one of the Viet officers bears a strong resemblance to the cân-bô they left with a dressing on Dominique II some weeks before. What's more, he is looking in their direction. Froissard, who had suggested 'finishing off' the Viet is afraid he'll be recognised. The sergeant reassures him: 'Don't worry. Not with that wound on your face. He won't recognise you.' On the other hand, the tall NCO does not pass unnoticed. He can see that the commissar has recognised him. Certain events inevitably leave their mark.

Late May 1954.

The prisoners are still walking. Froissard is managing all right, but the sergeant is ill, and walks with increasing difficulty. One afternoon he collapses. His companion tries to pull him to his feet again, but is not strong to raise the heavy body. Two guards come running up, and shoo Froissard away from his fallen companion. Froissard continues his march with a heavy heart.

Franceschi knows he is finished. He knows how it is. But against all expectations, as he prepares to meet his end, he notices some villagers coming towards him. One of the guards tells them to carry him to a hut. There, to his immense surprise, he is cared for, fed and left to rest until he is able to resume the march.

Years later, though he cannot prove it, Colonel Franceschi remains convinced that he was not treated like that by accident. Viet soldiers do not take that kind of initiative. The only explanation is that the cân-bô, having recognised him, issued an order. He, in turn, had saved Franceschi's life.

Exemplary behaviour, when elevated to the level of a strategy for action, also has an internal application which, though more traditional, is no less inseparable from the exercise of command. For the commander, the notion of setting an example, in the widest sense of the term, impinges on every area of daily life when in contact with subordinates: dress, attitude, competence, equity, style of command. Indeed, building on the theory taught in training, one's individual standards of behaviour are forged with reference to the yardstick of the example set by one's direct superiors. The first leaders one meets, often during the course of initial training, have a lasting influence on the moral standards of the men under their command.

Concern for his own dignity leads the commander to cultivate an exemplary attitude, which alone is capable of suggesting to the subordinate what his own attitude might be. The discipline and rigour he imposes on himself unconsciously encourages his subordinates to organise their lives in his image. But what is true in the positive direction is also true in the negative direction. Thus a temperamental leader, or one who lacks self-control, has every chance of unconsciously transmitting his faults to his subordinates, up to the point of depriving the unit he commands of the self-possession and harmony needed for action. How a leader behaves and the image of himself he projects will either consolidate or undermine his authority. [1]

Although the leader may exercise his authority and convey his ethics verbally, he conveys it all the more by the example he sets. In offering himself as a model, he is able to demonstrate that the ideal to strive for is achievable. The example he sets, even if not expressed verbally, is the most powerful instructor known. It is school of life, where teaching is by deed, always more convincing than words.

From then on, subordinates who witness actions and behaviour that can be appreciated for what they are, and who see the consequences for themselves, naturally develop a high degree of empathy with their commander. This imitation of behaviour enables doubts to be erased in those areas where education is lacking, and helps forge those certainties which the men rightly need most, moral certainties included. *Conviction comes from acting through empathy.*

That is why being a good leader requires rigour at all times. The least of his daily actions that causes him to deviate from his general rule, even in a trivial way, leads him off the straight and narrow, despite being held up as the reference point in every respect. The commander's behaviour has the greatest impact during operational missions, because it is precisely then that the leader confirms his legitimacy in the eyes of the men he commands. He owes it to himself to be particularly well prepared for this.

---

1. The exercise of command in the [French] army, 1993.

The five-star retired general Bertrand de La Presle confided to the officers at the Coëtquidan training schools how he prepared himself before leaving for a mission.

> *Before each one of my missions abroad, whether in Algeria, Lebanon or the former Yugoslavia, I always took care to arrange for a quiet place where I could shut myself away, so as to try to forge for myself a very firm personal conviction about my behaviour when faced, inevitably, with the risk of my standards slipping.*
>
> *And the notion of respect for mankind was obviously at the core of these resolutions, which I believe I was able to keep.*

In potentially destabilising operational circumstances, the exemplary model learned in peacetime is crucial. The necessity for the trust that arises from emulating the commander becomes even greater as the situation becomes more difficult. The expectations that subordinates have of their commander increase and he becomes the fixed point to which the men can hold fast at all times. The commander is someone to whom they can always turn. He represents normality in the face of absurdity and lack of meaning. He is an intangible rallying point in times of isolation. He doggedly explains the objective of the mission and ceaselessly gives meaning to what they are doing.

Thus, to him who is truly up to the measure of his task, to him who establishes his authority by example, his men will reply with trust and will tend to model their conduct on his. It is by following the ethical and exemplary path that the commander will be recognised as a model and a reference point. Moreover, that will give him the highest moral satisfaction, and will often be his greatest reward.

Whether directed outwards – adversary, population, troops, allies – or whether it applies to his own men, the strategy of setting an ethical example is not a long tranquil river; the possibilities of failure are numerous. Full knowledge of the risks and of how to avoid them – or to confront them – are the best ways to avoid giving in or being contaminated.

CHAPTER 3

THE CONTAMINATION OF FEELINGS

The battle within man is harsher than the battle between men.

Arthur Rimbaud

I N 2007, Doctor Patrick Clervoy, a senior professor of psychiatry and medical psychology, published an instructive article in the magazine *Inflexion* [1], about the events that occurred in Abu Ghraib prison in Iraq (the main points of his article are reproduced in Appendix 2). In it, he recalls that everyone has within him the same potential for brotherhood as for hate. Caught up in the extreme conditions of his commitment, a soldier can show himself at his best, as well as at his worst.

The facts are incontestable: the military personnel implicated in the Abu Ghraib scandal were *normal* individuals. Amongst them there were people who had behaved in a highly moral way up to that point, but the situation in which they had been placed inexorably led them astray. Something had truly *uncoupled their moral sense*. The soldier at war will always be liable to be overwhelmed by passion, a feeling of revenge, and the appeal of cruelty. In armies worthy of the name, it is right to require those who exercise command, at every level, to contain possible excesses of passion by their subordinates; for similar but more important reasons, it is essential that they prevent themselves using such excesses as a way of dramatically increasing their fervour in combat. The first eyewitness account entitled *Choice* provided an excellent illustration of this. It reminded us of the essence of the profession of arms, namely the responsibility

---

1. *Inflexion* is a forum for exchanges between civilians and the military, published by the French army. The article cited appeared in Issue 7, entitled *Le moral et la dynamique de l'action – Partie II*, [Morality and the Dynamic of Action - Part II] La Documentation française, 2007.

that the leader accepts for the use of force and the management of lethal risk. This commitment obliges him to answer alone for his decisions.

But the leader also has another responsibility, that of answering for the actions of his men. General de Maud'hui [1], whose testimony on command stands as a reference point, expressed this principle as follows: "Always stand by your subordinates when they have carried out, or believed they have carried out, your orders. "

As has been previously stated, this maxim is even more relevant in the French armed forces, where the lower ranks have considerable autonomy. This practice is founded on mutual confidence: the confidence the leader has in his subordinates to understand precisely what is expected from the mission, and the confidence the subordinate has in his superiors to stand by the choices he makes. Initiative, participation, respect for the same values and the mastery of force are not simply intellectual concepts, but shared principles for action, starting in peacetime.

However, having the confidence of one's commander and having the freedom of action stemming from such confidence, does not free the subordinate from his own responsibility. On this subject, everyone serving in the French armed forces is familiar with the Article of the General Statute [2] committing him to obedience, while simultaneously granting him the possibility, even the duty, of not executing an illegal order, because doing so would be contrary to the law.

Article 8

Armed forces personnel owe obedience to the orders of their superiors and are responsible for the missions with which they are entrusted.

However, they cannot be ordered to undertake, and must not undertake, missions which are contrary to law, to the customs of war and to international conventions.

This important feature of the Statute gives the serviceman or woman the right of 'non-obedience'. But it is essential to understand that while, in one respect, Article 8 protects the subordinate, it *de facto* reinforces individual responsibility. That is why, whatever the orders he or she may be given, everyone in the armed forces is recognised as fully responsible for their actions before the law and national and international conventions.

---

1. General de Maud'hui (1857-1921) left his "testimony on the subject of command" to the officers and non-commissioned officers of his regiment. The text, which retains much of its topicality, is reproduced as an appendix.
2. Article 8 of the General Statute of Armed Forces Personnel, codified as article @ 4122 of the Defence Code.

This essential feature of the Statute requires that everyone in the armed forces, of whatever rank, is capable of judging his actions and those of his equals. In other words, he must be capable of acquiring **his own autonomy of ethical judgement.** It is imperative that the soldier forges for himself his own ability to discriminate, before being picked for an operational mission. Such autonomy of ethical judgement is built not only by reference to legal benchmarks, but also to benchmarks derived from various studies of professional and personal ethics, which enable the soldier's thinking to go beyond what the rules specifically lay down. Before the commander leads his men into combat, he is entirely responsible for the effectiveness of the instruction he gives.

Today, there are still too many unacceptable violations of the principles of good behaviour in combat. We must have the courage to spot them, to acknowledge them and, finally, to learn as much as we can from them. This is precisely what this chapter proposes doing: to have an impact on thinking by drawing on real-life examples, some of which describe deviant behaviour. On each occasion, those who carried out the acts were severely punished by the military authorities. They were also punished by the law whenever it had been broken. We gain in moral stature by acknowledging our weaknesses, and it would be an act of cowardice not to draw lasting lessons from these incidents.

Mankind can and must be understood through our past, but our real interests lie only in our evolution and our future. It is in such a spirit that a commander must react when faced with transgressive behaviour: with the lucidity of knowing that no-one is immune from such acts being witnessed and with the determination to do everything to prevent them taking place or recurring.

*

* *

1. The loss of points of reference... which leads to deviant behaviour

> *Victory over oneself is the greatest of victories.*
>
> Plato

Losing one's points of reference is the main risk faced by the combatant immersed in a violent environment. When a soldier loses his points of reference, he irredeemably loses his legitimacy.

EYEWITNESS ACCOUNT [1]

Côte d'Ivoire: Rioters attack a French post

For almost four days and three nights we have been under attack by an out-of-control crowd. They are trying to break into our camp and indulge in looting and atrocities.

The very well-organised rioters have used every possible weapon – apart from weapons of war – to injure and try to kill the men defending the entrance to the camp. Violently thrown stones and ball bearings, shotgun rounds, assaults with iron bars, machetes, etc. Many men have been wounded, some seriously. Despite successive changeovers, the units are exhausted and I fear an escalation which could degenerate into even more violent clashes.

This morning, we sense that our aggressors are as exhausted as we are and on the verge of lifting their siege. The assaults are becoming less frequent, but increasingly violent. Fortunately we have obtained some defence dogs, and they are very effective.

A new attack is launched, one of the most aggressive so far. Too repel the attackers, the defending unit mounts a charge in response. The dogs are released. The assailants pull back. There are a number seriously wounded on each side. Several of the rioters are lying on the ground, lifeless.

As they retreat, one soldier takes advantage of his commander's momentary inattention, pulls the pin out of a hand grenade and tosses it at an inanimate body on the ground. The grenade explodes. It is clear what has taken place and who the culprit is. A few seconds pass in silence, then, as the crowd again prepares to attack, our men withdraw into the base.

The units are reorganised and a changeover takes place. I immediately call for the unit commander. I want to deal with the soldier's unacceptable act. The commander's initial reaction shows that he has lost his capacity for judgement. To my comments, he retorts in an aggravated tone, "They only got what they deserved!"

I interrupt him and take him aside. I remind him of the terms of his mission and forcefully make him see sense, recalling the elementary principles of respect for life and dignity. I continue, explaining to him the importance of correct behaviour in the 'management of the aftermath', which, apart from short-term emotion, involves weighing up the consequences of every action.

---

1. Account taken from *Le Code d'honneur en action, Opération Licorne au 2ᵉ REP (Régiment Étranger de Parachutistes)* ['The Code of Honour in Action' Operation Unicorn and the Second Parachute Regiment of the Foreign Legion], Preface by Colonel E. Maurin, SEPP, Toulouse, 2006.

After listening to me in silence, the captain realises his mistake and soon rediscovers his capacity for discernment.

He rejoins his unit and sets about disciplining this serious offence.

The soldier concerned was immediately relieved of his duties, severely punished and repatriated to France within a few days.

The unstructured environment in which the serviceman operates in times of crisis or war, can lead him to modify the framework of his peacetime system of reference. With the collapse of the normal distinctions between what is 'good' and what is 'bad', he may be prompted to alter his behaviour, whether consciously or not.

Isolation and being confronted with human distress, flagrant injustice and lack of respect for international conventions lead to serious mental disturbance and to the disruption of the standards on which individual morality is built. From then on, a feeling of revolt gains the upper hand, the boundaries defining what is forbidden become blurred, and cracks appear in the reference frame of human dignity.

In such circumstances the soldier is by nature inclined to intervene. He feels a willingness to act, strengthened by dint of being trained for action and by thinking that he can have a direct effect on the course of events. His action is all the more motivated because it appears to him to be legitimate, in view of the cruelty and injustice of the situations he witnesses. It is precisely for this reason, when all these conditions coalesce, that there is a risk of his behaviour departing from the rules of conduct hitherto constituting his frame of reference.

Yet the French soldier who is sent on operations has been specially trained and instructed to respect, through his actions, the values defended by his country. As the standard bearer of these values, he draws his legitimacy from the trust placed in him. As soon as he loses his ability to reason and to act in accordance with these standards, the grounds for his presence become questionable and his legitimacy effectively evaporates. He loses it in the eyes of the country whose colours he wears, he loses it in the eyes of the population among whom he is operating, and he risks compromising the legitimacy of the entire operation

HOW NOT TO LOSE ONE'S POINTS OF REFERENCE

* ***By recurrent ethical education***

> *A distinction must be made between education of the intellect and instruction. Whilst the latter supplies knowledge, the former shapes the mind and develops character.*

> Former French tactics course, 1922

Along with technical skills, life skills are the inseparable counterpart of individual instruction. They make up the 'education' element which today forms a large part of the syllabus for training officers, non-commissioned officers and other ranks. Life skills define daily behaviour in the exercise of the profession, the style of which must govern the relationships between commanders and subordinates. As well as knowledge of international conventions, acquisition of these life skills involves training in behaviour and moral education appropriate to the culture of the French soldier.

The requirement for ethical teaching at every level of the hierarchy is reinforced in our armed forces by the significant operational autonomy devolved to subordinate levels during mission execution. It is one of the strengths of the French system of command. The requirement for soundly based training is reinforced by the sociological changes characteristic of the young men and women who today put themselves forward for recruitment. These changes reflect the crisis of the common good, abandoned in favour of individual self-fulfilment. The sense of duty has given way to the defence of individual rights. A sense of service and of doing things without financial recompense is not widespread. However, education in collective values finds an echo in these young people in search of meaning. In fact, to claim that today's youth is individually less moral than their parents would be rash and almost certainly false. On the other hand, there has been an undeniable decline in the value of morality in society, both in theory and in practice. Without passing a value judgement on this change, I am forced to conclude that it is not leading toward the strengthening of social links. But the nature of the missions entrusted to the army involves the establishment of solidarity around a strong moral framework, to which every member freely adheres.

These life skills have long been handed down without being formalised. They were born out of what our forebears lived through and out of their humanity, forged in the heat of combat. They were skills nourished by the experience of the situations these men lived through and by their willingness to prepare others to confront – and if possible to avoid – situations of suffering. This training is difficult, for it is based on convictions that are more 'felt' than being clearly delineated, even though some officers have committed their experiences to paper. The compilation entitled *Réflexions sur l'éthique du chef militaire* [Reflections on the ethics of the military leader] edited by General de la Motte in 1981, while commanding the cavalry and armour training school in Saumur, is one such example. He tackles the subject of ethics with a very broad canvas, in times of peace as in times of war, providing a compilation of the main documents and writings on military ethics in the widest sense of the term.

- ***In the Army***

More recently, the French army has equipped itself with a body of dense and substantial texts for trainers to draw on. I would first of all cite *Exercising the Profession of Arms in the Army: Fundamentals and Principles*. This volume has allowed new professional soldiers to acquire a philosophical and ethical foundation in particular, capable of giving meaning to their actions and of inspiring their behaviour when faced with the chaotic character of the new situations confronting them. This work is complemented by the *Soldier's Code*, more accessible for the lower ranks, along the lines of the older *Legionnaire's Code*. Both these are reproduced as appendices.

Then, at the initiative of General B. Thorette, at that time chief of staff of the French army, these texts were completed by a compendium entitled *The Exercise of Command in the Army,* which deals with subjects related to and closely linked to ethics. Ownership of these documents by all those in the army is aimed at making these principles operative. All these are available as teaching materials for instructors in training establishments and regiments. General J.-R. Bachelet was one of the main editors. His many lectures and his personal involvement made a huge contribution to moving minds and behaviours forward. His writings have been gathered together in a book entitled *For an Ethic of the Profession of Arms* (published by Vuibert, May 2006), several extracts from which are reproduced in the following pages.

Over and above these reference works, a centre of excellence, Military Ethics and Deontology, was created in 2004 at the officer training schools, in the research centre at Coëtquidan, and is the core of the network of schools radiating throughout France and overseas. The creation of a 'research centre' on the same theme, directed by Professor Henri Hude, a philosopher, shows that training in this field today is not only ambitious but also, to some extent, proselytising.

Through these commitments, it is possible to prepare people's minds and to inscribe on their consciences strong convictions that will become the points of reference they can draw on in difficult situations.

Eyewitness account

A general confesses

I am a war criminal. I was directly involved in and complicit in a shocking massacre in 1992.

Having received the order to seize a settlement held by a rebel movement, I mounted an assault with two regiments, preceded by an artillery barrage worthy of the greatest moments of the Warsaw Pact. Right in the centre of town, without warning, on a civilian population. They were literally executed.

Happily it was an exercise.

Nevertheless I did do it

I was a young captain.

At the time, I was in charge of directing an exercise. I was in command of two regiments belonging to a division within the headquarters of the Rapid Action Force [1] (FAR), which had come to train for planning and commanding operations.

The details of the situation matter little. Just bear in mind that it unfolded in a typical African country (known as Green) dominated by a majority ethnic group. Taking advantage of a crisis, a neighbouring country (referred to as Carmin) had treacherously re-activated a rebellion. There was an insurrection in the province. We were perhaps not in a situation of outright war between the two nations, but it was at least the beginnings of a civil war, with the more or less overt participation of the neighbouring country. The French troops, at the request of Green, had deployed to try and calm things down.

At first, the exercise unfolded uneventfully.

Then, one evening, the directing staff simulating enemy forces announced that it wanted to wreck the FAR's plan – FAR was on exercise – in order to force its headquarters staff to carry out another complete emergency planning cycle. It was therefore essential that the situation, which we were bringing to life through our reporting from the field, would make the FAR aware of a major divergence from their operational plan and thus launch a new planning cycle.

It was therefore decided that the two regiments I was simulating would get into difficulty at the entrance to town P, necessitating a long manoeuvre – skirting, careful approach, attempt at negotiation –

---

1. The Rapid Action Force [Force d'Action Rapide – FAR] was an army corps created in 1984, in the context of the reorganization of the French army. It was intended for rapid deployment into external theatres of operation in the event of crisis. It was disbanded in 1999.

made to last all day, thus causing a delay of about 10 hours to the current movement plan and obliging the force to come up with a new one.

As agreed, we spent all the following day 'spicing things up', imperceptibly at first, then more and more obviously. At the crossroads controlling entry to the town of P, I reported observing the presence of armoured vehicles surrounded by a crowd, the origins of which it was impossible to determine, given the distance I was observing from. With the aim of 'providing accurate intelligence', I made the fun last all day, while having to put up with increasing irritation at the end of the line whenever I made a report. I stressed the wisdom of caution, specifying that in this manoeuvre we were still not in a situation of declared hostilities, and that neither party had opened fire on anyone. So prudence was not unrealistic in this context.

In the course of the evening, divisional headquarters staff became increasingly irritated and a colonel from the FAR gave me a really hard time on the radio "Must crack on!", "It's taking much too long!", "We're holding up the whole FAR!" No good arguing; he told me in words of one syllable that he had decided to 'get stuck in' and that I would have the benefit of massive multiple launch rocket support. That would sort out the problem and allow entry into the town. "Now we move into the attack – that's final!", he said, slamming the phone down.

Finally convinced I should obey, I went and saw the gunnery officer in the room next door. He was already on his feet, holding the telephone handset and looking at me with a broad grin. "It's done! I've just fired 12 salvoes of multiple-launch rockets! That ought to do the trick!"

It only remained for me to move my regiments on to the attack after the rocket launch, but I still had some hours to make up. I decided to transform the conquest of P into a humanitarian drama, and in order to treat the population of P, devastated by the artillery fire, I asked for the deployment of all the doctors and aid posts at my disposal.

During dinner, I mulled over what I had done. I had mounted an assault on a township, on an unarmed population, preceded by massive, even frenzied, artillery fire. In the real world, if that had really happened, there would have been a terrible massacre.

When I got back to business the next morning, the pressure had eased completely. The FAR was fully engaged in making a new plan and the situation was calm. At one point during the morning, someone quietly came and sat down next to me. He was a commodore, and was there as the observer from the chief of the armed forces. He didn't beat

about the bush. "Yesterday, the artillery fire unleashed on the popula-
tion of P, was that you?" "Yes, sir." "Tell me about it." While he took
notes, I told him the whole story. He asked me some questions of detail,
but made no comments, then left without further ado.

At the end of the exercise, a day or so later, the hot debrief took
place in the FAR command post. During the usual congratulations
about the excellence of the results, a discordant voice was raised,
asked for the floor, and abruptly poured cold water on everything.

It was the commodore representing the chief of the armed forces,
and he began by examining the politico-military consequences of the
force's action. And he did so mercilessly. In essence, he said, "Perhaps
the FAR's manoeuvre was splendid, but an action such as the destruc-
tion of P is a strategic defeat of the first order. We wanted to convince
those of ethnic Orange origin that their future lay in cooperating with
country Green. All they will remember of a humanitarian drama such
as occurred at P is that we liberated the province by massacring its
inhabitants. Gentlemen, I tell you that if we were in the real world, at
the present time the military victory in the field would count for little
when set against the media storm that would have been unleashed over
us. What's more, some of you would be liable to be indicted by an inter-
national criminal court to answer for your actions." End of message.

The psychological impact of such harsh criticism can easily be
imagined, coming as it did from the representative of the most senior
of all military officers, in public and in the final session.

Major-General Yakovleff, the author of this statement, concludes his
account by drawing from this revealing experience some lessons as to the
occasional lack of realism in training programmes.

It was only an exercise. But psychologically I found myself in the
position of a military commander subjected to great pressure, and
obliged to get a result, by whatever means. I am pleased to have expe-
rienced this situation while on exercise, and not in the real world. It is
a lesson I have never forgotten.

Later, I drew inspiration from it during my different training
appointments. I routinely introduced a concrete ethical issue into
every exercise. I arranged that a situation would deliberately get out
of control, so that the commanders would be obliged to think things
through on a level other than tactical theory. That allowed the develop-
*ment of what I call **ethical vigilance**. I realised that we were engaged*
in ethical teaching, unquestionably of a high standard, but once the
main principles had been specified, the lessons learned never had to
confront tactical reality in the field. There was an obvious lack of

pragmatism. For what use is an ethical sense, if it is only assimilated, even unconsciously, as a subject for seminars, and not as a continuous obligation, intrinsic to military action?

Consequently, the idea is that during every exercise, the personnel undergoing training tell themselves repeatedly that it is cannot be ruled out that a situation will imperceptibly veer towards the unacceptable. It is of the utmost importance that that they become aware of this shift and know how to forestall it. The commander owes it to himself to remain ever vigilant, so as to identify the moment when the situation might tip over into ignominy, not through insensitivity, but by mistake. This would not simply be a failure of training, but a potential disaster.

* ***In the air force***

In the Air Force Officer Training Schools (AFOTS), where the human sciences are most developed, much thought has been given about how best to teach ethics. As a result the time spent on this subject has been doubled, both in formal academic lessons and in instilling the moral codes every officer needs in his daily tasks. Indeed it is evident that, over and above lectures, ethics cannot be taught without continuous application in the realms of military, sporting, academic, social, traditional and family activities.

The lectures are entitled *Ethics and Command*. Moreover, it is not by chance that they are partly taught by the Training for Command division and by lecturer-researchers from the Air Force Research Centre. The schools attach great importance to showing that ethics is not just one academic subject among others, but that it is directly linked to the exercise of command. It must therefore inform every action in the lives of those in the military. There is an ethical dimension to all teaching, even special events such as the annual seminar on the law of armed conflict. Ethics is incorporated into most of the teaching, for it is a subject which requires an understanding of concepts that may be variously philosophical, sociological, ethnological, historical and religious as well as purely military, taught by the requisite specialists.

At the same time as they are assimilating moral rules of behaviour through the various courses they take, AFOTS students receive theoretical instruction that enables them to refine their understanding of moral concepts, ethics and deontology. With the help of these elements as a whole, they will be optimally qualified to make choices that live up to the expectations of the institution and of the country they have committed themselves to serve, while at the same time not repudiating their own opinions. [1]

---

1. Author's interview with the senior officer responsible for ethics training at the AFOTS.

Ethics as taught at the air force schools is formalised through a set of standards, such as 'ethical' codes, and rules contained within disciplinary regulations or in other regulatory texts.

This teaching generates a certain homogeneity of thought, thereby contributing to efficiency when those in the military act as a group, in a situation that has deteriorated. However, recourse to a 'checklist' of imperatives is not viewed as a solution in itself. Ethics is approached from more complex standpoints, such as the difficulty of overcoming the tension between the specificity of the profession of arms – killing, causing others to kill, dying, causing others to die – and Judaeo-Christian and popular morality, with their rejection of death, especially if violent and deemed unnecessary. The schools try to answer the questions raised by their students who, confronted by increasingly complex environments, are very often in search of meaning. As well as being aware of the meaning of their commitment, the students must also ask themselves questions about the meaning of the operations they are called on to lead.

The teaching of ethics in these schools is therefore largely aimed at making the serviceman or woman a 'good' leader: honest, responsible, exemplary and human. As such, ethics applied to command is taught mainly by using concrete examples from ancient and contemporary military history, with a view to illustrating theoretical concepts that are sometimes difficult to understand.

Ultimately, the teaching of ethics at the AFOTS strikes a balance between a varied theoretical component and a cross-disciplinary approach encompassing the widest possible range of elements, allowing in-depth personal reflection by each future officer.

- *In the navy*

As in the other services, ethics is a recurrent theme in the thinking and studies of the navy. Symposia, written works and press articles regularly deal with the subject. In the naval academy, the teaching covers two complementary themes: "The ethics of the military sailor: understanding the values on which the actions of the service person are based and the specificities of the navy, as well as life on board ship " in the first year and "The ethics of command: developing thinking about the military leader within the organisation and the society to which he belongs " in the second year.

Beyond the training schools as such, the attention given to this topic is reflected in a comprehensive and well documented special issue of the Naval Studies Bulletin titled, *The Sailor's Ethics.* Open equally to testimonies from service personnel and contributions from civil society, it opens with an in-depth interview with Michel Serres [1], who gives his views on the main aspects of ethics in war.

The main problem facing the military man is that he is ordered to:
"Kill! You must kill!" In every instance since Abraham, the rule is:
"You absolutely must not kill!". And it is the military man who must be
the exception to the rule "You absolutely must not kill!" He may even
become a hero for having killed.

[...]

What is war? There is no question about it: war is a lawful occu-
pation. It is a lawful entity. War is declared, follows a particular law
of the people and comes to an end by means of an armistice or the
signing of a peace treaty. It is therefore framed by rules of law. If you
take away that law, it is no longer war. You are no longer a combatant,
you are in a state of violence by everyone against everyone.

In the navy, ethical thinking is particularly well developed amongst
the officers in charge of nuclear armed ballistic missile submarines
(SSBN), responsible for the launch of nuclear weapons on the orders of
the President of the Republic. It is indispensable that each SSBN commander has conducted personal in-depth ethical reflection, before taking
command, so as not to fail on the day he is asked to implement the nuclear
firing sequence. One such officer, Admiral François Dupont, captain (C)
of the SSBN *Triomphant* in January 1995, spoke about this with Stéphane
Deligeorges (S), a distinguished scientist and journalist at *France Culture*
radio, when setting out on a mission in the Iroise Sea.

S. Let's come back to the role and place of the captain. How can
one experience the huge responsibility of launching a nuclear strike
and causing thousands of deaths, without it preying on one's mind?

C. That takes us to the heart of the matter, doesn't it?

S. Exactly.

C. Please allow me a somewhat lengthy reply, but this point is
worth the effort, because it takes us to the core of what constitutes the
military profession. I'll begin by reassuring you, by saying that one
does not accept this responsibility without it preying on one's mind, or
rather without fully appreciating the force whose possible use is
entrusted to us. We are entrusted with this responsibility by the Presi-
dent of the Republic – therefore by the state and the French people –
so that its way of life, even its survival can be preserved. The nature of
this mission is no different, whether one is commanding a SSBN or, as
today, trying to re-establish peace in Yugoslavia.

S. I don't see the connection between the two.

---

1. Historian of philosophy and science, member of the Académie Française.

C. In the one case you are deterring a serious and lethal attack against the vital interests of your country, and in the other you are intervening at the gates of Europe in order to re-establish peace and stability in a country which, because it is the scene of serious disruption, might, in the longer term, also be a threat to us. You will tell me that there are also humanitarian reasons for our intervention. That is quite true, but it should always be remembered that a well run state only is concerned about its own, egotistical, interests. There is therefore great similarity between a submarine on patrol hundreds of nautical miles from France and a light infantryman patrolling the Bosnian border. I would add that these two missions are mutually reinforcing, because when you expose a light infantryman to the situation there, you therefore run the risk of him dying. You demonstrate in this way that you are not sheltering behind protective walls, but that you are clearly intent on defending yourself and that the potential use of your nuclear warheads is real, not just for show.

S. I must insist: the light infantryman might have to use his weapon, but not you, since that would be, as you have already explained, the failure of deterrence.

C. You are both wrong and right at the same time. Wrong, because the French tradition with troops on operations is to make use of one's weapon as late as possible and in that sense the light infantryman is also a deterrent. Right, because with nuclear deterrence every day we manage a somewhat paradoxical situation: that of deploying a heavy and complex weapon system in the hope – and even the conviction – that the ultimate phase, that of weapon delivery, will never take place. But that probable absence of the final phase does not in any way give us the right not to have available a system that cannot, under any circumstances, be deficient.

S. Isn't it very difficult to be the head of a unit which, in the final analysis, will never go into combat?

C. What kind of combat are you talking about? That might be so if you are referring to exchanging salvoes of shells, or launching torpedoes. But if you bear in mind that combat can also be a perfectly executed patrol, undetected by a potential enemy, while getting the best out of everything a high technology platform can offer you, with a weapon system available 24 hours a day, a crew which remains motivated and willing and which also offers you personally a voyage rich in everything the sea can offer, believe me, combat is worth the experience.

S. We seem to be getting into philosophy here.

C. Yes, because the profession of arms cannot be undertaken without very much considering, with the help of philosophy, the place of man in the universe and the sometimes minor tasks with which each of us is entrusted. The SSBN commander is allocated a precise, perfectly defined task, which he cannot challenge without putting in peril the trust placed in him by the nation, itself a sacred cause.

S. *Would you say that you need a certain moral strength to be a SSBN commander?*

C. *Yes, if moral strength is what arises not only from a sense of commitment, of profound convictions, but also from the humility which life teaches you, and if that strength does not prevent you from also taking time to reflect.*

S. *It is either very late or very early, but for the day just starting, Captain, what is your programme?*

C. *To go to maximum depth, a depth much greater than that operated in by French submarines or even by any other western submarines.*

More generally, the French navy bases the development of its ethics on a long historical tradition of fundamental military values, and in close cooperation with land forces, with whom it shares the same perceptions.

The Navy is in complete solidarity with the other armed forces. Regiments of marine infantry fought in the trenches in 1914-18 and in the Leclerc Division in 1944-45. Then in Indochina, with the amphibious forces and embarked aviation dive bombers, and in Algeria with the DBFM [Demi-Brigade des Fusiliers-Marins – Half Brigade of Marine Infantry]. *Nowadays, sailors are side by side with their brothers-in-arms in Special Forces, on external and force projection operations. They are present in every joint organization, in the Defence Intelligence Directorate, the Joint Defence College, and in the major national, European, allied and United Nations headquarters. All this proves our unreserved commitment to the cooperation that has become indispensable for meeting the challenges of our times. And it is evidence of fidelity to the principles of intellectual discipline, one of the main foundations of the Navy's professional ethics* [1].

In all the armed forces, whether land, sea or air, educating one's subordinates in the principles of ethics is an intrinsic part of the commander's responsibilities. It allows him to be sure that his men will carry out his orders in the same frame of mind as his own. He will thus be confident in their ability to judge the significance of their actions, and to appreciate their consequences, and be sure he has done everything possible to pre-

---

1. Admiral Lacoste, extract from an article published in *Bulletin d'Études de la Marine nationale [Navy Studies Bulletin]* and later on the internet site *Regards Citoyens.*

pare them for the use of force, while respecting the principles defended by their country.

War is a state of utter brutality involving physical combat, the violence of which takes place in equal measure outside and within the combatants. Stéphane Audouin-Rouzeau [1] elaborates.

This leads me to make a confession to you, a confession which costs me dear, and which few combatants, for want of self-knowledge, dare make. War has turned us not only into corpses, but made us impotent and blind. It has also, in the midst of worthy acts of sacrifice and self-sacrifice, awoken within us, and sometimes taken to their very extremes, ancient instincts of cruelty and barbarity. For in this context, I am obliged to confess that I – someone who has never thrown a punch at anyone and is horrified by disorder and brutality – that I have taken pleasure in killing.

It happened during a surprise attack, crawling towards the enemy, grenade in hand, dagger between our teeth like assassins, fear gripping our guts, yet driven forward by an inescapable force. We surprised the enemy in their trench. We leapt down onto them, relishing the alarm of those who don't believe in the devil, but who suddenly see him towering over them! That moment of barbarity, that atrocious moment, for us had a unique flavour, a morbid attraction, as with those unfortunates who, using drugs, know the risks, but cannot prevent themselves from taking the poison.

On the same subject, Brigadier General Lecointre's testimony concerning the clash during the retaking of Vrbanja Bridge in Sarajevo in 1995 – reproduced here with his personal comments – once again highlights the importance of troops' ethical education in advance of combat, as an invaluable moral refuge when facing the grim reality of battle.

EYEWITNESS ACCOUNT

Sarajevo – May 1995

I was involved in a separation-of-forces mission at the head of my company in Sarajevo. We arrived in Bosnia at the beginning of May, just as the crisis had again begun to degenerate, despite a tenuous cease-fire that had done little to resolve the political deadlock. From the time my unit arrived, our combat posts was frequently subject to automatic fire and we had a number of seriously wounded men. We were consequently not seeing much combat. Although we were sup-

---

1. *Combattre: une anthropologie historique de la guerre moderne,* [Combat: an historical anthology of modern war], Paris, Ed. du Seuil. Extract cited in *Les guerres modernes expliquées aux civils et aux militaires,* Pierre Servent, Buchet Chastel, 2009.

posed to be defending democracy and human rights, the lack of action made us feel really useless. This feeling lasted until what has been called the 'hostage crisis' began, when the Serbs took a number of men hostage at one of the UN observation posts. At that point, I, with my company, had to retake the observation post now in Serb hands.

I would like to make you understand the great difficulty of being on a separation-of-forces mission, with its theoretical impartiality regarding Serbs and Bosnians. In point of fact, both sides showed equal hostility towards us and made clear they viewed themselves as our enemy. For us, the Serbian forces were unquestionably an enemy, since they had engaged in hostile action against us. Try to imagine our feelings: they are an enemy, but they are still one of the 'belligerents'. We are going to have to retake that observation post but, at the same time, we are not there to avenge our comrades who have been taken hostage. We have to defeat the enemy but, as soon as he has been defeated, he will once again become one of the 'parties present', having the right to our strict impartiality, because we are here to engage in combat 'for democracy and human rights'.

The first problem in a combat action, such as a classic infantry assault, is to conquer one's fear. Accordingly, one carries out tangible tasks, such as fixing the bayonet to the barrel, to give oneself confidence. With this basic and clearly visible piece of equipment in our hands, we'll be able to kill the person facing us.

Conquering one's fear, in fact, entails calling upon a sort of animal nature and violence that lie within oneself. I think it is deeply traumatising. In any case, that's how I experienced it. I felt disgusted with myself on discovering the horrendous bestiality active within me. The violence increased proportionally to the time taken for the assault. It lasted eighteen minutes. An initial rapid charge, and then terrible and interminable work, like in the trenches of the First World War: dislodging the enemy metre by metre.

This feeling of violence that one unleashes within oneself, this animal instinct, this evil that we possess and that possesses us, increases as a result of our wounded and our dead: of the thirty soldiers involved, we have two dead and fourteen seriously wounded.

Later, once this fury has built up, – one even finishes by feeling a sort of pleasure once the fear has passed – it is extremely difficult to stop it and to halt the assault when one considers that the set military objective has been achieved. It is extremely difficult to do, and it is a quite painful experience. One is drunk, one is ashamed, one tries to stop, but one wants to enjoy more of this drunkenness.

How can one stop? How does that work? As General Bachelot used to say, very surprising links are woven throughout shared professional life on operations: these questions and these shared doubts about the meaning of missions engender incredible mutual trust, a sharing, each man almost abandoning himself to the others. One relies on each other, collectively, one to another, and this feeling of absolute mutual dependence makes us a kind of primitive being, which feels and reacts as a single entity. However, within the entity, each person continues to act in an individual way, in accordance with his position, role and responsibilities. This occurs because the leader, at a certain point, manages to make clear that the unleashing of violence must cease. It also occurs because the leader feels obliged to do so: in the eyes of his men, he perceives that there is an ethical demand, which is a collective ethic, an ability to master collectively one's own violence and one's own strength. Because the meaning of our combat depends on it.

In fact, within the military institution, in our units, we engage in genuine education for combat for our men, for ourselves and between ourselves. Without this education for combat, there is no combat that respects our dignity and that subsequently allows us to relaunch an operation and, quite simply, to continue living.

HOW ELSE CAN THE LOSS OF BEARINGS BE PREVENTED?

• **By preparing for the mission in the right way and by strong group cohesion**

> *Moral strengths count for about three quarters in the final result: numerical and material strengths only count for one quarter. Morale and belief amount to more than half of the reality.*
>
> Napoleon Bonaparte

EYEWITNESS ACCOUNT [1]

Côte d'Ivoire. Bouaké Camp, 2003

I remember that evening. We'd been stood down, and I was watching a film with the platoon. During the screening, we heard the noise of a crowd and firearms coming from the road. We were immediately put on alert and the platoon was ready in a few minutes.

---

1. Account taken from *Le Code d'honneur en action* [The code of honour in action], Operation Unicorn and the Second Parachute Regiment of the Foreign Legion, Preface by Colonel E. Maurin, SEPP, Toulouse, 2006.

The situation was very tense: an enormous crowd of demonstrators was trying to invade the camp. The platoon was positioned in a defensive ring at the entrance to the camp. We soon became targets. Projectiles were falling on us – stones, metal nuts, pieces of iron... The man next to me was struck and fell to the ground, and was evacuated. Throughout the night we stood facing the demonstrators, having to put up with insults, a barrage of stones, and tear gas. We had to be regularly sprayed with water due the heat and the tear gas irritating our eyes.

In the morning, the crowd became larger and even more threatening. We were forced to throw offensive hand grenades to disperse it. I have never thrown so many grenades, but there was nothing to be done about it. At ten o'clock we were ordered to charge the crowd. We eventually established a measure of calm and were finally relieved by another unit.

In total, we remained for twenty-six hours without a break at the entrance to the camp. We were exhausted, but happy and proud to have fulfilled our mission and to have kept a cool head. We had been professionals.

In extreme situations, solders tend to draw resources from the strength of the group. Cohesion, friendship and solidarity cultivated as part of the daily routine generate the collective moral strength enabling the unit to endure, hold together and fulfil its mission. We call this the **brotherhood of arms.**

Unit solidarity is created at every level of the chain of command: platoon, company and, finally, regimental. This feeling arises through identifying the common values uniting all the individuals in the group and through the close relationship the commander is establishes with his subordinates. As shown by the previously mentioned account of the command post exercise, it has a direct relationship to effectiveness and performance when on active service.

Performance is undoubtedly at least as much the result of the moral strength of individuals and the groups to which they belong. This moral strength is based on two feelings that everyone has to possess deep within themselves: the feeling of belonging to a human community proud of itself and confident of its ability, and the feeling of a strong sense of responsibility towards comrades, commanders, the army, the nation...

With their self-esteem enhanced in this way, subordinates experience a profound satisfaction in serving, whatever their place in the hierarchy. From this satisfaction there stems the complete fulfilment of the men, the main source of their motivation and their desire to do well, revealing the impetus that can be given by enhancing self-esteem and conferring responsibility.

The desire to do well, catalysed by the spirit of solidarity, allows well-trained troops to surpass themselves. This form of group transcendence is known as *Esprit de corps*, an expression used in the original French by our foreign partners. General Jean-René Bachelet provides a particularly clear account of what it means [1].

Even within the institution of the military, the army remains the place where collective judgement has primacy over individual inclinations. This takes the form of 'esprit de corps', a network of strong relationships which takes the soldier beyond his mere self in the extreme situations confronted with; equally, and for similar reasons, faultless discipline is called for. For all that, superior effectiveness requires individual commitment, initiative, and a sense of responsibility, to the exclusion of any herd instinct or passive, robotic or, above all, fearful attitudes.

The brotherhood of arms, a subtle alchemy of interdependencies that are both horizontal – camaraderie – and vertical, through the exercise of firm, but attentive and benevolent authority, aims to resolve the problem.

The example set by commanders, their skill in the exercise of authority, their personal charisma are, in this respect, the determining factors.

The regiment, under the command of its colonel, is, we have seen, the setting par excellence for this alchemy.

In the way the humblest instances of devotion can come to be recorded as the most striking pages of military history. At the beginning of the last century, doctrine manuals were already evoking this French style of 'esprit de corps' [2].

When campaigning and on operations, esprit de corps is a powerful lever in the hands of commanders who know how to create and sustain it.

Its origin goes back to the humanity's distant past, when families and tribes were forming and were adopting individual signs and symbols to recognise each other, while at the same time forming themsel-

---

1. *Pour une éthique du métier des armes. Vaincre la violence.* [For an ethics of the profession of arms. Conquering violence], Vuibert, 2006.
2. *Les forces morales,* Tactics Course, Volume II, 1922.

ves into a unit. The war cry of the clan and the regimental song, the flag and the insignia by which legions recognised each other have a common origin.

Esprit de corps encourages a competition between units which has, in all wars, has led to countless acts of collective heroism.

Over and above heroism and surpassing oneself, group solidarity helps each soldier to find an anchor in the other, allowing him to retain his balance and not lose the his moral and psychological foundations. In this way he can preserve his capacity for judgement and keep himself from indulging in any excesses of behaviour.

ULTIMATELY, HOW DOES ONE KEEP ONE'S BEARINGS?

- *By keeping one's sense of humanity*

> *Each man is a whole human race, a universal history*
>
> Jules Michelet

The grandeur of humanity was affirmed at the moment when man was able to look at himself critically and to rein in his violent instincts.

Individual behaviour is conditioned by awareness of one's own humanity and that of others. If this level of awareness declines, primal instincts gain the upper hand, thereby giving free rein to the expression of brutal animal behaviours designed to ensure survival. To prevent this decline of awareness, the military leader must commit himself to preserving the humanity of his men, as the guarantor of their mental stability and their behaviour.

In the horrors of conflict, man has a natural tendency to protect himself, in order to no longer endure the sight of suffering. He tends to become harder, so as to desensitise himself when faced with reality. If nothing prevents this, he finishes by losing all potential for humanity towards his adversary. In abandoning this humanity, he loses all capacity for discernment, and tends to deviate towards illegal behaviour. He then finds himself caught up in a spiral of violence from which he finds it very difficult to extract himself. An Israeli journalist made the following bitter observation on this subject.

… There are moments when I do not understand my people. People I know so well, who I see moved by humanitarian disasters – such as the huge Asian tsunami – who I see dedicating themselves to ease the misery of unknown victims, are at the same time capable of acting with

the most pitiless cruelty towards their immediate neighbours. Many of them instantly lose all their humanity as soon as those they consider to be their sworn enemies are involved.

To retain one's humanity in a violent environment, it is first and foremost essential is to keep oneself from hating one's adversary. This demands preserving the capacity to see the sufferings of others – and to remedy them as far as possible – and leaving room for genuine moments of humanity during the daily routine of operations.

EYEWITNESS ACCOUNT [1]

Côte d'Ivoire – Duékoue Zone of Instability, 2002

One of the posts of the first section comes under heavy fire from rebels on the other side of Duékoue. The section is deployed in its combat positions. Everyone is keeping their eyes open: the fire is certainly going to come our way any minute now. Suddenly, 600 metres in front of us, a man breaks cover on the track. He is walking along, with no attempt to hide, and shouting. We can make out a suspicious bulge beneath his coat. Yet another Ivorian trick? On the face of it, he is alone.

An initial warning shot is fired to find out what he is up to. He stumbles on hearing the shots, then bumps into one of the chicanes and remains motionless. A group of soldiers makes its way safely to the man.

It turns out he is just a poor blind man and his presumed weapon is simply a stick. He must have been very frightened when he heard the soldiers running towards him. They bring him back to our lines, and he bursts into tears: he was abandoned by his own people a few days ago and handed over to the rebels. He is famished.

Released by the rebels and directed towards our lines, he followed the track, praying and singing hymns. The path he took brought him towards our positions. He was saved by the calmness of the section's soldiers.

It's the end of a nightmare for him and perhaps a splendid moment of humanity in this war.

In this critical situation, the men of the section, under the command of effective leaders, managed to retain their ability to feel for someone else. They thus were able use their discernment and, through this episode, gave even greater meaning to their presence and their action.

Humanity is a motive inseparable from individual mental balance. It is naturally advocated in the exercise of command.

---

1. Account taken from *"Le Code d'honneur en action"* Operation Unicorn and the Second Parachute Regiment of the Foreign Legion, Preface by Colonel E. Maurin, SEPP, Toulouse, 2006.

Commanders and subordinates are men who accomplish a mission together or collaborate in the building of a common entity. As such, they have constant need of each other. It is this mutual dependence on which the brotherhood of arms is founded, and which cannot flourish without the unequivocal expression of a profound humanity. Equally applicable to everyone, it implies that the commander does not reduce his men to one-dimensional subordinates and does not to deny himself their inner resources. It opens the door to enhanced self-worth on the part of each individual, whenever the commander shows initiative or demonstrates his own energy. The interest he demonstrates and the affection and respect given to him are, in the eyes of every subordinate, tangible signs of the principle of humanity. [1].

This style of command, which has to begin in peacetime when in barracks, maintains humanity between the individuals in the group. It nourishes, in the souls of men, the profound conviction in their equality when faced with the demands of human dignity.

In the daily routine of enduring conflicts, a discussion during a break, knowledge of one's men, debriefing as a matter of course on events the unit has experienced, and humanitarian assistance to the population, are some of the straightforward yet essential ways of keeping the men within their frame of reference. They also allow a 'moral breathing space', which is often needed to counterbalance inhuman situations or long-lasting confrontations.

*

*   *

2. Pride and the desire for glory... which leads to error

> *Pride is a swelling of the heart, which spoils all the good qualities of the mind.*
>
> Chevalier de Méré [2]

The first account in our compilation, entitled *Choice*, testified to the quality of a lieutenant who, in order to respect the spirit of his mission, resisted the temptation of a show of strength. Yet after the event, this officer felt compelled to explain, even to justify, his decision. In support of this recollection, he recounts:

---

1. Compendium on the exercise of command in the [French] army, 1993 (p22).
2. Antoine Combaud, Chevalier de Méré, (1607-1684) a French writer who was a contemporary of Pascal.

Some of my subordinates, having seen their dream of glory on that day fade, reproached me for my attitude... They could not bring themselves to understand my decision, still less to accept it. In spite of everything, looking back on it with several years' hindsight, in all conscience I believe more than ever how much I was right.

Seeking military success for the glory it confers is undoubtedly the least acceptable temptation for a military leader. It reveals a serious individual weakness, which might be the result of a misunderstood ideal or perhaps be provoked by external pressures. Military history has a natural tendency to glorify its heroes. For example, in schools, their example and stories of their military exploits are reference points for the transmission of the values of courage, honour and spirit of sacrifice. In the legitimate context of a duty to remember, the homage paid to them permits increased individual motivation and a better understanding of the notion of risk, even sacrifice, inherent in commitment to a military operation.

Some personality types, more affected than others by personal stories, tend to sublimate these values excessively and to build for themselves myths divorced from reality. The natural tendency is to transpose ancient feats of glory into current crises, while omitting to adapt the lessons learned to the new conflicts. In this way the unacknowledged desire to become a hero oneself, following in the footsteps of the great past heroes, can lead to the temptation to recklessly seek out opportunities for violent action or opening fire. This is the sin of pride: Henri Hude [1] explains its origin.

[...] pride makes a mistake when evaluating merit. It attributes an exaggerated role to the individual in the acquisition of his qualities or success – because luck may have played as large a role as merit – luck, or even education, or his colleagues [...] To know one's excellence and to enjoy one's excellence are perfectly reasonable in themselves, to the extent that such excellence is real. The error, or the lie, inherent in pride is that we love our excellence as if we were its cause, even though our family, our background and particularly circumstances have played an important part in the creation of what we are worth.

EYEWITNESS ACCOUNT [2]

Bosnia-Herzegovina – 1994

One of the units I was commanding had been given a very specific mission, which involved reaching an opposition position, searching the place, and possibly bringing back any abandoned weapons.

---

1. Henri Hude, *Dignité de l'homme,* extracts from the proceedings of the 2004 colloquium at the Saint-Cyr Coëtquidan military schools, p. 8.
2. Testimony recorded from General H. Gobillard.

In the command post (CP), I am listening on the unit's radio frequencies. I want to follow the operation in real time, as it is taking place in a very sensitive area.

The unit commander reaches the position without difficulty. As foreseen, the emplacement has been abandoned, but the former occupants only seem to have left the place a short time before. It's not long before their location is spotted; they are still in the immediate vicinity. The mission given to this unit is specific and limited. I therefore consider it accomplished.

I then hear on the unit's internal frequency – a frequency normally not monitored in my CP – a conversation between the commander and his deputy. The deputy has just located the exact position of the former occupants of the place and proposes pursuing them. The thinly veiled motive is to engage them and to justify this after the event under the pretext of a fire fight.

Motivated by the desire to pull off a coup, the commander intends launching an encirclement operation to win an apparently easy battle. This initiative, which goes beyond the orders given, is not only unnecessary but much riskier than he thinks, when faced with soldiers battle-hardened by long months of clashes.

I immediately have to intervene to stop this initiative. Not only does it recklessly put the lives of the men at risk and could compromise our neutral status, but its only purpose is to win cheap glory, merit and medals for those taking part.

The above event describes the temptation of a unit stopped at the last moment from exceeding its mission as result of the desire to achieve a military exploit. The commander, tempted by and the prospect of glory, was prepared to risk the lives of his men and to kill others, simply for the recognition of his worth as a warrior or to gratify an inflated ego.

The reaction of the commander who immediately put an stop to this action should not be interpreted as a rejection of the combat commander's initiative or as inhibiting tactical inspiration. These qualities, which have so often contributed to military successes in past conflicts, remain more relevant than ever, and the commander has a duty to cultivate them. But whatever the nature of the conflict, both the spirit and the letter of the mission must remain the absolute standards on the basis of which action is undertaken. The first eyewitness account in this book reminded us of that principle.

The ability to show initiative does not imply desire for conquest, and tactical inspiration must not be confused with an obsession with glory.

The exercise of responsibility in combat is more difficult now than in the past. Although current operations are often less risky and less brutal than those experienced by the veterans of former conflicts, they are undeniably more complex to conduct, because of the many factors and elements needing to be taken into account such as multinationality, the involvement of NGOs, interaction with media, overlapping populations, etc.

More generally, it must be clearly understood that the nature of today's operations has profoundly changed. They are undertaken in a much more complex environment, which often reduces commanders' scope for action when in combat. In this context, principles of good behaviour applied lucidly and consistently will provide support for initiative and situational intelligence, allowing a calm response to the unforeseen.

HOW TO PREVENT THE RISK OF PRIDE

- ***Though a culture of humility***

> *Humility is the antidote to pride.*
>
> Voltaire

EYEWITNESS ACCOUNT [1]

Rwanda – Operation Turquoise – 1994

In the early days of operation Turquoise, we were looking for evidence of genocide. Though widely reported in the media on the basis of a number of images constantly shown on TV, the reality of the situation had yet to be established. Every day, following intelligence reports, we moved a little further into unknown territory, eventually arriving at an isolated village.

We made contact with the local population, carried out discrete inspections and verifications, and had hasty discussions. While passing a hut, we encountered a doctor who circumspectly told us he was hiding four Tutsis – a woman and three children. We immediately suggested to him that we take charge of them and evacuate them to a camp where they would be safe.

At that precise moment we received a radio message from a captain, telling us that his team had witnessed a large-scale drama. As they were only five in number, they were unable to do anything, faced with thousands of people. We were therefore obliged to leave without delay to help our colleagues. We promised the courageous doctor that

---

1. Testimony by Commodore Marin Gillier.

we would return within forty-eight hours. He said firmly that, if we did come back, we should be extremely cautious and that he would prefer not to see us again, rather than run the risk of the villagers discovering his secret. He had no wish to be hacked to pieces.

Two days later, an opportunity presented itself and, to keep to our commitment, we asked for and obtained two helicopters. We had come up with a simple and effective plan.

The first helicopter landed in the centre of the village, attracting all the inhabitants. We assembled the population and gained some time by counting and recounting them, before proceeding to distribute foodstuffs. While we were busy doing this, the second helicopter landed behind a hill. Four men got out, carrying a padlocked chest. In the doctor's hut, they removed the padlock and the four Tutsis quickly took the place of a supply of medicines. Unseen and undetected, we pulled off an excellent extraction operation and saved four lives.

The press got wind of the resupply of the village, but obviously not of the rescue. They referred to it in a series of articles calling into question France's actions in Rwanda. These reports were subsequently referred to in parliamentary investigations [...]. In a context of extensive media coverage, we were summoned before the Parliamentary Defence Commission and questioned by the International Criminal Court, though without being able to defend ourselves on this controversial point in order to avoid putting the doctor's life in danger.

Having witnessed unbearably violent acts during this conflict and having risked our lives to save others, we had to put up with the suspicions and distrustful looks not only of those demanding that we account for ourselves, but also of our peers, who ended up by wondering about the possible reasons for such stubbornness.

Was it really necessary to put up with all this? And in the name of what?

Yes, it was necessary, in the name of our commitment, and to save another life, that of the exceptionally courageous doctor.

A sense of injustice is one of the most powerful motivating factors in human uprisings. To succeed in holding one's line under such conditions is evidence of exceptional strength of character and of equally remarkable qualities of humility.

Commanding men – in combat as in peacetime – does not naturally predispose one to humility. Giving orders, leading and persuading naturally involves reaching out towards one's subordinates, imposing one's will and situating oneself as the arbiter of the common good. The exercise of such responsibilities can therefore be accompanied by a certain personality cult, often sustained by the subordinates themselves.

However, when a unit commander is entrusted with the command of a regiment, his operations officer recites the ritual formula reminding him of the principles that must guide his actions: "The good of the service, respect for military regulations, observing the law, and the success of France's armed forces". In every respect, each link in the hierarchical chain has the same responsibilities and deserves to be similarly reminded of these, and only these, fundamentals for guiding action.

Cultivating in oneself, as in one's men, the notion of duty, together with the culture of service, enables the risk of pride to be counterbalanced. To be in the service of a country, a cause or a mission contributes directly to making one's subordinates understand that greatness resides primarily in the willingness of the act, and that reward lies above all in having realised their potential through motivated commitment. Of all the things that make the military noble, nothing is more ennobling for the individual than this simple feeling of duty and sense of responsibility, and is all the greater if he willingly commits himself to it.

The humility of a commander who makes the notion of service central to his actions is the finest example to give one's subordinates and is unquestionably the most effective of all the lessons conveyed.

- **By rewarding non-warlike acts**

> *Knowledge of having acted well is reward in itself.*
>
> Seneca

EYEWITNESS ACCOUNT [1]

Afghanistan – Kabul, Summer 2003

On June 7 the German contingent was attacked. One of Kabul's traditional yellow taxis, containing an estimated 300kg of explosives, exploded next to a military bus transporting soldiers, killing four of them. There were also a number of seriously wounded. This first serious attack against the multinational force abruptly increased the tension throughout the city.

As commander of the French detachment, some days later I go to Kabul. My vehicle is preceded by a lead car occupied by a protection team. Another team is following my vehicle, completing the convoy. All our vehicles are unmarked.

---

1. Testimony sent by General J. F. Hogard, when commanding the 3rd Regiment of Marine Infantry.

As usual, the traffic is dense, disordered, even dangerous, and threats can come from anywhere.

We are driving at reduced speed when a yellow taxi similar to the one used in the attack against the German contingent suddenly appears, driving at high speed towards our convoy. It appears to be heading directly for my vehicle. The bodyguard in the lead car reacts immediately: he leans out of the window and aims his gun at the taxi. From where I'm sitting, I can clearly see the 'red dot' of the laser sight on the driver's forehead. The bodyguard tightens his finger on the trigger, but he holds back from firing. He waits. Risking his life, he is taking the time to be sure about the reality of the threat. He has his doubts. As it happens, the taxi is full of women and children. I can see the bodyguard's face: he is concentrating very hard, looking out for the slightest change, entirely wrapped up in his mission.

He has left himself room for manoeuvre to hit his target, but this hesitation also gives the taxi time to crash into him and kill him.

At the last moment, the taxi driver becomes aware of the situation. In a terrified knee-jerk reflex, he turns ninety degrees into an alleyway. Initially taken for a kamikaze, he was just an ordinary taxi-driver in a great hurry, driving his customers to their destination.

The NCO bodyguard, himself a father and less than six months away from retirement, preferred to put his own life at risk rather than make a mistake. His concern for humanity, his consideration for others, his courage, and his reading of the situation led him to make the right decision. This courageous and generous act was not a matter of chance, but resulted from careful thought and a deeply ingrained commitment to exercise his profession as a soldier and be a decent man, respectful of life.

He earned my total admiration. For this and other similar acts during his mission he was awarded the Croix de la Valeur Militaire.

In recent years, the increased number of complex separation-of-forces operations has shown the relevance and importance of the qualities of self-control, discipline as to when to open fire, and negotiating ability. On many occasions, the courage not to open fire has been the key to the success of the mission, and has saved numerous lives, both civilian and military. The first official citations for coolness and self-control have begun to be awarded. In 2004, with the same aim, a decree [1] was issued modifying the awarding of the gold national defence medal, precisely in order to

1. Decree number 2004-624, modifying decree number 82-358 of 21 April 1982, which instituted the national defence medal.

broaden the circumstances in which it could be given in cases of heightened risk.

> *Article 5. The gold national defence medal may be awarded directly, without taking into account seniority and points, to active and reserve military personnel who have distinguished themselves while carrying out an act of heightened risk and have been awarded an individual citation without cross, delivered by the Defence Minister or, by delegation, by the head of the armed forces, the heads of Service or Directors-General.*

Being master of one's strength often calls for more courage than initiating an exchange of fire. This mastery does not mean systematically holding back on the use of force, but means being able to deploy it at the desired place, time and level. Every soldier should be aware that recognition of his worth is today no longer exclusively associated with firing his weapon. Their commanders will be able to recognise their real worth, because nowadays it is often more difficult to refrain from firing than to open fire.

*

*   *

3. Fear... which leads to blindness

> *True heroism is not the absence of fear, but the channelling of fear into action.*
>
> Doric German [1]

In combat, the soldier's first enemy is fear. The greatest warriors themselves admitted to being frightened.

– Henry IV (of France) acknowledged that "feared death" before each battle.

– Turenne cursed his "trembling carcass".

– "He who says he never experiences fear is three times a liar" wrote Marshall Ney, bravest of the brave, to himself.

– "I was", Marshal Canrobert wrote, "terribly old during the day and evening which preceded the assault on Zaatcha", and added "I do not believe those who claim never to be afraid."

Who in battle has not known fear? Finding oneself drowning in fear to the point of losing one's faculties is the most human, and certainly the

---

1. Canadian author born in 1946 and professor at Hearst University College.

most understandable, of risks. But giving in to panic can lead to even worse. That is why it is necessary to pay particular attention to becoming acquainted with this risk, the better to protect oneself from it.

Fear is an emotion that people have long analysed and whose implications they have most tried to understand. The previously cited 1922 tactics manual presents it as follows.

> *If one persuades a man that he can go into battle without apprehension, if one leads him to believe that he will be carried away by the sound of cannon and the smell of powder, that man will experience terrible and dangerous disillusionment when faced with reality. Astonishment on the battlefield means surprise, and surprise is very close to panic.*

The account which follows, over eighty years later, proves that this text has retained all its relevance.

EYEWITNESS ACCOUNT [1]

Afghanistan – Kabul, Summer 2003

> *A week after the previously mentioned yellow taxi episode, an American Humvee [2] on patrol in Kabul, found itself stuck in traffic behind the same type of taxi, also full of Afghan civilians.*

> *Although not directly threatened by this taxi in front, the vehicle commander became worried by the extremely erratic way it was being driven. Feeling very much under threat and probably inadequately prepared to cope with such stressful situations, the soldier allowed himself to be overcome by a panic attack and, for no apparent reason, treated the taxi as a target. From a few dozen metres away he fired a long burst with his heavy calibre 12.7 mm machine gun.*

> *It was total carnage.*

> *It was a perfectly ordinary taxi. All its occupants, men, women and children, were either killed or badly injured.*

> *It turned out that one of them was an officer of the Afghan army wearing civilian clothes. He was seriously wounded and had to have an arm amputated*

> *A political drama was thus added to the human drama, and for a long time exacerbated relations between US soldiers and the Afghan army.*

---

1. Testimony provided by General J. F. Hogard, when commanding the 3rd Regiment of Marine Infantry.
2. High Mobility Multipurpose Vehicle.

The panic attack of a soldier unable to find the will to regain control of himself led to a drama with terrible consequences. The notion of fear in battle has often been studied and analysed. It is worth taking a moment to consider this question.

Fear is natural in any soldier placed in a stressful situation. It is not abnormal, it is not intrinsically punishable, and it is even useful in the creation of the individual's psychological structure. A man without any fear whatsoever is abnormal, and liable to lose his sense of reality and proportion.

Fear should be viewed as a manifestation of the self-preservation instinct; it is useful because it allows people to act appropriately when threatened. However, when it completely overwhelms someone, it generates uncontrollable physiological phenomena, such as trembling and stupefaction, and even complete physical paralysis. As long as fear does not cross the boundary into abject terror, it remains under control, generating positive stress and allowing the self-preservation instinct to emerge. But as soon as it becomes panic, it acquires a pathological character and produces reactions that are dangerous both for the individual and his immediate environment.

Colonel Goya, an army officer, has written a fascinating work on precisely this question of behaviour in combat and reactions to stress and fear alike. Entitled *Sous le feu*[1] [Under Fire], he recounts eloquent testimonies, including an account of two 'poilus' [First World War French conscript soldiers] confronted by the fear of battle.

> *We naively imagined that the campaign would be a military walkover, a quick succession of easy and stunning victories. The first time you come under fire is therefore shocking: suddenly, shrill whistles ending in furious shrieks, hurl us down, face against the earth, terrified. [...] head beneath my pack, I glance at my neighbours, breathless, shaken by nervous trembling, mouths contracted in a hideous rictus, all of them with chattering teeth, their faces misshapen by terror, in that bizarre posture of prostration calling to mind the hideous gargoyles on Notre Dame. Arms across their chests, heads down, they look like tortured souls offering their necks to the executioner [...].*
>
> *How long is this torture going to last? Why don't we move? Are we going to stay here immobile, to be made into mincemeat?*

> Galtier Boissière in 1914

---

1. *Cahiers de la réflexion doctrinale du CDEF* (Centre de Doctrine et d'Emploi des Forces) de l'armée de Terre.
[Reflecting on Doctrine – Notes by the French Army Doctrine and Application Centre.]

While the phenomena of prostration and being reduced to a mindless state by terror described in these intense passages have only rarely been encountered in recent conflicts, they can nevertheless erupt again at any time during a brutal confrontation involving an exchange of fire. Such a confrontation still remains possible, or even probable.

Colonel Goya continues by analysing the particular difficulties soldiers have in withstanding the stress of modern conflicts, which though less extreme than experienced in high intensity conflicts is exacerbated by the constraining rules of engagement imposed on the force.

> *Frustration and psychological troubles are greater when one cannot act freely, or at least when one has the feeling of being unable to act freely.*
>
> *The men and women who have agreed to serve in the armed forces and under the French flag are often highly motivated, sometimes idealistic, and have a strong desire to carry out missions that live up to their expectations. Very often, the missions given to the armed services during stabilisation phases are bound by restrictive rules of engagement. As well as these restrictions there are also constraints linked to the international situation and to the complexity of local situations. These limits and constraints give rise to a kind of paralysis affecting the whole environment that the troops operate within. The forced inactivity resulting from these stabilisation phases is liable to generate intense frustration, and even to a feeling of abject failure with regard to what initially motivated their vocation.*

HOW TO PREVENT FEAR

- ### By developing self-control

> *Today's naked man loses control of himself when faced with steel or lead: the self-preservation instinct completely takes over. There are two ways to avoid or to lessen danger, and no middle way: fight or flight. So let's fight!*
>
> Ardant du Picq

Apart from the prostration effect described above, another combatant, Paul Linthier, an artilleryman in 1914, testifies that by making an effort of individual will power, it is possible to adapt minds and bodies to the terror of gunfire.

At first, the danger is unknown...you sweat...you tremble...the imagination exaggerates. You are no longer thinking straight...

Subsequently, you become discerning. Smoke is harmless. The whistling of a shell serves to predict its direction. You no longer turn your back needlessly, you only take shelter carefully. Danger no longer dominates us, we dominate it. Everything is there [...]. Each day trains us to be courageous. Coming up against the same dangers, the human beast irrupts less often. Your nerves no longer jangle. The deliberate and continuous effort to achieve self-control works in the long run. That is what a soldier's courage is.

You are not born brave, you become brave.

More recently, in so-called 'stabilised' separation-of-forces missions, which can acquire a certain routine, the problem is that the situation can suddenly change when least expected. And fear can erupt out of nowhere and in a totally unexpected way. Strength of character and self-control are then more essential than ever to prevent the situation degenerating.

EYEWITNESS ACCOUNT [1]

Côte d'Ivoire – Abidjan, October 2008.

In October 2008, a low-level human intelligence gathering patrol of the Unicorn battalion's armoured squadron is engaged in a mission in the Abobo Centre neighbourhood, to the north of the city of Abidjan. It comprises two P4 jeeps, an NCO [2] and five men, some of them on their first overseas operation.

The patrol stops regularly to make contact with the local population and various individuals – priests, shopkeepers, members of the neighbourhood councils, leaders of voluntary groups – with whom the French forces have been establishing links. Relations are normal and the exchanges cordial. The atmosphere is calm, as it has been since the start of the tour over three months ago.

Unconcerned, the patrol completes its work near a gendarme-commando base, then works its way around the perimeter, and finally leaves the area to head back to the Port-Bouët camp, where the French forces based in the Ivorian capital are stationed.

While going through a market, clearing a way through the crowd, the patrol is stopped at a crossroads by two pick-ups containing gen-

---

1. Testimony forwarded by Captain Augustin Delpit, commanding the 1st squadron of the 6-12 Lancers' Regiment.
2. Adjutant Clavero, (≈ NATO OR 8). His deputy is Brigadier Dauphine (≈ NATO OR-6).

darme-commandos. Two Ivorian soldiers get out of the first vehicle, weapons in hand. One of them, seemingly the commander of this small detachment, menacingly points his pistol at the patrol leader. The second gendarme, armed with an AK47, threatens the other P4, carrying the deputy patrol leader.

The patrol leader is petrified by the unexpected aggression. The muzzle of the pistol is inches away from his eye. In particular he sees that the weapon is cocked and ready for use. Throughout, the commander of the Ivorian detachment keeps up barrage of shouts and threats. Although it can have lasted only a few seconds, to the patrol leader it seems like an eternity.

The deputy patrol leader, an experience solider, analyses the situation coolly. To his eyes, the Ivorian soldier threatening him seems to be afraid. He orders the other men in the vehicle to discreetly cock their FAMAS [French assault rifle], but not to show their weapons and not to make any sudden movements. He is ready to act if the situation deteriorates.

The patrol leader recovers his wits. The danger is real, and the anger of the Ivorians could easily escalate into armed confrontation. He is worried about the lives of his men, as well as the hundreds of civilians wandering around near the vehicles. One shot and it will be a bloodbath. He sees that the crowd is beginning to move. Conscious of the danger, people are lowering their heads and running from the area. The tension needs be lowered. That is now the patrol leader's priority.

He waits until the Ivorian detachment commander complete his harangue and falls silent. Taking advantage of this pause, the patrol leader identifies himself and states the official reason for his presence in the area. He points out that the French forces have been granted free movement by the Ivorian authorities (the government and armed forces headquarters). But from where he is standing, he is out of radio contact with his superior office and in any case, can hardly pick up the handset with a gun being waved in his face. He is on his own.

At this point the gendarme notices the patrol leader's map of Abidjan. He tries to grab it. But the patrol leader manages to hang on to it, while continuing to talk to the gendarme.

Still angry, the Ivorian returns to his vehicle and starts talking on the radio. He comes back to the P4, again threatens the patrol leader with his weapon and concludes with the warning: "If you come back here, we will kill you". He issues some orders and the two vehicles leave the area.

The crowd in the market then begins berating the patrol, telling them to leave. Fear is inscribed on their faces. They cannot take a stand against the French army without putting themselves in overt danger. Although relations with this section of the population have been very cordial up now, the incident has completely changed the situation. "Go home, you have no business here!" The crowd gathers in large numbers.

The patrol leader orders his men to continue. The patrol returns to Camp-Bouët.

The incident has lasted no more than ten minutes.

In an echo of this account, let me once again quote Sun Tzu, who, several centuries ago, wrote in *The Art of War*: "Order or disorder depends on organization and direction, courage or cowardice, strength or weakness of tactical dispositions."

Strength of character and self-control are clearly among the indispensable characteristics of everyone with the responsibility to lead in combat. Although, like all intrinsic qualities, these are unequally distributed between individuals, they can, however, be easily enhanced: bravery and withstanding danger can be taught. Armies have long implemented such training and have further developed it in the form of 'battle hardening'.

The need to train potential combatants, to harden them to make them able to withstand all the vicissitudes of war, is as ancient as war itself. But the way to do it has evolved constantly over the centuries, no doubt at a similar rate to the various types of combat. These days, battle preparation is undertaken in specialist army training centres. It involves bringing men, in their own units, face to face with the greatest possible range of the physical or psychological conditions induced by undertaking missions in hostile conditions. Becoming battle hardened allows one to undergo physical and psychological preparation for combat, thereby increasing hardiness, endurance and resistance to fatigue and to climate conditions.

This type of training concurrently helps develop new social links between those who go into battle together, thus tending to reinforce the feeling of duty towards the group.

Moral obligation increases with mutual knowledge. There are very few people who are not sensitive to what others think of them. In a military unit, two feelings often arise through people interacting with each other: on the one hand, the fear of being seen as weak, fearful and incompetent and, on the other, the desire to prove oneself and be admired. [1]

---

1. Colonel Goya, *Sous le feu* [Under Fire] Cahiers de la réflexion doctrinale du CDEF.

Placed in situations similar to those likely to occur in real conflicts, the combatant thereby develops his strength of character, strengthens his team spirit and increases his ability to resist stress. Able to control his feelings of fear, he learns how to remain master of himself in all circumstances.

- **By solid group cohesion**

The previously discussed idea of cohesiveness is a 'cement' which enables one to avoid one being carried away by panic. Soldiers draw the energy they need to face up to the anguish of battle from the presence of others, and from the trust that binds them together. This is perfectly illustrated in this short, very honest account.

EYEWITNESS ACCOUNT [1]

Afghanistan – Nijrab, May 2009

I am having a discussion with one of the sentries at the Nijrab FOB. He mission is coming to an end in three weeks. He is twenty years old and is experiencing his first operation outside France. I ask him what his best memory is. Without hesitation he says, "The battle of Alasay!" The same question, but this time about his worst memory. With equal certainty, he replies, "The TIC [2] of 7 March at Shehkut."

I am a little surprised. Both were fierce battles in the Alasay valley. The young rifleman private explains that during the TIC on 7 March his platoon was separated from the rest of the company. For a while, he and his comrades felt that they might lose control of the situation. Moreover, the battle was taking place in the middle of a village. The insurgents were leaping out of doorways and windows barely a few metres from them.

"I saw the hatred in the enemy's eyes, that's what made the biggest impression on me. I was afraid and I saw that the insurgents were not afraid. At that moment I was able to appreciate how cohesion and the brotherhood of arms are one of the key ingredients of victory."

---

1. Reported by Colonel Le Nen.
2. TIC Troops in Contact. An operation which involves opening fire.

HOW TO DETECT FEAR IN ONE'S SUBORDINATES

• *By knowing one's men perfectly*

> *Combat is the ultimate objective of armies and man is the primary instrument of combat; therefore, nothing can be ordered wisely within an army [...] without precise knowledge of the primary instrument, of man and his moral state in that defining moment of combat.*

> Ardant du Picq

EYEWITNESS ACCOUNT [1]

Lebanon – Beirut, February 1984

Battles are raging between Christians and anti-government militias. The men in my platoon are occupying observation posts that are regularly attacked during violent battles. We reply with our FAMAS and our 50 calibre machine guns. The posts are often assailed at night, putting the nerves of my men under severe strain. Tension is very high and I do my best to do the rounds of my posts to reassure, to encourage and advise.

After one particularly violent attack, two of the enemy militiamen engaged in the assault remain lying on the ground. When the situation has calmed down and the rest of the militiamen have gone, I decide to take a close look at the state of the two men. We approach carefully. One of them is dead, but the other is still alive, though injured. My medic begins first aid. A corporal marksman has come with me. He is battle hardened and respected and has an impressive array of medals on his chest. He has been under fire in combat several times. He has the profile of a 'warrior', but he is also known for his irascible character and his moody and intemperate behaviour. He is certainly more feared than respected.

While we are busy with the wounded man, he goes up to the other militiaman and in a sudden crazed fit violently attacks the inert body, lashing out with his rifle butt and his feet. If the militiaman he was savaging were not already dead, there his no question that these blows would have finished him off.

It takes several men to overpower and disarm the corporal. I have him quickly evacuated to the aid post.

---

1. Account taken down by Colonel Pierre Hery.

I punish him severely for this act of madness. Subsequently taken into medical care, he is soon deemed to be unsuited to military life and is retrained.

The inquiry conducted into this incident in the days that followed revealed that the soldier concerned had suffered past trauma, the result of his African campaigns, which had deeply disturbed him. He had previously been punished for having cut off the ears of his 'enemies' killed in battle. His character and repeated outbursts of fury were well known, but no-one had dared to blow the whistle on him because he was considered to be a 'good soldier'. Medical examination revealed that he was suffering from acute paranoia.

I called myself to account, because I felt that I had not gone far enough in getting to know this man. His act of madness, on this occasion without consequences, could have taken place in any other circumstances and could even have been directed against his own comrades.

One can never know one's men sufficiently well.

I learned that lesson.

This example once again reminds us of the absolute obligation for a military commander to *know* his men. *Knowing* goes beyond being acquainted with someone, it involves getting inside the personality of the subordinate and understanding his nature and what motivates his behaviour. This is the very least consideration one can show to men whose very existence one might put on the line. This knowledge of the other creates the proximity for forging the close relationship needed for the exercise of command, founded on the brotherhood of arms. It is an almost intimate relationship that leads naturally to love of one's men.

Having delved deep into the personalities of those close to him, the commander is thus in a position to detect any changes of attitude indicative of a personal problem, distress or a more serious dehumanisation phenomenon.

Deployment on operations is a trial, and combat is a drama during which the commander demands enormous sacrifices from his subordinates: he must therefore be able to spot, almost instinctively, simply from a movement or a glance, a weakness, confusion or an expectation.

How can this be done, without a perfect knowledge of the deepest motives of other beings?

Do you believe that this knowledge can be acquired in the middle of a crisis?

Isn't it during the calm of life in barracks that one finds the opportunities to deepen this knowledge? [1]

It has been established that a well-balanced individual, possessed of all his physical and mental faculties, does not easily give in to panic. He has available the means to manage his apprehension and to keep it down to the level of 'fear'. In fact, a panic attack – equivalent to a psychological fracture – is a phenomenon that only occurs in individuals who are unstable or temporarily weakened. The sight of corpses or acts of violence, earlier traumas coming to the surface, bad news from the family left at the rear base or conflictual relationships within the group are events likely to destabilise soldiers and weaken them in stressful situations.

Keeping a regular watchful eye over his men, the absolute need to be available for them, and ongoing dialogue, enables the officer to find the right words in response to their questions and possible worries and, if necessary, to encourage them to see the detachment doctor.

*

*   *

4. Revenge... which nourishes hatred

> *Vengeance always arises from a weakness of the soul which is incapable of dealing with insults*
>
> Francis VI, Duke of Rochefoucauld [2]

Revenge contributes in part to the risk of losing one's bearings. It is linked to a sense injustice, which in turn engenders a seemingly legitimate feeling of revolt. The impulse to revenge is innate in everyone, but it can be and must be controlled by those bearing arms and responsible for justice.

EYEWITNESS ACCOUNT [3]

Chad – Abeche, French military encampment, 1987

In country for several weeks already, mine is the duty platoon this evening. About 23.00 hours, I hear voices shouting and people moving by the guardroom. I run towards it. On getting there, I see that the soldier on guard duty is being supported by a comrade. He is wounded in

---

1. The exercise of command in the [French] army, 1993.
2. Francis VI, Duke of Rochefoucald (1613-1680) was a writer, moralist and memorialist, especially well known for his Maxims.
3. Testimony recounted by General Emmanuel Maurin.

the neck, and is bleeding copiously and moaning. There is also a Chadian lying on the ground, held down by two other men. I am briefed on what has just happened.

The soldier on duty spotted a man inside the camp sneaking between the vehicles, probably hoping to steal petrol or kit. While trying to arrest him, the sentry was violently attacked and stabbed. Having alerted the guard, the post commander intervened with two men and overpowered the man. It was at that moment I arrived.

As the post commander finishes his account, the sergeant who accompanied me to the scene me begins repeating, "He wanted to kill him... he wanted to kill him... he wanted to kill him..."

He is speaking angrily, fists and jaw clenched. I suddenly see him take a knife from the sheath on his belt and advance on the Chadian, saying, "I'm going to kill him!"

I have only a few seconds to come between them and stop the sergeant. As a reflex, I punch him hard in the face. He falls to the ground. Shocked, he stares at me uncomprehendingly. After taking his knife, I give him a severe dressing down and immediately send him back to his room.

He remains antagonistic toward me for three whole days, not saying a word to me and going out of his way to avoid me. Since I'm busy with many other tasks at present, I put off seeing him until later. However, on the fourth day, it is he who asks to see me.

When we are alone, facing each other, he apologises and tries to make amends. He has recognised the seriousness of what he did and realised its far-reaching implications. He thanks me sincerely for having protected him and for probably having saved the life of the Chadian.

He was a good NCO and he deserved my trust. From then I considered the matter closed. The NCO went on to have a very good military career.

He and I have never spoken about the incident again, but when we come across each other, the memory is always with us. It has put the seal on a certain understanding between us.

As well as being in command on operations and acting as a catalyst for his troops, the commander needs to keep a cool head and remain an example of emotional stability for his men. He must do everything he can to ensure that violence does not get out of hand, especially if it is exacerbated by an adversary seeking to force him into making a mistake when the media are present. The commander has a fundamental responsibility in regard to any excesses on the part of his men – something, alas, that is always possible. Above all, he must never tolerate such excesses or, even worse, excuse them. In addition, there must be regular reflection with a view to respecting the enemy, controlling the use of coercive methods, setting uncrossable boundaries and ensuring that the rules of engagement are adhered to.

Since time immemorial, the military man has been the legitimate agent of might. It is not his responsibility to deal with 'bastards' or murderers. He is not the righter of wrongs. His role is clearly defined in the mission he is given. The way the mission is undertaken is bounded on the one hand by the rules of engagement – we have already referred to these in a preceding chapter – and on the other by rules of good behaviour. He draws his legitimacy from the scrupulous adherence to these two standards, as well as from respect for his adversary and his human dignity.

Eyewitness account [1]

Hélie de Saint Marc – Indochina

One of the most important airborne operations I participated in took place near Nghia Lo. This small town was a key outpost controlling access to the Thai hinterland and Laos. [...] The Thai hinterland also had to be protected at any price. That is why we were parachuted behind Vietminh lines. [...] After advancing through the jungle for two days, we hit the Vietminh rear positions. The CIPLE [Indochinese Company of the Foreign Legion] fought for several hours to gain a foothold. Lieutenant Lecoeur, a beanpole of a man over two metres tall, with a permanent smile, had his neck broken by a bullet. Lying on a makeshift stretcher, he began a time of agony lasting several days. Towards the end of the battle, I noticed that some wounded Vietminh had been finished off with a dagger. My NCOs found the guilty party, a legionnaire who had taken revenge, no doubt out of fear. On our return, he was dealt with in accordance with military law. Such men had no place in my company.

To speak about the dignity of the enemy is also to affirm that man, whatever his choices and his position, always possesses inalienable rights. In the same spirit, this amounts to saying that those in society who have been given the power to use force, also have duties towards those who confront them. They must therefore guard against any propensity to hatred and any temptation to act vengefully.

---

1. Hélie de Saint Marc, *Les Champs de Braise* [The Fields of Embers], Perrin, 2002.

Action is given meaning through continuing explanation, education and example setting. The meaning thereby conferred enables one to struggle against humanly unacceptable situations using acceptable means.

HOW CAN THE TEMPTATION FOR REVENGE BE COMBATTED?

• *By the leader's total lack of ambiguity*

If the preceding example has shown the total absence of equivocation in that platoon commander faced with an attempt at revenge, the following account highlights the need always to issue very precise orders in situations where there is a latent risk of things taking a wrong turn. Leaving the slightest room for doubt or interpretation is not only a mistake, but it can also be a weakness, or even an act of cowardice.

EYEWITNESS ACCOUNT [1]

Chad – Pacification campaign, 1970s

I am the commander of a platoon which, on the day in question, is isolated in a desert area far from anywhere. To my great astonishment, when crossing a wadi, we surprise a small group of lightly armed rebels.

We respond immediately. An exchange of fire takes place and without any serious difficulties on our part – and without loss on our side – we neutralise the enemy. Several of the rebels are dead and one is seriously wounded. He has been hit in the stomach. It is a horrible wound and his intestines have spilled out.

The platoon medic, trained on the job as were all our medics at that time, does what he can. For my part, I recall the guidance learned in medical training: don't try to push the intestines back in, and don't give the person anything to drink. But it's over 40 degrees in the shade!

I report the contact and ask for an emergency CASEVAC (casualty evacuation) by helicopter. The reply from headquarters comes without delay: the CASEVAC is refused, for reasons which I am not given.

It is patently impossible to transport the wounded man and we only have a few doses of morphine. I am in an insoluble situation: what must I do, what can I do? I can see no answer other than to wait, in the hope that a solution presents itself. Initially, in the hours that follow, like all Africans, he is hardened to pain, and does not complain... But

---

1. Account recorded by the author.

before long, he starts groaning and moaning because of the now unbearable pain.

My deputy, an old and experienced NCO with whom I have a real relationship of trust, tells me there is only one way to stop his suffering and to enable us to continue with our mission: to finish him off. I can still remember his words. "If you move him into the truck, he will suffer terribly and will die long before we reach camp. If you abandon him, you will be an even greater hypocrite because, once night falls, he will be eaten by hyenas or jackals".

I refuse: perhaps I hope that a helicopter will finally arrive or that he will die naturally. To save time, I leave with two groups to reconnoitre the wadi on foot.

After half an hour, my deputy calls me on the radio to report on the suffering of the wounded man, which has become unendurable. I talk it over with him, but do not agree. I eventually break off the conversation. I decide I have been away long enough. I have a vague feeling that I have not done the right thing by absenting myself, and I fear I have not been very clear in my radio message.

On my return to the platoon, I look for the wounded man. I learn to my surprise that the man is dead and that my men are already burying him. My deputy had not told me of his death.

I am perplexed.

I am tempted to take my deputy to one side and ask him for more details about the circumstances of the death, but possibly I am afraid of the reply.

Were my orders clear enough?

I am not sure what exactly I said, but all the same... I like my deputy, but all the same... like a coward I console myself, but all the same... I prefer to convince myself that his death, in any event unavoidable, was nature taking its course.

The platoon moves on. I wonder whether I am the only one asking himself questions.

The years have passed: this memory is still with me.

I am still asking myself questions... and not without self-criticism.

It is difficult for someone who has not lived through the situation, so succinctly described in this testimony, to answer these questions. However, if this officer is still asking himself questions many years afterwards, it is probably because he believes that he did not fully shoulder his responsibilities, in a situation calling for a strength of character that he did not yet have at that time, and the outcome of which has never allowed him to be at peace with his conscience.

On operations, the serviceman's field of action is indistinct and complex, confronting him with ambiguous situations where there is neither a single interpretation nor an ideal solution. Yet in such circumstances, the leader has to make choices. These often difficult decisions must leave him at peace with himself, but they must also conform to the ethical principles he has laid down for himself. The first ambiguity, the smallest double meaning, the slightest unspoken word, and the leader runs the risk that his orders will be misunderstood or not followed correctly.

The often invoked loneliness of the leader is a daily reality on operations. In the realm of ethics – as in decision-making – the leader is alone. This solitude is the price to be accepted to protect subordinates from their superior's possible moods. In fact, whatever the environment and the savagery of the situation, it is crucial that the leader keeps any doubts to himself. Even if he wants to show his subordinates that he is not ignorant of their own feelings of injustice and revolt, he may only do so in order the better to remain faithful to the rules of professional ethics he is bound by. He cannot let himself share the slightest confidence; he cannot leave room for the slightest doubt. How could he publicly express a vengeful attitude toward the enemy one day and expressly demand that his integrity be respected the next? In this area more than any other, the leader must accept his solitude or – if he cannot do so – turn to his superior.

Clarity of orders given, absolute respect for the rules of engagement, and regular explanation of instructions on behaviour are principles governing action that have demonstrated their relevance and allow the commander to make it clearly understood which path is to be followed, with no deviation tolerated.

A former lieutenant in Algeria, General Pierre De Percin elaborates.

In a climate of violence and tension, soldiers can be worried, frightened or even, in cases where the platoon has lost some men, be seeking revenge... The commander must be endowed with great authority in order to prevent his men from being carried away by the law of an eye for an eye. In Algeria, I commanded a platoon of Algerian riflemen: I had to display a great deal of authority and deploy considerable energy to bring our prisoners back alive on the day following clashes that had resulted in a number of deaths in our ranks [1].

---

1. Pierre Servent, Les guerres modernes expliquées aux civils et aux militaires, [Modern wars explained to civilians and militaries], Buchet Chastel, 2009.

HOW CAN ACTS OF REVENGE BE PREVENTED?

- *By never covering up the mistakes which arise from them*

> *Hatred is the trap which binds us too closely to the adversary.*
>
> Milan Kundera

EYEWITNESS ACCOUNT [1]

Bosnia-Herzegovina, 1994

One evening, during my time as the senior military officer in Bosnia-Herzegovina, my headquarters reports a serious matter to me. Two French soldiers took a Bosnian fighter prisoner and, motivated by revenge, locked him inside a metal cupboard, into which they then threw two live grenades, killing him instantly.

I know that the soldiers of the separation-of-forces mission harbour considerable resentment towards the different communities in whose midst they have intervened, and they have reasons to be angry. Snipers from all sides have no hesitation in firing on the blue helmets here to help them, and others fire on their own populations – women and children – under the eyes of the media, while claiming it was the work of their adversaries. The environment in which the troops under my command are moving is one of extreme cruelty and seems not to be governed by any principles of justice. I understand the disgust and the feeling of injustice gripping my soldiers.

But nothing, absolutely nothing, can excuse the actions of these two men, whatever horrors this prisoner might have perpetrated. I cannot accept that they behave with the same savagery as those we loathe and denounce. I also know that this murder, still confidential, will in any event become public knowledge and that it must be decried.

I therefore make the only possible decision, the only acceptable one, the only honourable one.

I make contact with the top Bosnian politician and call a press conference for the following day. In front of him and the assembled journalists, I outline the facts, express my regret for them and in the name of France offer an unreserved apology to the Bosnian community. I also commit myself to relieving the two men from duty, returning them to France and to handing them over to the courts. This is what happened: the men were judged in accordance with the law and severely punished on their return.

In that particular theatre, we heard no more of the affair.

---

1. Testimony recorded from General H. Gobillard.

Standing by one's men when they have carried out orders means accepting responsibility for actions carried out in good faith, but it also not tolerating excesses in the name of a supposed brotherhood of arms. Accepting responsibility does not entail accepting every action, and certainly not atrocities that breach the most basic of human rights: respect for life.

France is too ancient a nation not to know where the limits of force lie. In the course of its history, French soldiers have committed excesses that have marked souls and consciences. Like them, France has not forgotten. The wounds may have closed, but even now the scars let us know exactly where the right choice lies. That is why, buttressed by such memories, no leniency can be shown to those who violate the ethical rules. It is a matter of being fair, but also of making the punishment fit the crime, to ensure its seriousness is understood. Punishment is only of value when it generates lessons for the person involved and those around him. Disciplinary, administrative or criminal sanctions must be taught and understood as such. Clemency shown for such serious acts can only breach the very principles that the acts themselves violated.

Nowadays, ethical principles of behaviour possess a sort of moral authority, based on their universal recognition. No derogation can be allowed when putting them into practice: this, in fact, is their greatness and their strength.

*

* *

5. Detachment... which leads to indifference

> *Increasing the distance from a horror suffices to make it disappear. This historical distance has a little in common with the innocence of someone who releases a bomb at 10,000 metres.*
>
> Marc Augé [1]

The perception of combat is profoundly influenced by one in particular of the five human senses: touch. Touch is in fact the sense *par excellence* of the military's *contact* arms – infantry and armour. The physical approach of the enemy increases the feeling of impending action as well

---

1. Born in 1935, Marc Augé is a French ethnologist, author of many works and currently director of studies at the School of Higher Social Studies. This quotation is taken from the review *The World of Education [Le monde de l'éducation], April 2001.*

as of danger and possible death. Yet it also contributes to empathy and a sense of responsibility towards others. Other arms engage in combat at a greater distance and are therefore more liable to *detachment*, which tends to distance the soldier from awareness of the consequences of his actions.

Let us look at the impression gained by Bernanos [1] in 1936 of this combat from a distance, presaging the horror that the blind bombing of civilian populations would provoke in a future conflict, at that time still hypothetical.

> *Tomorrow, the best killers will kill without risk. At thirty thousand feet above ground, any foul engineer, nice and warm in his slippers, surrounded by specialist workers, will only have to flip a switch to assassinate a town and then head quickly for home, his only fear being that he will miss his dinner. Obviously, no-one will call this employee a soldier. Does he even deserve being called a serviceman?*

These few lines were written almost a decade before the terrible bombings of Dresden and the nuclear infernos of Nagasaki and Hiroshima. They reflect the fear of seeing some of the military involved in warfare becoming detached from the consequences of their actions and sowing death and terror with total indifference, because they are not in direct contact with their adversary. Such is the risk of detachment, of killing at no risk to one's life. Hélie de saint Marc analyses this risk very critically [2].

> *The means of combat have changed. The bombings of Serbia, Iraq and Afghanistan raise a serious ethical problem. The American concept of warfare developed after Vietnam consists of causing death without suffering human losses: pilotless planes, drones and missiles. But from time immemorial, the soldier's legitimacy comes from his acceptance of risk. He has power, beyond the normal limits, to kill, but he risks his own skin. Thus he is not an assassin, but a combatant.*

> *As soon as the soldier ceases to come close to death, but he dispenses it by pushing a button, he loses his claim to be a soldier and becomes an executioner.*

> *No-one has yet asked the question, when faced with this new concept, as to what becomes of the soldier's conscience?*

This well-identified possibility clearly applies to pilots, be they air force or navy. It can also apply to the sailor on board his ship when he is not engaged in naval combat, but is ordered to engage in long-range naval

---

1. Goerges Bernanos, *Diary of a Country Priest* [original French title: *Journal d'un curé de campagne*].
2. Hélie de Saint Marc, August von Kageneck and Etienne de Montety, *Notre histoire 1922-1945* [Our history 1922-1945], Les Arènes 2002.

gunfire towards the coast. It also concerns, as a direct corollary, all soldiers who use indirect fire weapons: artillery, rocket launchers and missiles. Several of the testimonies recounted in this book suggest that this acknowledged risk is, however, less blatant for those in the army who might succumb to it, because they are to a greater extent directly involved in land operations. As for the navy, the subject was raised in *The Ethics of the Sailor*, a remarkable special issue [1] of the *Naval Studies Bulletin*, in which several facets of this topic are developed at length.

"For the pilot or the sailor, the target is often far distant and, except for air force commandos or naval marines, there is little likelihood of direct contact with the enemy. But the impact on the conscious mind, and sometimes also on the subconscious, is unfortunately very real. In terms of ethical teaching, the army is developing a centre of excellence at Saint Cyr Coëtquidan under the direction Professor Henri Hude and has produced a 'soldier's code'. The navy too is as equally concerned, and its CD 'Make a Success of your Life' clearly indicates the interest of the armed forces in ongoing thinking about ethics [...].

Honour, homeland and discipline are, for a Navy seaman, ethical landmarks, the meaning of which he must make his own [...]. Thus, the ethic of the sailor is similar to that of all human communities which care about liberty and solidarity. This ethic is neither different, nor specific, but it expresses itself covertly in the very particular daily universe of the warship, whether surface or submarine. Aboard his vessel the sailor spends weeks, even months, far from family and friends, in a confined and potentially dangerous space, subject to the vicissitudes of the sea. At the same time he is undertaking a mission which, in extreme cases, may requires him to sacrifice his life – a duty, albeit uncommon, demanded of all those who, like him, serve the state with as servicemen or servicewomen.

In the last paragraph, Commodore Olivier Lajous makes clear that the sailor's risk of detachment is counterbalanced by the communal life of the crew in an often hostile maritime environment. The length of the mission, the cohesion of the group and the permanent operational atmosphere render the phenomenon of detachment less potent, because they preserve a sensitivity to what is human and to the perception of danger.

The air force is undoubtedly more affected by the problem of 'distance'. However, it has, through a series of studies, shown a specific interest in the subject over the past few years. One of these studies, with the

---

1. *Ethique du marin* [The ethics of the sailor], The Navy Studies Bulletin no. 43, September 2008.

evocative title *Too near, too far: changes in the perception of combat by fighter aircrew* [1] devotes a hundred and fifty pages exclusively to the subject. The study brings together a number of testimonies and statements from fighter pilots, several of which have been included here to illustrate the theme of this chapter. They are often very direct and extremely frank and outspoken, as shown by the following extract on the subject of detachment.

> *What is sure is that in the air force we don't go into a village and kill men with bayonets, we don't storm a trench. It must obviously be understood that, in terms of how we see things, we are in a completely different position from ground forces.*

> *You don't see guys being blown up because your bomb has fallen on their head. That makes it much easier to do – that's for sure. What you are doing is making a technical adjustment, to have best possible aim, to fire within the time window, and you're happy when you hit the target, but obviously you're not there to see the people you've blown to pieces with a 250kg bomb.*

The firepower of new weaponry allows ranges of several tens of kilometres, thereby increasing the distance between the firer and his target. In fact, the technique of fire and forget, the increase in effective range and the increasingly technical nature of war mean that it is now possible, from the pilot's seat, facing a computer screen and from over 50 kilometres away, to cause the deaths of hundreds of the enemy. Some pilots even consider that with automation the difference between good and bad pilots is tending to decrease. But being a systems manager carries the terrible risk of **no longer being a combatant.** And to no longer be a combatant is to renounce not only the courage to confront the enemy and the experience of coming face to face with death, but even more so the idea at the basis of an ethical relationship: preserving one's own life must not become more important than protecting the lives of others or more pressing than the imperative to complete one's mission.

This phenomenon, which the Air Force and the Naval Air Arm are very much aware of, has been accentuated by the conditions under which the first significant air campaigns since the end of the Algerian war have been carried out. Apart from a few interventions on the African continent, the French Air Force was not involved in combat from the 1960s – the end of the Algerian war – to the early 1990s – the first Gulf war. In 1990, the first combat mission – in which a formation of eight Jaguars clashed with

---

1. C2SD Study (Defence Social Sciences Study Centre) [Centre d'étude en Science sociale de la Défense], Gérard Dubey and Caroline Moricot, 2008.

Iraqi ground troops – was a rude reawakening to the reality of war, after decades of training against a virtual enemy. But the rapid collapse of the Iraqi army and its ground-to-air defences did not allow this reality to be assimilated by a good many pilots.

Then came the Kosovo war. Although this conflict saw pilots back in combat, the conditions under which it took place did not allow much attenuation of the detachment phenomenon. Two aspects probably even exacerbated it: first, having the planes take off from a base in Italy, far removed from a combat situation, in country at peace, where even the families of the pilots were able to join them and, second, the nature of the targets attacked. Indeed, when the French aircraft and their crews were based at the Italian airbase of Istrana, several pilots mentioned the difficulty of moving, with no transition period, from a state of peace to a state of war.

We were based at Istrana, near Venice, and it was normal to see families arriving, because Italy is fun. That created a fracture between the everyday life that we were living there and the few hours we spent above hostile territory dropping bombs [...]. So, we had families arriving just like that, they were there, they saw the pilots fly off [...].

As regards the identification of the targets, another recounts:

[...] In Bosnia, in Kosovo, we fired on vehicles, bridges, buildings, shelters, built-up areas, things like that [...]. Perhaps we fired on people, but people we couldn't see, hidden in a factory. We didn't go any further to see if there really were any people [1].

In becoming more technical, conditions for combat have been established that put the enemy at an ever increasing distance and, as a corollary, decrease one's own exposure.

Nevertheless – and every day the conflict in Afghanistan proves this to be so –, air combat can still put one's sense of self-involvement to the test, even to the extent of paying the ultimate price. For the introduction of various changes to operational deployment have enabled the phenomenon of detachment to be either averted or at least reduced.

---

1. C2SD Study op. cit.

HOW CAN DETACHMENT BE AVERTED?

It is easy to be brave from a safe distance.

Aesop

- **By placing bases and pilots right inside the operational zone, thereby reducing physical distance**

In Afghanistan, the arrival of French aircrew at Kandahar base allowed closer contact with the coalition's armed forces, especially the army. The aircrew's view of the war changed as a result and, by decreasing the distance that had been built up technically, gave them greater exposure to it. Even though the Air Force's aircrew had a special relationship with French Special Forces – a detachment of which had been stationed on the Tajikistan base to facilitate the preparation and conduct of the operation – their arrival at Kandahar was seen as a high point by all those participating in this crisis since 2002. This physical proximity both to scene of combat and to those directly involved on the ground changed how the war looked to the pilots and their teams as they went about their daily tasks.

In the Kandahar region, fierce battles are an almost daily occurrence and the base itself regularly comes under rocket fire. The airmen, whether pilots, engineers, intelligence personnel or support crew, thus experience and to an extent share in the arduous life of ground combatants. They now often meet up to prepare or debrief missions, or simply to exchange points of view and, when appropriate, thanks and congratulations.

> *At Kandahar, we no longer have that distance, because we are mixed in with the combat infantry and the Special Forces. We live with them, we go to the mess with them, we can brief missions with them, and at that point we begin to think of foot soldiers as human beings. Those little black dots we can see on the ground, we start to find out who they are, how they interact with their environment, and so forth. All this makes the war more believable, more real.* [1]

EYEWITNESS ACCOUNT BY A PILOT [2]

> *I am in the operations room when a Canadian captain arrives, accompanied by one of the unit personnel. He is looking for the crews he worked with a few days before. They are airborne, so I ask him the reason for his visit. It turns out he was their JTAC [3] during a difficult*

---

1. C2SD Study, op. cit.
2. Testimony from Captain Gaviard.
3. JTAC: Joint Tactical Air Controller, the ground-based controller responsible for guiding aircraft to their targets.

mission. Several live passes had been required to enable the Canadian troops to extract themselves, before opening fire on the positions held by the insurgents. The captain says that without the involvement of the Mirages neither he nor his 'combat buddies' would be here to talk about it.

His French Canadian accent and Quebec expressions somehow made the event seem less serious without, however, altering the solemnity of the moment. He took a number of gifts out of his bag for the crews who, following his guidance, had opened fire. He also said that some of the windows in his vehicle, previously weakened by the enemy fire, has been blown out by the blast from the French bombs. I realised that he must have been quite close to the target and that it could not have been easy for him. For it is always very difficult to intervene when troops are in extremely close proximity. In fact, the JTAC has a hard time providing good guidance when under fire. Moreover, it is much more often guidance problems that hinder air arm involvement rather than overlapping forces. There are always some enemy elements – snipers and basic artillery [1] – located some distance away and it is important to destroy these. It's clear that this man knows his job, as he succeeded in guiding the French aircraft to enable the disengagement.

He and I continue our discussion throughout morning, then in the evening we have dinner with him and the air crews engaged in the operation. He tells us how important it is for them to hear the sound of combat aircraft when they are under fire, alone, somewhere in Afghanistan. He also says that they still expect a number of deaths in their regiment in the course of their tour, due to the type of operations they are undertaking. His words made all our pilots think about the meaning of our mission in Afghanistan.

A further testimony from the same man shows how the presence of pilots in a danger zone allows them to become aware of the reality of the terrain and the humanity of their mission.

On that day, two of the unit's pilots are having a discussion near the rest tents, close to a group of personnel tasked with support for the French detachment based at Kandahar. Suddenly the siren warning of incoming enemy rocket fire starts up (launch is detected by sensors). Given the great size of the Kandahar base, it is unusual for rockets to be really dangerous – the previous fatality was as far back as 2003. Because these French personnel have been deployed for several

---

1. The insurgents use mortars and RPGs as artillery support.

weeks, they have been through this routine a good many times. So, no panic, despite the unnerving whistling sound associated with the Doppler effect as the rocket flies through the air. On this occasion, the tension rises because the two pilots quickly realise, from the increasing frequency of the whistling, that the rocket is heading their way. "Damn, this one's got my name on it", one of them thinks. Everyone dives to the ground and waits for the impact. As it happens, the rocket lands a few metres from them without exploding. The two pilots look up and see the rocket buried in the ground, with its propellant still belching smoke. In a single movement, they get up and run to shelter behind one of the concrete bastion walls situated inside the camp to contain rocket shrapnel.

This particular rocket does not explode and the two pilots return to flying the following day.

Though not a combat zone, Kandahar base is located in a dangerous province, where airmen, like everyone else, run the risk of being fired on, even though it is less frequent and less dangerous than when on foot patrol.

There is therefore a sort of convergence and closeness between airmen and ground forces as, under a table in the mess or in a shelter, they wait for the siren to stop. We can well appreciate the dangers of ground combat, since we can watch it through our on-board cameras. The insurgent who walks into friendly machine gun fire, rounds from Apache helicopters or 155 mm artillery fire causing considerable damage, mortar impacts, screams over the radio.

Finally, an account by a pilot comparing two large deployments of operational air bases in Kosovo and Kyrgyzstan reveals that the way pilots live on a daily basis influences their perception of war.

My two experiences are very different from each other. In the first we were living in a four-star hotel on the Adriatic coast – there were really no ground operations and we saw people living normally. This certainly created a discrepancy with our mission [...]. It was like we were a little further away on a business trip [...]. Whereas in Afghanistan, we were in a camp, there were military personnel, we were accommodated on site, sometimes in a hotel – but that was unusual – and then in a very different environment. In other words, Kyrgyzstan is not Italy. In Italy, there are two, more obviously separate worlds and our access to communications was also perhaps a little less easy. It was more like war in Afghanistan. [1]

1. C2SD Study op. cit.

The location of the air arm, now based in Kandahar, in the middle of Pashtun territory and at the heart of the war, is a break with decades of operating from a distance. War has once again become a concrete reality, and this contributes to the re-personalisation of war and to the prevention of certain trivialising effects. Personalisation concerns friend as much as foe: it becomes possible to put faces to those asking for air support. Communal life in a closed and hostile environment reinforces ties and facilitates solidarity and the sharing of experience.

IN WHAT OTHER WAYS CAN DETACHMENT BE PREVENTED?

- *By developing collective solidarity to prevent the pilot being isolated*

We have seen in previous chapters how group solidarity is vital for building up esprit de corps and thereby maintaining individual equilibrium. The pilot's problem lies in his solitude when in action. In practice, the pilot is alone at the controls of his aircraft and, even if he always flies with a wingman (or crewman for two-seat aircraft), he remains isolated in his cockpit. This feature of combat in three dimensions shapes the pilot's psychology.

> *This is what people told me about the profession of fighter pilot when I was very young. One shares a great deal, but it is mainly egoistic. One is alone in one's plane. And in the final analysis one will always be alone, whatever might happen if there is a serious problem [...]. Certainly, there will always be a sense of sharing and brotherhood with the unit formed for purposes of war. But the medals go to the pilot and not to the mechanic, because the tricky part is releasing the bomb, not getting it into the plane. Loading the bomb is a standard procedure, there is no particular stress, even if it requires some commitment, and the mechanics were expected to do it frequently during that period.* [1]

Alone when in action, alone when making the final decision, alone when returning from action, the pilot nonetheless needs a community to re-establish his personal equilibrium and to eliminate stress. It is important not to underestimate this need and to do everything to encourage times when he can develop emotional bonds with the human environment around him. This communal level will initially be embodied by his Flight. Created to undertake missions, the Flight will also help build the confidence needed to perform well, both in the air and outside the mission period as such.

---

1. C2SD Study op. cit.

The idea of a Flight at war was something quite new for me. Four people going to complete a mission, which is not an insignificant thing for them, or for others. It was absolutely essential that the group worked well outside missions because on detachment we were living, if not quite on top of each other, in two-man rooms. Moreover, these combat missions called for a certain trust, and the trust required for a training mission is not at all the same as that needed to undertake a combat mission. The level of trust must be much higher, making the bonds between people necessarily closer [...].

Above the level of the Flight, it is the entire squadron embodying the group and it this the pilot will be able to rely to on preserve his equilibrium. Words are not enough; it is above all the sharing of what one feels when airborne that creates bonding.

Trust when in an operational theatre is necessarily also linked to the way people already know each other, in the squadron, from day to day.

This means that squadron life has the particular feature, it seems to me, that we don't talk about serious matters too intimately. But there is nevertheless great closeness stemming from being people 'of the air', from collectively experiencing the same sensations, from all being moved by the same passion, and overall having a psychology that exhibits common characteristics.

In the way these pilots express themselves, we find a search for a common identity, the need to recognise in each other the same passion, the same sense of action.

We are not far from the esprit de corps often referred to in the army or the crew spirit found in the navy. This communal closeness can break through the isolation stemming from the pilot's professional activity, and counterbalance the insidious and sometimes involuntary tendency to detachment.

TECHNOLOGY CAN ALSO HELP PREVENT DETACHMENT

- ### *Technological developments in observation allow the target to be re-humanised*

We saw in the introduction to this chapter that the advanced *technicisation* of how and when to open fire allowed pilots to distance themselves from their target and thus contributed to their dehumanisation.

Technology has today attained such a level of precision that it has in the end resulted in an unexpected effect, diametrically opposed to the preceding one. The quality of fire control optics and optronics now allows one to approach visually to within only a few metres of the target, while remaining at a much greater distance physically. This capability has the positive consequence of bringing the human being back into the pilot's immediate field of vision, and thus finally leading to a *rehumanisation* of the target.

> *Being able to see, in a laser designator pod, a man walking or a bus crossing a bridge, while monitoring the area or guiding the weapon – this is something very new, and in my view it is a really important change [...]. The pods are more and more accurate, and when the weather is fine, whether by day or by night, one can see much more, such as what the man on the ground is doing. In addition this has the advantage of making us realise that, in the final analysis, if we are there, it is also for the benefit of those on the ground. You don't just see the bad guys on whom you are going to open fire; you also see those who are trying to live in the environment that, as far as possible, you are trying to improve. This helps us in our combat, because our motivation is strengthened by the reality of what we can see: life trying to begin again here and there* [1].

Thanks to their new laser designator pods equipped with high magnification day/night cameras and their gyrostabilised goggles, fighter and helicopter pilots, navigators and drone operators achieve a remarkable level of discrimination of ground targets and their immediate environment. Low altitude passes, although at high speed, also give pilots the opportunity to come close, reinforcing the notion of proximity. Night vision goggles make it possible to pick out all exchanges of fire, generally very intense, at night during clashes between friendly and enemy ground forces. The airman, if he is not completely at the heart of the battle, is generally just above it, ready to intervene and to support the forces engaged, and he feels himself to be even more involved by virtue of exchanges over the radio with the forces engaged on the ground: screams, shooting as background noise, shouts of relief, and so on.

EYEWITNESS ACCOUNT BY A PILOT [2]

Afghanistan 2006

> *We have just received the order to head towards a new area further south, although we had been working in support of Dutch troops in Uruzgan for over an hour. We therefore head towards the region of Helmand, where we are asked to make contact with a British JTAC.*

1. C2SD op. cit.
2. Testimony of Captain Gaviard.

We get to the area in about ten minutes. The British JTAC asks us to observe two people suspected of planting an IED [1] on a road leading out of the town. As well as binoculars, we use the laser designator pod to observe their behaviour. We see that they are digging by the roadside with spades. For long minutes we study their various movements, which we report by radio to the British forces. Their behaviour, as well as that of other personnel detected close to a nearby line of trees, soon makes us sure that this is not merely a case of bomb planters, but a full team of insurgents ready to act. Our analysis of the situation is informed by a number of conversations we have had on base at Kandahar with Canadian specialists in insurgent behaviour. However, designation of a target and the authority to fire come from the senior officer on the ground.

We therefore await their orders and the go-ahead, which in our opinion will obviously not be long in coming. There is no doubt that we will open fire once, or several times, on the men we are watching and that they will certainly die. From that point on, observing them takes another turn. Yes, they are enemies, but we can see them talking, walking and digging under a baking sun. For several minutes, we continue scrutinising their movements, but also life around them. In fact, not very far from there, we can see the movements of civilian vehicles in town, cyclists, and people walking around. It is obvious that the proximity of civilians is giving the leadership on the ground pause for thought, even if in this case a burst of cannon fire along a precise bearing should prevent any collateral damage, and would conform to the rules of engagement.

Those long minutes of waiting are harrowing, because we are waiting, and waiting is never good when the situation is clear and one knows with certainty that one should shoot to kill. One should not close one's eyes to the fact that if we have to act, it would be to fire on those insurgents, on those men [...].

Finally, the British JTAC informs us that he has no further requirement for our services. We are surprised. Our first thought is that he has not understood what we had explained to him in English. To no avail. Following our orders, we leave the area and land at Kandahar. As soon as we have done so, we send the video to the British troops, so that they can go and check the road. They find two bombs buried in the ground.

Later, I draw a parallel with marksmen. We were in a similar position and we acted and certainly thought like a sniper from a combat

---

1. Improvised Explosive Device.

unit deployed on the ground, with the difference that we were at a safe distance, but also that we could unleash much greater firepower.

Now so close to the pilot, the enemy's face becomes visible to him and he cannot ignore it completely. The way the enemy physically stands out and can be seen in detail on the cockpit displays fractures the ability to keep people and objects at a distance. Such ruptures enable the crews to judge the extent of their sensitivity and humanity.

Through their ethical teaching, the studies pursued and the manner of their deployment in Afghanistan, the French air force and naval air arm have shown that they have taken fully into account the risk of the pilot being too far distant from the reality of the conflict in which he is likely to intervene. Pilots are made to understand that allowing themselves to be contaminated by detachment is to run the risk of indifference, the risk of abdicating from the courage to directly encounter the adversary. But the warrior's ethic is to a large extent built on freely accepted individual exposure to danger which may result in death. Particularly close bonds may be formed and relationships of trust can be built around fear experienced directly and through the shared communal waiting when units are based in the area where the operation is taking place.

For a pilot, the right distance seems to be that which makes intervention possible, but does not dehumanise the person carrying it out. It entails a continuing search for balance that each individual must learn to manage. Instructors training crews for air combat, no matter what their country, should always be aware of this basic requirement.

*
*   *

6. Brutality... which leads to torture

> *The soldier who can no longer control his violence loses his meaning. War is then irremediably engulfed by absurd killing.*
>
> Hélie Denoix de Saint Marc

"Your book has made me feel guilty."

The comment came out of the blue, in a tone devoid of reproach. It was the first time my father [1] had said anything about my book, though it had

---

1. General Pierre Royal (1928-2009).

been published eight months previously. His confession took me by surprise, because I had only very rarely known my father confide in this way.

He was suffering from advanced cancer. We knew it was incurable. He probably felt that too, but without daring to admit it.

For a few seconds I was speechless, then, trying to avoid a display of emotion that would interfere with the rest of our conversation.

"Oh, really. Why is that?" I said

'Because of memories to do with Algeria," he answered after a pause. "Your book is of your time. It could not have been written in my era."

"Yes, I'm with you on that point, but isn't it precisely because we have been able to draw lessons from history, including those from Algeria, that it is possible today to take a clear position on these sensitive subjects?"

That particular telephone conversation was taken no further. I had to wait until the following month when, taking advantage of a period of remission between two chemotherapy sessions, he continued confiding in me, telling me about the whole of his military career in a way that he had never done previously. I had gone to see him in his home at Saint Georges-de-Didonne. My son Thomas, aged 22, was sitting on a sofa next to us. He could tell we were approaching an important moment. A moment which he did not want to disturb, but did not really want to be part of either. He seemed engrossed in reading a newspaper, but I knew he was totally focused on our conversation. Yet he shared in it completely, for almost two hours, without daring to move. I was happy to know he was there, a witness to this handing down between generations, of which he too was one of the links. Wholly absorbed, he listened to what his grandfather had to say, while I took a few notes, so as not to forget anything. Today, though, I have no need of my notes: my father's words are engraved on me as clearly as the events that had seared his conscience with sorrow and remorse.

His Algerian experience began as a young infantry lieutenant in the 2nd and 3rd RIC [Marine Infantry Regiment] in the region of Constantine; then, having earned his wings, on a second tour as a helicopter pilot posted to the village of Djidjelli. Djidjelli... a word I am able to write without hesitation, because this was the village where I was born in 1960.

He gave me the following account of the incident that had brought about his feeling of guilt.

It took place in Algiers, where I had gone on a liaison visit. An Algerian suspected of knowing the location of a future attack, or of being in contact with those planting bombs, had been arrested. I knew the horror of the situation in Algiers, the attacks, the civilian victims cut to pieces almost every day, the children, the women... We despe-

rately needed intelligence. I was present at the interrogation. The pri-
soner was extensively beaten up and tortured. I did not like what I was
participating in. But I did not see how we could do anything diffe-
rently. At that time, I did not view what we were doing as reprehensi-
ble. We were caught in the trap of a situation that left us no other
choice: we absolutely had to stop the carnage and I knew of no other
way to achieve that.

The man in charge of the interrogation was a 'pied-noir' [French
settler]. That was a mistake. He was too involved and it didn't go well.
The man being interrogated was quite old. He couldn't take it. He died
as a result.

During the interrogation he confessed to nothing, and for good
reason: he knew nothing. That was confirmed to us later. There had
been an error in the assessment. Despite this new information,
although I was very ill at ease, I believed that in the event we had no
alternative.

Today, I am not so sure.

This discussion was the last time my father directly confided in me; as
I have already said, he was not much given to introspection. I could see
how much he had been marked by the events, of which he had imparted
only a few fragments.

This unexpected confession echoed an incident during a speech given
several weeks earlier in Toulon [1]. Together with an air force officer, I had
been invited to speak about the thinking on ethics in our respective services. No sooner had we finished our presentations than we were taken to
task by a member of the audience. Requesting the microphone on the pretext of asking a question, he began shouting at us angrily. He read out a
long, evidently prepared, diatribe. His voice was shaking. He recounted
how, as a young pied-noir child living in Algeria, he had seen his mother
killed before his eyes, blown to pieces by bombs in her kitchen, in the
course of an attack by French soldiers. Was it an act of war? An instance
of dreadful collateral damage as a result of a targeting error? An operation
gone badly wrong? We shall never know. That evening, he expressed a
real hatred for the French uniform, as a result of a terrible trauma from
which no-one can really recover.

---

1. Speech given in the framework of the '*Thursday Ethics* series, a joint initiative of *Marians in the Var, Greater Toulon Lions' Club* and the *Higher Institute of Electronics and Computing*, the object of which was to organise, on a Thursday evening several times a year, panel discussions, conference-debates or events aimed at defining the role of ethics in commerce, finance, industry and society, when faced with the changes linked to globalisation.

He finished his declaration with a stifled sob. There was total silence. The atmosphere had suddenly become oppressive.

What does one say in response to such a statement? I could only express my compassion and my sincere personal regrets for the human drama he had suffered. Without paying any heed to what I said, he again challenged me, reproaching me for the lack of any reference to the Algerian period in my speech.

After what the French army did over there, how can you talk about ethics? And the torture practised by both sides? You don't even talk about it. It's easy to expound high principles when you forget the past. Algeria is a taboo subject in the army, I know that. You don't even dare to look the past in the face. For my part, I have never forgotten.

It was obviously impossible to engage in any debate with him. The man's understandable revulsion left no room at all for calm discussion.

As for his first cause for criticism, he was not wrong. I had, until then, blanked out the Algerian period from my thinking. This incident, and my father's testimony, made clear to me that change in this respect was overdue. Any study of military ethics worthy of the name could not ignore a period of history that gives rise to so many questions, especially if it claims to be intended for future generations. In fact, how could educational ethical reflection on the use of brutality in modern [1] conflicts be undertaken without addressing what took place during the Algerian war?

As the son of a serviceman, born in Algeria during the war, I belong to what I call the 'first generation' of Algerian combatants. Our fathers, and those close to us, were actors in or spectators of the drama, whether at close quarters or further away. We grew up sufficiently distanced from the events not to have directly suffered traumatic effects, but sufficiently close to those who paid the price to have felt their wounds. Whenever they were willing to open up, we heard the words from their own mouths, and we understood that only they had the right to pass judgement on them. Only they could decently draw any conclusions, with the calm of hindsight and the distance that allows events to be viewed with a degree of perspective and discernment.

Military chaplains have been foremost in expressing how harsh things were in the field. 'Shepherds of souls', as they are pleased to consider themselves, they were the first to witness the torments of conscience engendered by the implementation of the principles of revolutionary warfare. As early as 1959, Father Henri Péninou, reserve lieutenant,

---

1. Conflicts which took place after the creation of international humanitarian law and the laws of armed conflict.

paratrooper and auxiliary chaplain of the 25th Parachute Division, produced a first *spiritual guide*. This pamphlet, of which a hundred copies were initially roneotyped, was written as a response to his colleague in the 10th Parachute Division, Father Louis Delarue, who had tried to legitimise the use of torture. Péninou's text appeared as *Reflection on the Duties of the Soldier*, and was reprinted under the same title in 1999 by Montpellier Paul Valéry University.

In 1962, François Casta, paratrooper chaplain from the Army vicariate, in turn published some fifty copies of *Le drame spirituel de l'Armée* [The army's spiritual drama]. At the time, this compendium provoked a veritable outcry and was even banned initially. He focussed on describing the reality of the situation and the complexity of the dilemma facing the combatants. The full implications of *Le drame spirituel de l'Armée*, striking in its maturity, is clear fifty years later [1] in the current context of the struggle against terrorism, where the methods deployed are comparable to those used by the FLN (National Liberation Front). Offering the beginnings of an ethical response to the adversary's violence, it can be transposed to the military operations of our era, marked both by their growing complexity and by a fashionable relativism that tends to erode standards and to trivialise ethical standpoints.

Many other authors have subsequently written on this sensitive subject. The writings of Major Hélie de Saint Marc have won numerous awards and been frequently cited as reference points. Another, very exhaustive work on this conflict is the *Le livre blanc de l'armée française en Algérie* [White Paper on the French army in Algeria]. Prefaced by a listing of 328 officers who served in Algeria, it was published in 2002 in response to a particularly aggressive media campaign, itself echoing the publication of the memoirs of General Aussaresses in 2001.

To talk about this conflict and to summarise the aspects of it involving torture, I have therefore deliberately chosen to draw on the richness of these testimonies, giving the floor to those involved and who have had the courage to speak out, so that their commitment should not have been in vain and the lessons they learned should not be lost. I trust that readers – particularly those involved at that time – will be convinced of the integrity of this decision, which seeks to understand these events by means of real-life experience, with a view to building up individual and collective consciences, present and future.

It is therefore be a matter of offering a dispassionate summary of the historical events which led to the use of brutality and torture in Algeria, so

---

1. Republished in 2009, with the addition of a biography *Homme de Dieu... Homme de guerre,* [Man of God... Man of War], Esprit du Livre Editions, 2009.

as to allow younger generations, fortified by the lessons learned, to understand why it would not be acceptable for us to use the same methods – and make same mistakes – today.

In choosing to tackle the Algerian war in this way, it is clearly not a matter of using the one issue of *brutalisation* to sum up the entire conflict. This neologism, taken from the historian George Mosse [1], who specifically examined the issue of escalating violence in combat, characterises the pernicious spiral that can be triggered by the use of excessive violence during a conflict, whatever its nature. He describes how the use of brutality, elevated to the level of an operative principle, can generate a trivialisation of violence, a hardening of hearts and souls that can extend beyond the military field and affect whole sections of society, even many years after the combat had ended. Over and beyond my focus on this totemic aspect, I am well aware that the Algerian war was highly complex and that more than a half century after its conclusion is still very difficult to tackle dispassionately, when faced with the pain of the victims of attacks, misconduct and mistakes. I am well aware of the suffering of a million civilians repatriated so badly, as well as thousands of abandoned *harkis* (Algerian soldiers who fought on the side of the French). Nor do I forget the military actors – career, conscript or recalled to service – who were often shamed or ignored by people in metropolitan France prejudiced by political passions and who have never really recovered from a war so quickly decried and one that many of its participants prefer never to talk about, even today. I am also aware that to a very great extent what primarily characterised the actions of the army in Algeria was precisely its struggle against all forms of torture, assassination and ideologically motivated and systematically organised crimes. I wish also to spare a thought for the many outstanding acts of devotion by those who believed in a peaceful solution and sacrificed themselves for it.

To conclude this necessary preamble, it is not a matter of confusing or inverting the order of victims and executioners, but of seeking to look at the military history of our country unflinchingly, so that we can build a future that takes account of its lessons. Analysis of the past is essential because it holds the keys to tomorrow, particularly in the field of ethics.

*

*   *

---

1. The concept of *brutalisation* was introduced by the historian George Mosse in his book *Fallen Soldiers,* published in French as *De la Grande Guerre au totalitarisme*. It refers to the idea that the extreme violence experienced during the First World War had repercussions for inter-war society and that it engendered great political and social conflict, with serious repercussions for subsequent history.

Introductory proposition: the phenomenon of brutalisation is not innate in soldiers, but primarily stems from the violence of war.

Odile Roynette [1], a historian known for her work on conscription, explains that the drift into *brutalisation* is characteristic of war itself. She has shown that violent armed engagements tend to trigger a dynamic of violence in many combatants that may be gratuitous and result in aggressive behaviour lacking any tactical or strategic utility. For example, such is the case with wartime rape, committed in enemy territory by soldiers driven by the terror of combat. These odious acts have more to do with humiliating the enemy by imprinting on the bodies of their victims the reality of conquest, rather than serving any military objective. Such brutality feeds off the cruelty of combat, the horror of certain situations and sometimes the atrocities committed by the adversary.

Hélie Denoix de Saint Marc, witness of and participant in the last three wars France has fought, makes the following bitter observation on the subject [2].

> *In war, there are horrors. The Allied bombings of Germany were the application of a kind of terror. Ultimately, if I returned from deportation, if the camps were liberated in time, it is arguably because allied air power had, at that point, launched blanket bombing raids on Dresden, Cologne and Hamburg, massacring hundreds of thousands of innocent people and permanently mutilating children. There is no clean war. One finds in it a reflection of human life, good and evil cohabiting. Sometimes it is a combat between one good and another, if not of one evil against another.*

Even if the use of brutality during the Algerian conflict originated with a very specific operational objective, it was inevitably suspected and accused of being gratuitous – though it never liked to admit as much – to the extent that one can never be certain that those charged with acting with brutality in the field avoided the inevitable excesses it engenders.

In Algeria, despite atrocities by the FLN, French servicemen did not immediately begin using torture and excessive violence. It was at the time of the battle of Algiers, during implementation of the concept of 'revolutionary warfare', that these were increasingly used.

---

1. Odile Roynette, a historian known for her work on conscription and its relationship to the shaping of masculine identity in French society during the Third Republic.
2. Laurent Beccaria, *Hélie De Saint Marc*, Perrin, 1999.

A brief historical [1] recapitulation will help to place the events in context. At the end of the Second World War, Algeria was at boiling point. By virtue of the sacrifices made during that long conflict, the Muslim population was demanding reforms, but the French government paid little heed to their aspirations and harshly repressed demonstrations. Nationalism, mainly embodied by the National Liberation Front (FLN) grew rapidly and, after the French defeat at Dien Bien Phu in Indochina, its emboldened militants took up arms against France. From 1954 to 1956 the fighting took place mainly in the Algerian *djebel* (mountains).

In 1956, two years after the start of the clashes, the leadership of the FLN turned to a plan for an urban offensive based on terror. In their view, targeting towns with more spectacular attacks than those carried out in the countryside would strike at the heart of the colonial apparatus and would sensitize public opinion to the cause of independence. On 30 September 1956, three bombs exploded in central Algiers, injuring over sixty people. In the following weeks and months, the lives of people in Algeria were punctuated by a succession of murderous attacks. No less than twelve hundred attacks in the month of January 1957 alone turned the Algerian capital into a bloodbath. Strengthened by its successes against an ineffective police force, the FLN planned an insurrectional strike at the same time as the much publicised UN debate on the Algerian situation. But the French minister for Algeria, Robert Lacoste, wanting to address the UN under the best possible conditions and realising that the police force could do no more, decided at that point to hand over the maintenance of order to military units.

Accordingly, he assigned the 10th Parachute Division (DP), commanded by General Massu. This unit had just arrived in back in France following the Suez intervention. Initially envisaged as a general reserve for the Algerian theatre, the parachute division was finally used to restore order in Algiers.

The following three historical factors explain the spiral leading to the implementation of the principles of violent action in the battle of Algiers.

1. *The inadequacy of the police force.*

When the FLN decided to take the battle from the countryside into the main Algerian urban centres, it set about creating a 'bomb network' intended to increase the number of attacks in Algiers and spread terror. This

---

1. The historical recaps used in this chapter are translated directly from the excellent memoranda of the CDEF – Centre de doctrine et d'entraînement des forces de l'armée de Terre, (the French army doctrine and force training centre) – *La guerre révolutionnaire. Succès et ambiguïté. Le cas des batailles d'Alger*. [Revolutionary war. Success and ambiguity. The case of the Battle of Algier.]

network was responsible for making explosives, then transporting and planting them. It proved particularly effective.

The forces of order in Algiers were soon overwhelmed. Not only were they incapable of combating independentist violence, but were also totally ineffective against random punitive expeditions, triggered in response to the tragic event that brought 1956 to a close. On 28 December, Anédée Froger, a respected figure in Algiers, veteran of the First World War and Chairman of the Algerian Mayors' Association, was assassinated by the FLN. At his funeral, the government representative was verbally abused by anti-FLN European extremists following the cortege to the ceremony. These extremists then took advantage of the situation by ransacking shops, setting fire to cars and beating up anyone they come across who appeared to be Muslim. Officially, four Muslims were killed and fifty people, including three Europeans, injured. While all this is happening, the police took little or no action.

The event was emblematic of the security situation in Algiers. The police, taken by surprise by the internal reactions and faced with an enemy about which they knew nothing and were powerless to fight, were incapable of maintaining order. Used to dealing with criminals in peacetime, they were overwhelmed by an organisation bringing a climate of war to the city. There was widespread questioning of their orders by the police and a general refusal to go into action against a crowd of Europeans like themselves, who had taken the law into their own hands.

The political authorities therefore decided to turn to other agents of state power. Recourse to the army appeared to be the only alternative.

2. *Political responsibility unloaded onto the military*

On the morning of 7 January 1957, General Massu was summoned to the seat of government by the minister for Algeria. "Massu", he announced, "I am going to entrust you with order in the department. You have total power. With your division, you are going to regain complete control."

In this way, the commander of the 10th DP received the order to pacify Algiers and the entire north of the country. Powers were delegated to him, based on the law of 16 March 1956, known as the Special Powers Bill. It is easy to imagine what the idea of "total power" might mean at that time, in a territory far from France and in the grip of unbridled violence. Hélie de Saint Marc recalls that very unusual period at the beginning of 1957 [1].

---

1. Hélie de Saint Marc, *Les Champs de braise* [The Fields of Embers], Perrin, 2002 p 214.

With nowhere to turn except the army, the political authorities had decided to give the 10th parachute division complete power over Algiers – on condition that they sorted things out. It must be clearly understood what it meant for the French government at the time to transfer complete civil and military power to a few thousand paratroopers, ordered to clean up a city the size of Algiers. In reality, every officer was given the power to enter the home of any inhabitant of Algiers, interrogate him and place him in solitary confinement for an indefinite period, and all that without the slightest supervision, except possibly after the event, with all the difficulty that entails.

The transfer of civil power to the military leadership required them to exercise a new profession, for which they had been neither trained nor prepared. Much more than a delegation of power, this hastily taken decision represented a real leakage of power from a government apparently overwhelmed by events.

The Catholic Centre for French intellectuals wrote:

The army has more often than not been abandoned to its own inspiration, without receiving from the state, from public opinion or from the other manifestations of the nation, the impetus and orientation which would not have been lacking had the army and the nation been in step with each other. Turned in on itself, the army had been led to create for itself, with the means at its disposal, a morality and a politics, and sometimes also a religion [1].

To have mastered such a delegation of power would have required specific legal training and a system of control intended to limit potential excesses. But the political leadership deliberately gave full powers to men of action trained to wage war, because the problem in Algiers 'needed to be sorted out'.

Philippe Conrad [2], historian and joint editor of the *Livre blanc de l'armée française en Algérie* [White Paper on the French Army in Algeria] describes the extremes to which such political abandonment led the military forces, trained to complete their mission at any cost.

Those in the military do not deny that the battle for Algiers led them to break the rules of war in order to undertake police work that was

---

1. François Casta, *Homme de Dieu... Homme de guerre*, [Man of God...Man of War] Esprit du livre publications, 2009.
2. Professor of history (born in 1945) and lecturer at the French Joint Defence College, Conrad has been editorial director of *Histoires Magazine* and *Terres d'histoire*. He is chairman of the committee for editorial continuity of the *Nouvelle Revue d'Histoire* (NRH) and contributes to the monthly *Le Spectacle du Monde*.

not within their competence. However, they stress that this 'dirty work' had to be done to save the population of Algiers from attack. They only carried out the orders of the political authorities, the government of the socialist Guy Mollet, the longest lasting administration of the Fourth Republic. Even if they state – as Bigeard will later say – that the battle of Algiers 'was shit and blood'.

3. *The willingness of the military commanders and the search for effectiveness at any price*

Having been given a mission, the 10th DP equipped itself with the means to complete it successfully, for, like all military units, it had been trained to win, whatever the cost. Thus, in between terrorist attacks and policing operations designed to stop the attacks, the battle, which the 10th DP began in Algiers, was the direct application of 'revolutionary war' to an urban environment. General Salan's Directive Number 1, of 18 December 1956, setting out the paratroopers' objectives, specified the three aims of the new plan of action to be implemented by the parachute division: "The hunting down and destruction of the adversary's political structure; human contacts that benefit the local population; and rallying cries to common sense, which are in the interests of all those here".

The city of Algiers thus became a proving ground for new concepts of repression, combining winning over of the population with the destruction of the enemy, and made the acquisition and analysis of intelligence the spearhead and capstone for effectiveness in the field.

The leadership of the 10th DP threw themselves into the battle of Algiers as if they were mounting a new operation, in accordance with the principle of effectiveness at any price, which was their hallmark: dividing the town into sectors, infiltration of informers, rounding up of suspects, interrogations, passing information up the chain, crosschecking information, reconstitution of networks, etc. The majority of my friends who stayed with the 1st REP [1st Foreign Legion Parachute Regiment] took part in this work reluctantly. I met them at divisional HQ, set up in a Moorish villa on the Algiers heights, permeated by the scent of orange trees and exotic flowers. They all said the same thing: "This is not soldiers' work." One of them, who had the job of crosschecking the information gathered, told me with a grimace of disgust: "The politicians are offloading the responsibility onto us. Every day we discover new evidence of complicity in odd places. Save us from this, for goodness sake [1]."

---

1. Hélie de Saint Marc, *Les Champs de braise* [The Fields of Embers], Perrin, 2002 p 214.

The journalist Antoine-Pierre Mariano also refers to the impasse in which the combatants found themselves [1].

For the French army, it was a terrible ordeal. The straightforward soldiers involved were not prepared for it. It is counterproductive to use a paratrooper, who has been trained to assault a fortress under enemy machine gun fire, to search a neighbourhood of alleyways too narrow for two donkeys pass each other, where all the houses are intercommunicating and where the population is basically hostile or at least uncooperative.

The armed forces were thus confronted by insoluble dilemmas. Nonetheless decisions had to be taken and orders issued.

With heavy hearts and a divided conscience, the army did not hesitate to fully accept its responsibilities in a policing operation that had nothing in common with its traditional role. For us, it was no longer a question of confronting clearly defined battle lines, but of trying to destroy an extensive operation of generalised and organised assassinations. Against an unscrupulous adversary, we were defenceless. For the enemy, any method was acceptable. To achieve their aims, the killer became an essential cog in the system. All this explains, even if it does not entirely justify, the sometimes atrocious excesses we committed. It created a real ambiguity [2].

These testimonies inevitably invite comparison with the terrorism with which our modern societies are confronted today. Faced with an adversary without scruples, without law and without morality, the questions remain the same. But the forces fighting terrorism today benefit from the support of public opinion, whereas the French military in 1957 was isolated in its task. They did not even enjoy the support of their own population, which had distanced itself from them, leaving them alone to deal with a merciless and unscrupulous adversary.

Given such an adversary, the army faced the question 'Within what moral framework can we operate?' Throughout its long history, it had never encountered a comparable difficulty in establishing the limits of such a framework. In accordance with the moral code of warfare, a long military tradition had required men to fight with a degree of loyalty, whether that of the uniform or the weapons used, or in the identification of targets and combatants. Very quickly, an experience to which we were not accustomed was bound to reveal that the 'moral

---

1. *Livre blanc de l'armée française en Algérie,* Editions Contretemps, 2001, p. 136.
2. François Casta, *Homme de Dieu... Homme de guerre,* [Man of God...Man of War], Esprit du livre publications, 2009.

code' was not only no longer applicable, but was being ignored by an adversary who wholly rejected it. For the enemy, all blows 'below the belt' were allowed. Its ideological victory was largely based on the clear and flagrant violation of the defined and respected laws under whose protection the whole population lived. Here, the end justified the most atrocious means. Throughout this period, the forces of law and order remained confined within their scrupulous legal and moral conventions (or conformism).

Terrorism views this clash between two opposing sets of rules to be one of its main strengths. This war is like a game of cards between two players, of whom one gives himself the right to choose his own cards, but cries foul and demands justice whenever his opponent glances at his hand – intentionally or not. One fights as a maverick, tramples the Geneva and other conventions underfoot, orders or knowingly tolerates theft, arson, lying, murder, assassination, but will not allow himself to be dealt with except by judges, lawyers, prosecutors, and according to the rule of law. The other fights in uniform, respects the Geneva convention, the rule of law etc. [1]. *"*

After several weeks of operations in the field in Algiers, the first assessments made it clear that the means employed had resulted in unquestionable tactical success. But the methods used were already being contested and beginning to be condemned by public opinion.

After ten months of clashes, the 10th DP seemed to have succeeded in its mission: in October 1957 Algiers suffered just one attack, and none in November and December. The FLN was decapitated and Algiers was restored to peace. The feeling of an unassailable success was shared by most of the military leadership. They were convinced that it was possible to defeat urban terrorism, on condition that military means are used and that intelligence services are well coordinated. As a result of this tactical success, the Battle of Algiers became a template for revolutionary warfare in an urban environment. The model was soon being taught in military academies and was again applied in Algeria, particularly in Constantine, in 1958. It was even be exported to other countries. But from 1962 it began to be condemned following debates on torture that shed light on the methods used to win the battle. These methods are recalled by Hélie Denoix de Saint Marc in his first book of conversations with Laurent Beccaria in 1999.

---

1. François Casta, Homme de Dieu... Homme de guerre, [Man of God...Man of War] Esprit du livre publications, 2009.

The battle of Algiers came to an end with the death of the reclusive Ali la Pointe, tracked down during the night of 7-8 October 1957. Where everyone else had failed, this was a total victory for the paratroops, crafted by Massu, Bigeard and Jeanpierre, heroes to the pieds-noirs of Algiers, now able to begin living normally again. France breathed again. The press played up the myth of the strong, violent and implacable para. In the field, decimated and discredited by the flight of its headquarters staff in mid-battle, the FLN was a spent force in the Algiers region for many months. However, this crushing victory hid a number of serious threats. Although denied by the chain of command, the disappearance of suspects, the use of torture and excessive repression was a casus belli, and resulted in to a groundswell of rejection by part of the nation critical of colonialism. Though still a minority, they were young and intellectual. There thus began a long battle of opinion, with newspapers and books as intermediaries, in which each side hurled corpses at the head of the other – the body of Professor Maurice Audin[1] justifying the victims of the Corniche casino and vice versa. While torture did not disappear with Algiers, 1957 left festering wounds and had a profound effect on people's thinking[2].

François Casta echoes[3] Major de Saint Marc.

To obtain intelligence, it is hardly likely that the suspect will confess spontaneously. The heart of the matter is therefore to loosen tongues. We know they will not loosen themselves. Given this fact, one found oneself forced into using a number of procedures that are not altogether legal, if not an oblique way of getting around the law.

At what point, therefore, do the recommended methods become intrinsically illegal? A technique is neither moral nor immoral. Only its use and the intention behind it determine its morality. There is no well established rule to determine the exact moment at which an act, which is in itself neutral, becomes intrinsically bad. For example, at what point do kicks or blows with a truncheon become torture?

Torture. Even the word makes one shudder because it harks back to the dark days of the occupation and to the methods used in French prisons by a shameful enemy. It is therefore not surprising that the revelation of its use during the battle of Algiers was a bombshell in mainland France.

---

1. Maurice Audin, born in 1932 in Béja (Tunisia) who died in 1957 following his arrest in Algiers, was a lecturer in French mathematics at Algiers University, a member of the Algerian Communist Party and a militant in the cause of Algerian independence.
2. Laurent Beccaria, *Hélie De Saint Marc*, Perrin, 1999, p. 180.
3. François Casta, Homme de Dieu... Homme de guerre, [Man of God...Man of War] Esprit du livre publications, 2009.

However, in the field, in the months that followed, the situation to some extent moved on. Historically, the Battle of Algiers is in practice divided into two periods: the first, from January to March 1957, the second following the reorganisation of the FLN networks between July and October of the same year. Following the incontrovertible initial victory in early April 1957, calm returned to Algiers. However, the brutal methods used by the parachute division to achieve the victory were beginning to be a problem for the political leadership. The 10th DP itself was keen to change mission, and as a result three of the division's four regiments were ordered to leave Algiers. Aussaresse's special team remained in place, although its methods and the lack of transparency of its actions were already being seriously contested.

Hélie de Saint Marc again addresses this sensitive topic.

Let us first of all come to an understanding about words. Roughing someone up during questioning, a bright light in the face and a few punches: that is not torture. It is practised by police all over the world. That said, torture did exist. The men who resorted to it were not particularly perverted, but were following orders. The command chain at every level, as well as the political authorities, covered up the practice. It was the end product of a spiral, of which not only the ultimate practitioners at the end of the line should be accused. One must also put oneself back into the atmosphere of a city subjected to terrorism where, once or twice a day, men, women and children were torn apart by bombs.

In September 1986, Paris was in a truly psychotic state of siege, even though the attacks were much less well organised and systematic – and above all much less bloody – than in Algiers in 1957, where the tension at every street corner was palpable. Then it was a trial of strength between the FLN and the paratroops. In that sordid atmosphere, does the person responsible for maintaining order have the right to mistreat men whom he knows for a fact are harbouring intelligence? Basic morality says no. When one talks about it calmly in a tranquil city and in a nation at peace, it is not possible. When one is immersed in it, I just don't know. It is not as simple as saying 'I am against torture' – everyone is against torture. I think that there were surely some interrogations which should not have taken place. But truly, fundamentally, I have not yet found a satisfactory answer [1].

Alas, despite that initial period of calm, the attacks began again in Algiers in the summer of 1957 – less than two months after the force

---

1. Laurent Beccaria, *Hélie de Saint Marc*, Perrin, 1999, p. 176.

levels were reduced. The FLN had in fact reorganised itself, in an attempt not to make the same mistakes as the first time. To find the FLN bombs, General Massu entrusted command of the Algiers Sahel sector to his deputy, Colonel Godard, a man critical of the first battle of Algiers, who wanted to introduce new methods of working.

For the great majority of the military present in Algiers, the second battle of Algiers greatly resembled the first. The soldiers and the non-commissioned officers carried out searches, arrests, surveillance of FLN caches, and guard duties on the roofs of the casbah. But the arrival of Colonel Godard marked an important break in the way intelligence was acquired, because he was unhappy about urban warfare and its excesses. He later explained this in several accounts.

> *The carrier of bombs or the thrower of grenades always knows at least his commander and often a great deal more, in spite of the precautions and the dead ends of a compartmentalised organisation. So should a confession be forced out of him? I say no.*

> *First of all, because such a method is contrary to the military tradition that prohibits the mistreatment of adversaries taken prisoner. Over and above this immutable principle, I say no for more down-to-earth reasons: dragging out confessions by suffering very often leads to fantasy confessions, whose use results in mistakes.*

> *Brutality serves the propaganda purposes of the enemy who, by exaggerating it – experience proves this – stirs up the opinion of decent people not hitherto inclined to subversion. Brutality allows those who spontaneously confessed to subsequently retract their confessions, claiming that they spoke under torture. Furthermore, those who talk of their own volition when under threat of arrest are much more numerous than is generally thought, and I am speaking from experience.*

> *No limited torture either, under the pretext of not attacking the physical integrity of the individual. That is playing with words and starting down a slippery slope. So, if intelligence is necessary and no suffering can be caused, what then is the solution? There are no good solutions in the struggle against subversion, which can only be a dirty business.*

> *My solution is probably the least bad; warning the enemy that any terrorist caught red-handed will be shot if he has not, within a period of twenty four hours, given up his secrets willingly* [1].

---

1. *Livre blanc de l'armée française en Algérie [White Paper on the French Army in Algeria.]* Editions Contretemps, 2001, p. 117.

Continuing his earlier 1999 narrative, Major Hélie de Saint Marc further elaborated in 2002, in *Les champs de braises,* the work by which he became known to the wider public, and which was awarded first prize in the Army's newly created literature competition, the Prix Erwan Bergot.

In Algeria, France responded to the height of terrorism by the height of repression. I continually run and rerun in my head the film of these tragic events and the system that, little by little, was put in place. I remember the day when we learned of the first 'official' use of duress [...] during a number of interrogations. The results were impressive. Like all clandestine organisations, that of the terrorists was at one and the same time both powerful and fragile. It was enough to pull on a few well placed threads to unravel the whole web, and in doing so to save tens of victims, unknowing passers-by, women or children. In the thrill of the moment, few leaders had any crises of conscience. The parachute division, especially the 1st REP, followed his orders in a disciplined manner. Jeanpierre's division was just like him – effectiveness was everything. My former commander took responsibility for his decision, to treat prisoners violently in certain cases in order to make them give up vital information, on condition that that he always remained in control of such violence.

Throughout this whole period, I was detached to General Massu's personal staff, so I benefited from the victory without being confronted with a choice during interrogation sessions. That is why I will take care not to present myself as whiter than white. I have a horror of those who polish their good consciences while denouncing others. I have known too many former deportees, protected in high level administrative jobs during their 'postings' to the camps, from whom, after the war we have had to suffer flights of oratory about the unshakeable dignity of man and resistance to humiliation in all circumstances.

[...] Apart from the people affected, the battle of Algiers raised an issue of conscience. How can it be denied that actions of which current morality disapproves took place under the army's responsibility? Beyond a condemnation in principle, always easy in the abstract, the drama was obvious. Leaving examples of easily reprovable individual behaviour characterized by vice – human nature is such that we sometimes have difficulty controlling the power we are given over others – judgement of the great mass of interrogations carried out 'under duress' is a matter of a scale of values.

[...] When I told one of my comrades who had stayed with the 1st REP about my unease, he flew into a rage: "Where is honour, Hélie? Here we are not waging a war wearing kid gloves. You've read the FLN's communiqués... 'the Dien Bien Phu of the rue Michelet'...It's

them or us. When I am alone in my company, in front of the clandestine organizational chart we've reconstituted, with only three or four key pieces missing, I no longer know where honour is. Should I hit, scream insanely at, and threaten with the worst acts of brutality the prisoner in my office, in order to break him? His confession might enable me to prevent new attacks and to save lives. Or perhaps I should refuse to participate in this degrading war? I have made a decision. It is the FLN who chose the weapons and the battlefield. They wanted the casbah and bombs. If I refuse this trial of strength, I acknowledge the superiority of terror."

I understood my comrade's anguish. It was cutting him to the quick. But I also discussed it at length with Jacques Morin, who had stayed with the 1st REP and shared my unease. We thought that certain interrogations were taking place for no reason and that more explicit boundaries should have been drawn up. Common morality was absent from our reasoning. When good is no longer faced with evil, but evil is faced with something worse, the conventional fixed points of morality are no longer any help. From our spell on the German plains to the villages burned by the Vietminh, we had seen so many unjust deaths that universal concepts of good and evil evaporated in the face of a personal reflex, an instinctive reticence, against the use of duress on an already submissive man. Is not the violence one inflicts primarily an evil inflicted on oneself?

I know officers who were by no means those most involved in the interrogations, yet who took two or three years to get over them. Afflicted by doubt, I searched to hang on, despite everything, to the military ethics that had accustomed us to other situations [1].

This long testimony explicitly reveals the dilemmas of officers responsible for intelligence missions and the matters of conscience that can result from them. However, despite the number of officers who remained loyal to their principles and refused to give in to physical repression, the violent methods made public during the first battle of Algiers and exploited – in the media and politically – by an adversary carrying out actions a hundred times worse cost the French army dear.

Media exploitation of the use of torture by the French army hastened the political and strategic stalemate in Algeria. Yet many of those who used these brutal methods suffered serious consequences which to this day, more than fifty years later, have left them badly scarred.

---

1. Hélie de Saint Marc, *Les Champs de braise,* [The Fields of Embers], Perrin, 2002 p. 216 et seq.

Informed, or misinformed, public opinion distanced itself from the nation's soldiers and the conflict.

Although the methods used in Algiers were by no means unanimously supported in the army, public opinion ultimately learned of them and called the military authorities to account.

Indeed the FLN, by skilfully manipulated the media and drawing on 'war of liberation' ideology and the strongly anti-colonial French elites, conducted a very effective denigration and condemnation campaign against the French army. When in trouble on the military front, the FLN nationalists and their supporters in mainland France deployed a diplomatic and political strategy consisting of systematically publicising instances of military misconduct. Little by little, the questioning stirred up increasingly indignant public opinion. The use of media coverage as a weapon by the FLN marked an important change in the Algerian war.

Condemnation of the methods used was first heard in the press. From mid-February 1957, *Témoignage Chrétien* [Christian Witness] began publishing the files of Jean Müller, a former scout leader killed in Algeria, who spoke of his discouragement faced the growth of military violence. Shortly afterwards, a pamphlet titled *Les appelés témoignent* [The Conscripts Testify] appeared, supported by the *Committee of Spiritual Resistance*, of which the historian René Rémond [1] was a member. Simultaneously, the publishing house Editions du Seuil brought out *Contre la torture* [Against Torture], a compendium of testimonies with an introduction by the Catholic writer Pierre-Henri Simon. Finally Jean-Jacques Servan-Schreiber, director of *L'Express,* wrote a series of articles in that newspaper based on his own experience as a lieutenant in Algeria.

The decision to send conscripts to Algeria opened the way for public exposure of the methods used in counter-insurgency warfare. The first conscripts returned to France and some of them, shocked by their Algerian experience and once again civilians, began to speak out, adding to the unease of a public already cool towards the conflict. Debates about the use of the 'question' divided the French nation. The publication of such incidents in the press brought the horrors of the war into French homes and strengthened the anti-war camp.

Taking advantage of this current, as well as of intense diplomatic activity and information (and disinformation) campaigns directed at French and international opinion between 1958 and 1960, the FLN chipped away at the consensus around the war. Public opinion in mainland France began wondering about its relevance. The French no longer recognised themselves in their army. The military, for its part, felt that its legitimacy in the

---

1. René Rémond (1918-2007) historian and political scientist, member of the Académie Française.

eyes of its fellow countryman was increasingly being weakened. But popular support plays a key role in winning a 'weak against strong' type of conflict. From then on, despite the victory in Algiers in 1957, successes in the countryside with the Challe plan and blockades of the Moroccan and Tunisian borders, all of which seriously weakened it militarily, the FLN was inexorably heading for political triumph. The twofold feeling that the war was illegitimate and that civil war was imminent grew in mainland France, swelling the camp of those opposed to the conflict. A gulf was developing between mainland France and Algeria. The referendum of 8 January 1961 on the question of self-determination, a solution suggested by General de Gaulle as a way of getting out of the conflict, won 75% of the 'yes' vote in France and 72% of the 'no' vote in Algeria.

Thus success in the field turned out to be of no avail, since the political decisions that followed ultimately led to the Evian agreements, without any lasting benefit – strategic or political – from the victories in Algiers or in the *djebel*. Worse, it unleashed a serious moral crisis in France and a considerable deterioration of the army's image in the eyes of French public opinion. This legacy weighed heavily on the French military for a long time, and most particularly on the Army.

Traumatic experiences increased the number of revelations and stigmatised the methods used.

I began this chapter with my father's testimony. For him, the passage of time did not allow him to cope with his memories, which became a matter conscience. Was it really the role of the military to do the dirty work, as recalled by those who felt they had the duty to accept responsibility for that role? Was it really up to them to pay the price, with their remorse and their contrition, for the political mistakes in a conflict that did not put the nation in danger? In the light of the testimonies of all those who have never recovered from it, the question deserves to be put. If torture, the ultimate form of brutality, destroys those people subjected to it, neither does it spare those who use it. In Algeria, it deeply marked its perpetrators, in a way that cannot be summed up in terms of profit and loss.

I fought for thirty months in Algeria, under the command of Colonel Flour. What I did was noted and I was even awarded a medal. But I didn't accept the medal. I gave it to one of my subordinates. My captain had told me: "Here are two medals for your platoon. One for you and one for whomever you choose in your platoon". But I didn't want to keep the medal. I didn't like the memories associated with it. I was not proud of all my actions. Because there were some actions which did not deserve to be honoured with a medal: those involving torture which I had cause to do myself and to order my men to do.

It is because of those actions that I left the army after the war. I lost confidence in the system. But I would have liked to become a colonel. I have a military mindset, I love my country and I want to defend it. But after that war, I needed to find my bearings elsewhere.

I do not know if we could have acted differently, without relying on torture. Those were the orders, and we obeyed them because we did not know how else to stop the clashes. When you see your comrades being tortured, dying in unspeakable agony, because of disgraceful torture committed by the enemy, you are both revolted and sad at the same time. And you are scared of dying in the same way.

The fear of dying in combat can be conquered. But dying under torture is something else. We wanted all that to stop. So we tried to obtain all the intelligence that could help us end it all. And when prisoners refused to talk, when reasoning served no purpose, when verbal violence was ineffective, when rough handling had no effect, then one doesn't know what else to do to make them talk, except more force, more violence. And we ended up with torture, through hopelessness, faced with our powerlessness to make them understand our objectives. We had nothing else. At the start, one tells oneself: "It's not that serious, he'll pull through, even if it's hurting him at the moment". But finally, it always ended up in a summary execution. The road to hell is paved with good intentions, that's for sure.

Recorded by the author, these comments were made by an officer who wishes to remain anonymous. He has never recovered from what happened then. Extending what resembles a spontaneous confession, he continued his testimony with a poignant introspective analysis, a genuine testament addressed to current generations on the subject of torture.

Torture does not make revulsion or sadness disappear. Nor does it satisfy the desire for revenge. On the contrary, it adds to them a fear of oneself, of what one can become capable of doing, and the shame of denying the principles one learned through one's education and that one is defending by fighting for France. Moreover, it leads to the committing of serious mistakes in regard to innocent people. But it was only afterwards that we sometimes knew they were innocent...

And then one adds self-disgust to it all...

But how could things have been done differently? In particular, our anger gave us the courage to act with violence and against our principles. And that anger was constantly revived by the actions of the fellahs against our soldiers, our friends, who were horribly tortured. And we became just as savage as them. We no longer knew how to contain our anger against them.

I did it because I believed it was essential for maintaining French Algeria. Because the political speeches told us that was the objective and that these means were part of the way to achieve it. And the army obeyed that order. Everyone believed it. Afterwards, we were told to stop fighting for that goal.

Everything was done for no purpose. The politicians did not even give us the means to pardon ourselves for what we had done, by claiming the victory that had justified these acts. They moved on to other things. We could not erase these memories from our minds. You cannot be proud of yourself, looking at a medal which reminds you of all that guilt, all that lack of restraint.

History is not an abstract subject, nor a theoretical debate. Hélie de Saint Marc states that it is more often a field of embers through which we must move forward. Algeria is a part of that history, and the servicemen, appointed by the political authorities, committed themselves to it willingly and courageously. Many of them burned their souls there and the scars will mark their consciences for ever.

CONCLUSION: EVALUATION AND LESSONS

What assessment can be made of the use of brutal methods in a conflict?

Within the institution of the military, two main arguments are invoked against the use of violent methods, such as those used in the battle of Algiers and in the months that followed. The first relates to morality, the second to military effectiveness.

1. First of all, as we have seen, the methods of 'revolutionary warfare' generated profound moral and ethical conflicts in a great many military commanders. On the one hand, they were obliged to execute their mission and carry out their orders when faced with lawless adversaries who indulged in horrific indiscriminate acts affecting both civilians and the military. On the other hand, they had to respect the law – national or international – that forbids brutal procedures and torture, thereby restricting the implementation of certain types of activity in the field. Moreover, the violence perpetrated against suspects gave rise to unease, inseparable from a particular concept of mankind and of its rights in our own country, rights those in the military were supposed to be to defending. Faced with this dilemma, many commanders had to choose, as their conscience dictated, between tactical effectiveness and repugnance toward the use of prohibited methods. The battle for Algiers shows that simply seeking immediate tactical effectiveness, at the

expense of an officer's sense of morality, inevitably carries within it the seeds of the mission's political failure. It also accounts for, though in no way justifies, the inevitable terrorist reactions. This idea is reinforced by the memory of the Second World War, when France opposed a Nazi regime that oppressed its enemies and its own people while presenting itself as a country defending civilisation and human values. For a many of the combatants who experienced Gestapo prisons, it was unacceptable to stoop to the very methods we had so often condemned. For others, such practices also ran counter to personal notions of mutual relationship, whatever acts may have been committed.

2. The second argument is that, with hindsight, the tactical effectiveness often invoked to justify methods such as those used in Algiers is questionable. Like many other officers, Colonel Goddard has clearly challenged the reasoning that interrogating one man using excessive violence allows a hundred lives to be saved. In fact, it seems that, given the compartmentalisation of enemy networks, there are very few cases in which a prisoner has access to such important intelligence. How many men, therefore, were wrongfully mistreated? Moreover, the reliability of confessions obtained through brutality is very unpredictable and the information gleaned is very often retracted subsequently. To obtain quality intelligence, many other options exist and many officers believe that torture adds nothing. In addition, some leaders who have studied the doctrine of revolutionary warfare in depth, see in these procedures the very negation of the slow 'population structuring' process, with the aim of winning over the population in order to counter enemy propaganda. Finally, the history of the battle of Algiers demonstrated – and not for the first time – that tactical successes won through violence are very short-lived and in the long term always end with a price to be paid in terms of unexpected effects, even to the extent of wiping out the original gains. Marshal Lyautey taught us that every decision in the field, even at the most elementary level, must always be taken with a very long-term perspective: *the aim, always the aim*, he insisted. In an impatient world, where decisions favour the immediate future rather than the longer view, this lesson is of prime importance.

What ethical lessons can we draw from this today?

Without claiming to summarise in a few lines all the lessons to be drawn from the extreme complexity of the Algerian war, two important ones are relevant to the ethics of the soldier, the specific field we have focused on. These lessons touch on the nature of the relationship between politicians and the military and on the role of democracies in irregular warfare.

1. Historically, relations between the politician and the soldier have always been complex. In our democracies, the indisputable supremacy of the former over the latter is an intangible guarantee of legitimacy. Within that framework, the decision to involve the armed forces – equipped with lethal weapons – in the maintenance of order is a final resort, freighted with meaning and consequences. Consequently how and under what circumstances the armed forces are used needs to be studied and framed with care. The events in Algeria remind us that when such a choice is made, responsibility for its implementation under military authority must be shared with the civilian authorities, who cannot be absolved from it.

    Military and political leaders move in very different worlds, but worlds which cannot ignore each other. Long before the Algerian conflict, in the *Le Fil de l'épée* [The edge of the sword], the then Major de Gaulle said of the politician and the soldier: "They will go two by two,[…] step by step, side by side." The arrangements for the defence of the nation are defined within this relationship. They are not determined without altercation and debate, but at the end of a necessarily collaborative process, the final decision remains in the hands of the politicians. If each party is subsequently required to work within its own area of competence, the involvement of both in the initial decisions implies a considerable overlapping of their respective responsibilities, which cannot be abrogated to the other party. This is why ethics concerns both parties and cannot be viewed separately. When political ethics weakens and defines rules outside the norm, it often drags the military establishment with it, or else leaves it to make its own choice. To repeat what we have already said: there can be no military ethics without political ethics. In exceptional circumstances, when for example the armed forces need to be used for maintaining order, military commanders must be firm in asking the politician responsible for a clear definition of the mandate, the final desired effect and the means granted to achieve this. In turn, military commanders must take care not to allow themselves to be carried away by a search for tactical effectiveness at any cost, which will contravene international laws and conventions signed by their country and which would repudiate the political values through which their fellow citizens recognise themselves. In the eyes of history, in a democracy worthy of the name, and in the final analysis, ultimate responsibility will always be shared.

2. What is at stake today in the debate about brutality goes well beyond a single controversial page in the history of our nation. It echoes the struggle of democracies faced with lawless and unscrupulous adversaries lacking all common decency. It is a clash between two different concepts of human society. On the one side, there is a political system based on principles and values – therefore on ethics – which it is bound to respect at the risk of losing its own legitimacy, and on the other, there is an adversary for whom the end justifies the means, and who will seek to drag its opponent into its own system of violence, in order to compel him to repudiate his principles. A democracy which stoops to using the same means will sooner or later hand victory to its adversary. Does warfare against lawless opponents justify the abandonment of the principles that have characterized the history of our civilizations? Were the Geneva Conventions conceived just to regulate traditional military conflicts and should one be absolved from them in all other cases? Should we reject all humanitarian law and the 150 years of effort to try to 'civilize' armed conflicts, at least a little, on the pretext that we cannot respond to barbarity other than with barbarity?

Over and above the arguments, the question is in fact crucial: faced with terrorism, blackmail, all sorts of mafias, what weapons does democracy want to use to defend its citizens? The answers already exist and to some extent are being implemented. They are necessarily international and collective and must be seen within a long-term perspective. Happily, they are different from those of the adversary. They touch on the ethics of civilizations which place man at the heart of their design. Who today could argue, judged against the yardstick of history and its consequences, that brutality and its extreme form, torture, are a not dead end for mankind? A nation worthy of the name does not base itself on a dead end for mankind.

*

*   *

A nation must be able to accept responsibility for its past and to ask questions of itself about its shadowy periods. Without undue contrition, an examination of painful events with eyes wide open, as we wanted to conduct with the discussion of the use of torture in the Algerian war, can allow the past to become a reference point, a resource, a source of knowledge. "Experience cannot be transmitted, but it can be recounted. Because only in the retelling can it be understood, which itself will propel forward the generations which follow [1]." May the keys to our future, on

---

1. Hélie de Saint Marc, August von Kageneck and Etienne Montety, *Notre Histoire* [Our History] *1922-1945*, Edition les Arènes, 2002.

this subject, remain those of total and definitive rejection and refusal of the use of torture in all places and under all circumstances.

To CONCLUDE THIS CHAPTER AS A WHOLE

To win the support of the population means presenting them with a military force beyond reproach, or at least devoid of any intention to engage in unworthy conduct. The struggle against the main weaknesses, both for oneself as an officer and for one's men – the loss of one's bearings, pride, fear, desire for revenge, and brutality – requires the development of strength of character, itself based on great emotional stability. The conjunction of these two qualities creates the moral strength lying at the root of the greatest acts of heroism and the humblest acts of courage.

A harmonious amalgam of will, intelligence, moral and intellectual perspective, and moral strength allow one to keep one's head in destabilising situations, to cultivate humility so as not to succumb to a temptation for false glory, to develop one's courage so as to conquer one's fear, and to never give in to hatred.

But it would unfortunately be an oversimplification to suggest it would enough, 'however difficult it might be', to remain true to a given direction, in order to find comprehensive solutions to every crisis and war. Reality, alas, still gives rise to situations without solutions. We must look for answers elsewhere.

CHAPTER 4

THE QUESTIONING SOUL

Responsibility cannot be shared.

Robert Heinlein [1]

T HE exercise of responsibility is consubstantial with the role of leader. From the moment he earns his first stripe, the enlisted soldier changes state: he becomes the guarantor of something or someone. Within the military more than elsewhere, the exercise of command, however minor, only has meaning in relation to the freedom of each person to accept or refuse such responsibility. But while accepting one's responsibilities in the first instance means taking decisions for others, and subsequently seeing that they are carried out, it also involves – and perhaps above all – being able to take sole responsibility for all their consequences.

We have already noted that a commander who measures his own thinking against the yardstick of ethical principles commonly held to be just, rightly feels able to accept the outcomes. By showing himself capable of questioning himself about the value of his actions, he *de facto* asserts his own dignity and imbues his command with its full value.

For all that, experience shows that it is not always enough to set out a code of conduct recognised as just for confronting with equanimity the ambiguities that can characterise forceful action in combat. A number of questions often remain unresolved.

Who is able to foresee all the possible consequences resulting from a command decision in combat? Who is in a position to grasp all the factors influencing the infinitely complex environment of zones of conflict? Is it possible to believe that every decision taken in accordance with these

---

1. The American science fiction writer, who began his career in the United States Navy. This period left its mark on his subsequent writings.

principles can unquestionably be deemed 'good', whatever the result might be? Is there not also a risk of dogmatic intolerance, in claiming that the principles adopted are absolute?

It therefore seems worthwhile, by means of further testimonies and reflections, to use the above questions as a yardstick for evaluating the convictions outlined in the preceding chapters. It is clearly not a matter of calling them into question, but of convincing the reader that, even when it comes to ethics, it is necessary in all circumstances to show the greatest modesty. The principles described previously, even if they are points of reference or stability in situations of turmoil, do not always shield the commander from issues of conscience. Even if the commander can chart a route through most situations by drawing on these principles, grey areas will always exist, where he will never be entirely sure of taking the 'right decision'.

An order, issued in perfect coherence with these ethical reference points, may have unexpected consequences that run counter to the goal being pursued. It may also happen that the choice facing him is so difficult that the commander is unable to draw on any of his convictions in coming to a decision. Finally, in certain extreme cases, the commander may even be obliged to issue orders that can briefly run counter to one particular principle in order to respect another, or to save the lives of innocent people, or to complete his mission.

The military commander is at the very heart of these dilemmas and will often have to confront them alone.

1. Grey Areas

The term grey area refers to circumstances where no solution stands out clearly but where the commander nonetheless has to make a choice and take a decision. The grey area is the risk zone, the fog of war. Many officers have experienced it and some have recounted how they managed to find their way in this zone of uncertainty.

EYEWITNESS ACCOUNT [1]

Afghanistan – Southern Region

On one occasion, I deployed to a tactical CP in the mountains, to command an assault at the head of a Special Forces unit against a group of rebels. During our infiltration, we came across one of our assault teams that had turned back. I stopped the vehicles and asked why they were leaving the operational area. They had a militiaman

---

1. Commodore Marin Gilliers.

with them, whose lung had been perforated by a bullet. It was impossible to obtain a helicopter to evacuate him. The doctor had done everything possible to keep him alive, but his chances of survival were not good if he was not quickly taken to hospital. The team leader gave the order to evacuate him. The poor man was in a bad way. I caught his eye: he knew where he stood.

The mission we had been given was to infiltrate on foot for 24 hours across very difficult terrain, then to observe, attack and subdue. The enemy was not expecting us, but was in a strong position and undoubtedly equal to us in number. The full complement of men are needed to complete the mission, otherwise the rest will face great risks if there are not enough of them. The ratio of forces is basic in this sort of situation. I ordered the team to turn back. Protests erupted from sides. I cut them short. I had too much respect for the enemy not to. The silence was filled with grim accusatory looks. I gave the order to press on and the team departed after leaving the wounded man in a neighbouring village.

On their way back through the same area three days later at the end of the operation, the team collected the man they'd left in the village. He was still alive. We managed to evacuate him by helicopter and save his life.

I believe I made a good choice in this situation and that I was right. But if he had died in the meantime, would I have been wrong? On the basis of what criteria? In my opinion, I opted for mission success and maintaining the ratio of forces – and therefore in favour of saving the lives of my soldiers – as opposing to safeguarding the life of that one militiaman. His survival had been the priority criterion for the group. But not for me.

A month later, we heard that the militiaman had been assassinated, because of his links with us.

In the final analysis, should his life been the dominant criterion?

Finally, returning to the region some time later, we came across him again: he was alive and well after all! It was a pleasant surprise and, grateful for having been saved, he was a good source of intelligence!

So what was the right criterion? Was this militiaman worth the risk of the mission failing and perhaps the loss of several of my men as a result of the absence of an assault team? Do some lives have greater value than others? For what, and for whom, am I primarily responsible, and up to what point?

The answer is not in the rule book. It lies inside each of us.

The officer asks the right questions: how does one choose? how does one decide where the truth lies?

Each one of us has the answer. It is perhaps to be found within our own personal logic, in our own capacity for discernment, deep inside oneself. Whatever decision the commander might make in these grey areas where things are neither black nor white, following his conscience probably counts for more than the consequences of his decision. If the commander is responsible for the lives of his men during the mission, is he the complete master of the events that govern their destiny? For what consequences is he really responsible?

Professor Henri Hude gives a philosophical, but nevertheless practical, answer to these questions.

We are fully responsible for our 'voluntary effects'. [...] For example, bombing a military target can cause collateral damage [...]

On the other hand, we can be the material cause of certain effects and not be held morally or legally responsible for them, because they were not caused 'voluntarily'.

The main matters of conscience are of three kinds:

a) when, in order to achieve a good result, it is necessary to use means that are not good;

b) when, to implement one value (for example, justice) it is necessary to sacrifice another value, very much in opposition to it (for example, clemency);

c) when the implementation of a good means to achieve a good end or to produce a good effect produces, within a given period of time, a bad effect.

Even at the time, our actions often have a double or triple effect. Furthermore, the effects of our actions stretch virtually to infinity, like the ripples spreading out on the water when a pebble is thrown in. [...]

A classic problem in ethics is knowing under what conditions a decision resulting in a 'good' primary effect and a 'bad' secondary effect can be justified. [...]

How far then does our responsibility really extend?

In his answer, Henri Hude draws on another notion: intention.

Undertaking a good act, the immediately intended aim of which is good, but from which a bad consequence results, does not seem morally permissible except when both the following two conditions are met:

a) there is sufficient reason to run the risk of the bad consequence

b) the intention applies only to the good act and its good consequence.

Thus even the most determinedly objective ethical code, the code most desirous not to let the person concerned get bogged down in psychological complications, cannot disregard intention.

This approach, which takes intention as its point of departure, brings us back to the very first testimony in this book, headed *Choice*. In accordance with his conscience, the young lieutenant decided not to engage in battle, a decision that led to the surrender of the Chadian rebel group without fighting. Unfortunately, this seemingly unambiguous example had a tragic ending.

The author recounts what happened later.

Some months after that Chadian troop had been converted into a nomad guard and my unit had left the area, the situation was turned on its head, as is often the case in Africa. Power changed hands. In the days immediately following, incidents of scores being settled and atrocities against troops loyal to the previous authorities proliferated. The excellent unit we had won over was horribly massacred by those now in power for having rightly chosen to join us.

Was I responsible for this? Should I have regretted my decision? Could I have guessed the future? I have never really asked myself such questions, because this outcome, sad as it is, does not change that fateful moment when, faced with that troop at bay, I listened to my conscience and took full responsibility for my decision – a decision that for me was the best one at that precise moment.

What happened subsequently, though it does not leave me unmoved, was no longer my responsibility. I have no regrets as to the decision I took.

Undeniably, there were unquestionably no negative intentions behind that decision, and it is therefore beyond reproach. The morality of the decision was good, as was the intention. This is undoubtedly why the officer who took the decision expressed no regrets.

EYEWITNESS ACCOUNT BY A PILOT [1]

Afghanistan – 2006

We have just arrived in the new area assigned to us. Contact with the British forces is going well. The radio exchanges are clear and the JTAC [2] gives us the impression of being on top of things, even though

---

1. Captain Gaviard.
2. JTAC Joint Tactical Air Controller: the ground controller responsible for guiding aircraft to their targets.

the situation on the ground is chaotic: there are several dead and wounded as a result of an insurgent attack. On the other hand, the British JTAC does not have sufficient information on the positions of the various friendly combat units deployed on the ground and has trouble guiding us.

We suggest to him that we make a low-altitude high-speed pass over the battle to weaken the enemy's morale. He likes our suggestion and gives us the go-ahead. So a few minutes later we overfly the contingent, having carefully picked out the Predator drone and the Apache helicopters in the vicinity and making sure we stay clear of their airspace.

By the time we have climbed back to our working altitude, the British JTAC tell us that he now wants destructive fire on a building. He uses the standardised target designation protocol with great thoroughness and exactitude, confirming his competence and professionalism. But in every action in war, there is almost always a grain of sand in the machinery. This becomes apparent when the JTAC specifies the target in his protocol: he uses the term 'school'.

It immediately worries us. Even though a lot of restrictions in the rules of engagement are lifted when friendly troops are in grave danger under fire, the designated target seems nevertheless to be a Koranic school, or madrassa, likely to be occupied by civilians. In any case, it is impossible for us to verify who is in the building. I curse inwardly, because in this type of case there is really no solution.

To do nothing might be to pass sentence on some British soldiers. To fire might involve killing Afghan children and could incite others to join the Taliban and seek revenge.

The target seems to me to be too sensitive to be managed only at our level. I therefore ask the British JTAC if he has authorisation to open fire from a higher level. Although he has a delegated authority to assign targets within the strict limits of the rules of engagement, I point out that this is a very sensitive type of target and that we need confirmation from higher authority. He says he will seek further information about obtaining a clearance – in other words, authorisation to open fire from a higher level than his own. For our part, we too contact – via the control centres – the relevant decision-making authorities in the Air branch, who are responsible for authorising our use in support of the ground forces as well as the which targets can be engaged. Two requests are now being processed, and I wonder what I am going to be able to do.

Several minutes pass. Then the British JTAC advises us that he has not received authorisation from his superiors. A little later, the 'air' control centres we had contacted inform us that permission to fire has been granted, in view of the situation on the ground [1] and the losses already sustained.

In the end, the British JTAC does not require us to open fire, although I have been careful to inform him that the 'air' chain of command had agreed. He considers that there is still doubt as to the location of friendly positions, and he will not take the risk of committing us. Was this a mere pretext or really the case? We never knew.

It did not change anything for us. We knew that once the doubt had been lifted we would have agreed to open fire, if he had asked us to. Once we received authorisation from the decision makers, we 'compartmentalised' our worries. In other words, we put our initial questions and our reticence behind us, thinking at that point that the impending action might exceed our own convictions.

We raised these questions on that occasion because we wanted to be sure. No-one holds it against us. On the contrary, we could have been taken to task for not opening fire without first asking questions, and could have been required to give an account of ourselves had we opened fire immediately. Potentially, both courses were open to criticism.

Even after numerous missions, even after having opened fire on several occasions, I still say it is extremely difficult to be sure of the right solution. The pressure is immense, mistakes are often made, and people's convictions vary. But when the outcome is favourable, we should remain modest, telling ourselves that we did our best, while staying within our own internally imposed boundaries of behaviour.

In this particular case, the target of opportunity assigned during a ground support sortie raised doubts in the pilot. He could find no immediate answer, neither in the rules of engagement, nor in his own personal idea of what constituted an act of war, to the questions worrying him. He had to make a decision in a state of uncertainty, in an emergency and under the pressure of events. This is still the risk zone.

This testimony shows that it is important to leave the door open to questions and to doubt – in other words to be able to ask oneself questions about the action, once it is revealed in its complexity. Under such circumstances, doubting does not mean equivocating or fretting about the meaning of one's actions. Rather it means, over and beyond procedures and instructions, by

---

1. This took place in 2006. The same decision would certainly not be taken now.

drawing on the principles on which everyone has forged their own moral code of behaviour, that one must be able to leave a space for *questioning*, for the possibility that there is a different way, perhaps for *instinct,* which might lead to a way out of inextricable situations.

A commander who has inscribed ethical reflection into his personal culture and his preparation for combat need not be afraid of reacting instinctively and can trust in inspiration. Napoleon had the habit of saying to his generals: "In battle and the brouhaha of combat, the happiest of inspirations is often no more than remembering." This is why a decision made in an emergency naturally tends to be connected to the most profound reference points and instinctive reasoning of the person concerned, whose capacity to adapt has often made all the difference.

Eyewitness account [1]

Afghanistan – October 2008, in the middle of a densely populated wooded valley

That day, the battalion was carrying out a large scale operation. Two companies are combing sections of a water course. The infiltration began during the night. Despite the weight of their protective gear, the men are not suffering too much from the heat, for we are already well into autumn. The insurgents have not shown themselves and we can see only a few groups of suspect individuals with no visible weapons moving around the area.

About 10.30, the situation is normal and the operations officer lines up the contingent, with a view to crossing a wide stretch of open ground. One section has taken up position on a barren hilltop in support of the traversal. It is preparing to fire Milan missiles at a previously spotted combat position about 1800 metres away, which is likely to be hiding a heavy machine gun.

Then in a few seconds, the situation changes. Men carrying guns break cover to the east of the open ground and engage us with fierce and very accurate fire. At the same time, they open fire on the support section on the hill. The men hunker down, take cover as best they can, and fire back at any of the enemy they can see.

At this point someone opens fire on my support section from the mountainside to the north of the valley.

A few minutes later, this time to the south, another enemy group breaks cover. They had been hiding in two kalat – houses surrounded

---

1. Colonel Jacques Aragones, at that time commanding the 8th Regiment of Marine Infantry (8e RPIMa).

by high compacted earth walls – between the two companies. They are also concentrating their fire on the support section, whose position is becoming untenable: it is caught in crossfire from three different directions. It is a real ambush.

As best they can, and putting into practice the infantryman's basic techniques, the section manages to withdraw. But it is under such heavy fire that it is forced to leave behind an anti-tank firing post and two missiles that too heavy and too unwieldy to be transported when withdrawing under such conditions. We are now under fire from a good hundred enemy combatants. The battalion's advance has been stopped in its tracks.

The intensity of the battle redoubles. By now, we have been fighting for over two hours. One of my companies manages to neutralise one of the three enemy positions, while mortar rounds fired by support artillery rain down on another of their fire positions.

Twice during this battle, the support section has tried to retrieve its firing post and two missiles. Taking enormous risks, its men have managed to bring them about half way down the hillside. During the last attempt, two soldiers are hit. Bullets rip through the trousers of one man and the other's boot. The two men are only grazed: they were lucky. The section commander reports in and is ordered by the captain to start withdrawing and abandon the weapons. I support the decision. Is not the life of my men worth more than a firing post and two missiles? I know they will obey my orders if I send them back, but I am responsible for their lives. In my heart and soul I know that what is at stake is not worth the price.

The captain then decides to try and destroy the abandoned kit with an air strike. An American A-10 bomber has been on station above us since the fighting began. He is in support but has not yet been able to open fire.

The bomber makes two passes, but reports that he is still unable to open fire. There is a house less than 100 metres away from the abandoned kit. It is probably inhabited. A family may have taken cover there, waiting for the fighting to end.

Two Kiowa OH-58 helicopters, also on station in support, attempt an approach, but also confirm that firing is too risky.

It is still possible for me to call for 120 mm mortar fire. Here too, despite the excellent work of the artillery section, I know that the inevitable fragmentation of the shells when they hit the ground makes the risk of collateral damage extremely high.

If I consider that the lives of my men are worth more than a Milan firing post and its ammunition, how can I put civilian lives at risk for the same purpose? I am here to pacify the country, not to kill its inhabitants. That is not the way to win the hearts and minds of the population and carry out my mission. The battalion therefore resolves to leave the kit where it is, in the hands of the enemy, who will inevitably retrieve it.

I had very little time to weigh up the risk of their possibly deploying it against us. Using such kit is not that easy. A trained operator is needed to use it effectively. And again, once the firing post batteries go flat, they cannot be recharged. The kit will then be unusable.

Some time later, I asked myself this question. If it had been a matter of easily reusable kit and ammunition, would I have taken the same decision? Would I have run the risk of possibly letting the enemy turn them against us on another occasion?

At that particular time, and in the conditions of that mission, it was not worth risking the lives of my men and innocent Afghan civilians for that reason or that risk.

While I was reading out this testimony as part of a speech I gave last year to an audience of young officers [1], a captain, very sure of himself, said: "If I had been in the place of that unit commander, I would not have made that decision, because I believe that abandoning one's weapons to the enemy is a grave error."

I told him that one must be careful not to pass judgement in terms of *good or bad solutions* when confronted with this type of dilemma, and that the whole point of these testimonies was to encourage their readers to ask certain questions, prior to being confronted with them in an emergency and under fire.

I then asked him if he had ever been in the position of having to ring the doorbell one morning, accompanied by a gendarme and a representative of the town hall, to inform a mother or wife that her son or husband had just been killed in action. In the ensuing silence, I added that if, on such a day, he would be able to explain the reasons for his decision to that widow or bereaved mother, looking her in the eye, without blushing, he could to conclude that his choice had been made in good conscience.

This does not mean that soldiers' lives must always be protected at any cost. As we have already said, once a soldier ceases to risk death, he no longer merits the title of soldier and becomes someone merely following

---

1. Officers of the rank of captain and major, during their course at the [French] army headquarters' staff school.

orders. The commander has the power of life or death, both in regard to enemy or in regard to his men. His decisions must take precise account of the consequences of this responsibility, in relation to the mission he has been given.

This type of situation allows us to put our finger on the sometimes awesome complexity of the choices facing the soldier. General Bachelet comments:

> The soldier is a litmus paper for the human condition, in its tragedy and its grandeur; the extreme situations which can be the soldier's lot, where even life itself is at stake, are indicators of those moments when, faced with the alarming complexity of things, there is no correct solution. But he must choose, decide and act, as a fully free man [1].

Thus, even if the action ordered does not conform to one's usual convictions and does not completely exempt its author from inevitable questioning, the right intention can be a way of guiding one's conscience in the grey areas where the commander is alone, confronted by the need to choose.

2. The Ethics of Responsibility

The German sociologist Max Weber was the first to introduce the notion of the ethics of responsibility.

> It is essential that we clearly recognise the following fact: every activity guided by ethics may be subordinated to two totally different and diametrically opposed maxims. It may be guided according to the ethics of responsibility or according to the ethics of conviction [2].

In brief, he explains that on a day-to-day basis the rather theoretical ethics of conviction comes up against a sometimes divergent reality, which forces the individual bearing heavy responsibilities into a state of resignation, and obliges him to modify his personal ethical principles. In Weber's view, states possess the "monopoly of legitimate physical violence" and there are grounds for believing that an "ethics of responsibility" can be distinguished from an "ethics of conviction".

Is such an ethics of responsibility, sometimes used – but not uniquely so – in the military sphere, still defensible today, after the sinister experiments of totalitarian states, especially Nazism, and faced with the proof of the ravages caused as much by a deficit of state power as by an excess?

---

1. Jean René Bachelet, *Pour une éthique du métier des armes. Vaincre la violence*, [For an Ethic of the Profession of Arms. Conquering Violence] Vuibert, 2006.
2. Max Weber, The Vocation Lectures: Science as a Vocation, Politics as a Vocation.

Making a distinction between the two types of ethics opens the way to introducing unacceptable *restrictions* on principles. There is therefore a high risk of justifying deviation in the name of the responsibilities exercised. Rather than an ethics of responsibility, others put forward a more subtle notion, that of "applied ethics".

> *An ethic is not easily constructed. It comes up against hesitations, tensions, labyrinths, as it were. [...] In applied ethics there is never a pre-prepared and definitive solution. Invention, trial and reworking are necessary. There is finally, in the best sense of the term, an element of cobbling things together in applied ethics* [1].

For example, for someone in the armed forces holding religious beliefs, the simple fact of killing already runs counter to the first principle of all religions: "Thou shalt not kill". Agreeing to kill is already a derogation of those beliefs. On the other hand, making it a rule to fight and to kill only when necessary, and limiting the level of violence wherever possible, offers a way of maintaining one's beliefs and even gives any derogation a measure of meaning. Those bearing responsibility have to find, within themselves, ways of accepting their burden, for it is always very dangerous simply to say "it is my duty" or to downgrade principles in favour of an "ethics of responsibility".

An ethics of responsibility is risky, because it can justify any decision *a posteriori*. It is a temptation to accept that *the ends justify any means*, since it offers the possibility of favouring tactical effectiveness at any price. Our previous discussion around *brutalisation* endeavoured to show the dangers inherent in this approach.

Commenting on the subject of justice, Aristotle maintained that judges dealing with responsibility should use the same rule as architects. In ancient Greece, the architect's rule, unlike one made out of wood, was not rigid. Because it was made of lead, it was to a certain extent flexible and could be fitted to various shapes – for example, in measuring the curve of a portico or the reliefs of a column. Ethics follows the same model. It can be adapted by means of reflection and discussion – very often by trial and error, and with due caution. It is a matter of adapting the rule, but not of modifying or changing it. In reality, no ethical question can be asked in an all-inclusive way. The question always concerns particular events, different environments, different relationships with others, and varies according to circumstances. Every type of situation calls for a kind of adjustment that takes account such variables. This is particularly so in professions where

---

1. Roger Pol Droit, *L'éthique expliquée à tout le monde*, [Ethics explained to Everyone] Éditions du Seuil, 2009.

great responsibility is exercised and where decisions have a direct impact on the development of individuals and on their physical or moral integrity. This is why contemporary ethical reflection is very often marked by a certain internal tension, that arises when there appears to be no clear or absolute solution, and a compromise solution is therefore called for. Finally, in addition to this tension, the commander has to live with the fact that he alone is ultimately responsible for the decisions he takes.

The following testimony illustrates in a particularly revealing way what an *applied ethics* might be or, with the above-mentioned caveats, an *ethics of responsibility*.

EYEWITNESS ACCOUNT [1]

Indochina – Talung Outpost – Chinese border, 1948

Another day, the partisans brought me two men, their hands tied behind their backs, their faces swollen. They were spies planted in our ranks to provoke trouble, encourage desertions and, in the last analysis, kill Europeans. Some of partisans had allowed themselves to be approached, the better to expose the infiltrators. The two men had confessed. They were the lead elements of a large-scale operation. We had come very close to disaster. The two spies lowered their gaze, like all prisoners. They were at the mercy of my verdict. The partisans, with their high cheekbones, were standing around me impassively, their eyes narrowed, awaiting. my decision. It was not possible to lock the men up. We didn't have a cellar or cell. And transporting prisoners was out of the question. I knew I must not be weak, and I wasn't. The whole situation in the valley depended on what I did. The responsibility still haunts me sometimes, especially in the light of our final abandonment of the terrain.

But in front of those Thos gathered around me, men from whom I had demanded absolute trust, who had saved me after I was wounded and who risked being massacred by the Vietminh because of their involvement, I did not hesitate.

So how does one find peace? How does one know if one has made the right decision? Once again, the answer is an individual one, to be sought deep inside oneself, in one's heart of hearts. It is not a question of devaluing the principle of correct behaviour, but of making individual choices in a given situation. Moreover, despite its profundity, the preceding testimony is emblematic of an old-style war, with which it is difficult for today's young military commanders to identify. The next testimony,

---

1. Hélie de Saint Marc, *Les champs de braise* [Fields of embers], Perrin, 2002.

recounted by Lieutenant Colonel Jaminet on his return from Côte d'Ivoire, has more in common with situations likely to occur in modern operations.

EYEWITNESS ACCOUNT

Côte d'Ivoire – November 2004 – Town of Bouaké

As we leave Bouaké on the morning of 7 November, I have two certainties and a host of questions.

The first certainty is that the mission assigned – to get the battle group back to Abidjan as quickly as possible – may lead us into battle against those opposing this redeployment. The time for dialogue came to an abrupt end the previous day, when our logistics base was bombed by an Ivorian Sukhoï 25 and we suffered nine fatalities and about thirty seriously wounded.

My second certainty is that the squadron is not engaged in a punitive expedition. This is very clear in my mind and I know that is also true for my marines. The exchanges we've had exchanged since yesterday have been entirely professional. Surprising though it might appear to an outsider, we've been never in that frame of mind. A soldier does not seek revenge; he carries out his mission. He imposes his will on the adversary. That is his honour and his strength, because hatred distorts judgement, changes one's thinking and, in time, probably leads to a dead end. The attack by the Ivorian air force has also acted as a real catharsis. This action has restored meaning to what we are doing.

But there are still many questions. The situation in Abidjan is at the very least confused. The type of opposition we might meet is equally unclear. Will the loyalist Ivorian units fight or let us through? We estimate their strength at about at a battalion, located in the village of Tiébissou, about an hour from Bouaké by road. And have to go through the village. We are therefore likely to be spotted very quickly.

Half way to Tiébissou, we are stopped by Moroccan officers from UNOCI[1] who warn us that the FANCI[2] have set an ambush for us in Tiébissou. We know nothing further. From this point onwards, I'm anticipating a classic ambush scenario. I'm also worried about how well some of our armour will measure up against RPG type rockets. Not an attractive prospect.

---

1. United Nations Operation in Cote D'Ivoire.
2. Cote D'Ivoire National Armed Forces.

At the approach to Tiébissou the road from Bouaké, there is a long, straight descent for about two kilometres, giving us a perfect view. Very soon the lead tank reports by radio that the entry points to the town are blocked. A crowd, difficult to estimate in terms of numbers, is agitatedly bustling around a barricade composed of a pile of assorted objects jumbled together. In the middle of it some tyres are burning, and the resulting thick black smoke blocks visibility beyond the barricade. After observing the scene for a while, the lead tank reports that the large crowd is made up a mix of armed Ivorian military in uniform and many civilians, including women and children.

I quickly decide to 'sort' the leaders from the led. I devise a manoeuvre with a view to discouraging the less determined members of the crowd, thereby giving me more freedom of action regarding the tougher ones. The two lead tanks (AMX 10RC) will therefore make a dash forward, sirens screaming, and as soon as they're close enough fire their machine guns over the heads of the crowd.

The outcome exceeds my expectations. Within seconds, the barricade is abandoned by its occupants. With the road now clear, we must exploit our advantage and press on without delay.

I therefore advance my platoons so they can fill the gap between the vehicles and break through the barricade in a single group.

Unfortunately, there are numerous obstacles, many of them on fire and obstructing visibility. Slaloming around them, one of the tanks lifts up a blazing tyre, which impacts a lighter vehicle (a VBL). Off balance, the VBL lurches and tips over, landing violently on its side. The other vehicles stop. My platoon's situation is now considerably weakened. The column has been split into two by the barricade and I have three slightly injured or at least badly shaken men to extract from the vehicle, and they will need medical treatment. There is also weaponry, ammunition and a vital radio set to retrieve from the VBL. All this is going to take time.

This situation will embolden our adversaries, who have been watching our advance from a distance. They can see we are now in a weak position. A group forms and, spurred on by their leader, advances towards us. The tanks protecting my injured men report back to me immediately in regard to this potentially very dangerous situation. If the crowd returns, it will tie us down where we are. Anything is then possible: our injured men might be lynched, the armoured vehicles might be set on fire... I don't want to have to fight under these circumstances. I will probably lose some men – not an idea I can happily entertain – and I will certainly be obliged to inflict loss of life on our adversaries – something I want to avoid if possible.

The report coming over the line is very clear. The leader has been identified and his position is known. Following an exchange by radio with the unit commander, who is with the column, and on the squadron radio net, I give the order to neutralise the leader. I no longer recall the exact wording of the orders. But I have absolute confidence in those who are going to carry it out. I am conscious of the commander's professionalism, and the accuracy of his gunner – he is one of the best. In my mind, it is not an order to kill. I know that, in the situation my unit currently finds itself, legitimate self-defence can include actions of this kind. My intention is to wound the leader, thereby breaking our adversaries' will to take things further.

From my VBL, I hear a short burst of machine gun fire from the tank. The situation report follows immediately: "Leader wounded in the left leg. He is being retrieved by the crowd, which is pulling back and dispersing."

Exactly what I had been hoping for.

A while later, the VBL crew is on board, together with as much of its kit as could be recovered. The column resumes its journey southward, with the town of Yamoussoukro as its next objective. But the consequences of the clash at Tiébissou do not stop there.

A few minutes after leaving the town, we receive a piece of intelligence from the helicopter preceding us in our direction of travel. Right now, even though it will still take us just under an hour to reach Yamoussoukro, several thousand people are waiting for us at the northern entrances to the town. Their intention, as at Tiébissou, is to prevent us from going any further on our march towards Abidjan. Mentally, I prepare myself for confrontation. I anticipate that this time it will be harder, and that I must not rule out the possibility that shots will be fired at us.

It turns out to be a very bad appraisal of the situation. In actual fact, we pass through a deserted town of Yamoussoukro without hindrance. The thousands of people spotted by the helicopter have literally disappeared into thin air. Why?

It seems that the telephone link between Tiébissou and Yamoussoukro has worked very well. Our adversaries have apparently analysed the situation and concluded that our determination to complete our mission is greater than theirs to stop it. The wounded man at Tiébissou has acted, from a distance, as a powerful deterrent on the leaders at Yamoussoukro. He has undoubtedly prevented many further injuries or worse.

Yes, the order I have was the right one. The application of perfectly controlled force by soldiers allowed it to be so.

EYEWITNESS ACCOUNT BY A PILOT [1]

Afghanistan – March 2002 – Operation Enduring Freedom

Operation Anaconda is in full swing in Afghanistan. The troops on the ground are being supported by numerous fighter-bombers.

That morning, an E-2C Hawkeye [2] from the aircraft carrier Charles de Gaulle's air group is controlling air traffic. Delegated by the CAOC [3] it is responsible for the tactical control of air assets in the South Afghanistan area, like its equivalents from the US Navy or the British and American air forces. At that time, the terrain in Kandahar is still unoccupied and impassable. Control is therefore exercised from these aircraft.

A section of US Marines is involved in a violent engagement in a valley and asks for immediate support. The section commander on the ground has taken over from the usual controller – the JTAC – for unknown reasons. The situation is confused; shooting and shouted orders can be heard very distinctly over the control frequency. The transmit button of the other radio often remains pressed down for long periods, evidence of the officer's tension, as if to keep a link between his world and that of the aircraft.

Very soon the mood becomes anguished, as the section commander announces "ten KIAs" (ten killed in action) and renews his urgent request. Two F 15 Strike Eagles complete their refuelling and are quickly over the area. But on the ground, the friendly and enemy combatants are now really at close quarters, with less than 100 metres separating them. The rules of engagement do not allow the aircraft to release their GPS guided bombs, because the safety distances are not large enough. Moreover, the very low altitude prevents the use of the aircrafts' cannons, because of the risk of ground-to-air missiles. The dive profile for deploying the cannon would place the aircraft in the acquisition cone of an anti-air missile, several of which have been fired in the preceding days and weeks.

Conscious of the critical situation, the flight commander asks the French E-2C Hawkeye for permission to engage.

On this particular point, the rules of engagement are very clear: in such a case, formal authorisation must come from the CAOC director himself, located several thousands kilometres away. Unfortunately, no radio contact can be established with the next level up. The mission

---

1. Captain (Navy) Zimmerman.
2. The E-2C Hawkeye is an airborne surveillance and command aircraft carried on aircraft carriers.
3. CAOC, Combined Air Operations Centre.

commander and the aircraft captain are therefore alone, faced with this decision.

After a quick consultation, they agree that the only option is to risk using the cannon: the section is being overwhelmed.

The French E-2C therefore authorises the transfer procedure of the F-15, permitting them to engage ground forces. Visual guidance is the responsibility of the section commander [...] The two F-15s exhaust their ammunition, making several passes and firing with impressive mastery of their weaponry. The radio operator rejoices into his microphone with indescribable enthusiasm and relief.

When the firing is over, the section manages to fall back; it is now in a better position. The Taliban withdraw leaving many of their number on the battlefield. In the meantime, helicopters have taken off from a base located about thirty nautical miles from the action. A recovery operation is launched to retrieve the bodies of those killed in the section. The tension again eases. The crew of the E-2C are overcome with emotion when the section commander thanks the F-15s over the radio and says to the E-2C, "Merci, la France, merci les français, merci la France, merci...". Those simple words still resonate in the memories of those involved.

The F-15s climb back towards a tanker, having consumed a great deal of fuel in 15 minutes of flight at very low altitude. The E-2C switches back to its control frequency.

This episode is one example in which the French E-2Cs, undertaking the function of tactical controllers of coalition assets, were confronted with decisions relating to the theory of the rules of engagement. The situation was made even more difficult by the topography and the lack of direct contact with the operations centre (CAOC). Luck was with them, however: no collateral damage or friendly fire marred their record during the hundreds of missions undertaken in the seven month deployment of the Charles de Gaulle.

Upon analysis, how could two senior officers, in positions of responsibility in their units, have gone beyond their orders and authorised a risky attack by the two F-15s?

Even though it was limited, the risk to the fighters was not zero. The loss of a fighter would have been a major event in terms of media coverage of what happened and could have had serious consequences. In other respects, what would have been the crew's responsibility, and consequently France's, in the event of friendly fire or collateral damage during this sort of action, using coalition assets, most of them American, placed under the tactical control of a French crew?

In this specific instance, the crew at the controls explained that the *ethics of obedience* was confronted by the *ethics of duty*. Conscience suddenly asserted itself as the only guide for action. One has to admit that the reality of combat and the complexity of military-legal situations make prior in-depth personal reflection indispensable. Not everything can be written or transcribed in words or language.

The officer giving this testimony concluded his account with the following comment.

> *On only one occasion did I see a general officer, a 'great man', acting as tactical commander in the area, make this speech before an engagement. "You are going to find yourselves alone, faced with situations which you will not find in the rules of engagement cards. You are perhaps going to have to act in accordance with your soul and conscience, put your life in danger to perhaps save others, and on occasion risk opprobrium... and that is what differentiates an aircraft pilot from a drone. You will have to accept responsibility for your choice, whatever it might be... and I will accept my share of responsibility for your act and your decision." These were not casually spoken words.*
>
> *In his own words, he was repeating Marshal de Saxe's famous maxim: "In war, the heart is the point of departure for everything."*

The courageous statement by this general, committing himself to support the future decisions of his pilots to open fire, reveals another facet of the problem of military ethics, that of the commander situated outside the centre of the action, but whose overall responsibility is exercised through the decisions of his subordinates. **To command is also to accept responsibility for the decisions of one's subordinates when they have carried out one's orders.**

To conclude – for the time being – this subject of the ethics of responsibility, let us hear from the officer, one of our predecessors, whom I asked how the consciences of young commanders should be guided in cases where they had no answer.

> *In the moments of solitude, when I was in a situation of doubt, where even the ethical principles that normally guided my choices were not in themselves up to the task of helping me to answer my questions, I established for myself the following standard of behaviour: if you are able later to recount the memory of this to your grandchildren without shame, you may consider that your decision will have been as just as possible.*

CONCLUSION

*Ethics precede, accompany and follow
the action. They are at the same time a
factor of balance and a condition of evolution. The fruit of past experience, they
are indispensable for the action to come.*

General de la Motte [1]

As a fully fledged citizen of today's society, the serviceman cannot decently exercise his responsibilities without prior thought and without regular self-questioning.

In this manner, soldiers of conviction and experience have extended the humanitarian philosophical movement and its legal applications, in order to determine principles of behaviour concerning the use of force. They have inspired a state of mind in combat built on teaching and setting an example: the ethics of behaviour in combat.

However, in conclusion to this compilation of testimonies, it is essential to recall that emphasising the importance of guides to ethical behaviour is not about calling into question, by implication, the primary purpose of the armed forces. Armed action is, and will always be, undertaken with the aim of winning. There are many cases where the involvement of military forces leads to crises of unimaginable violence. This possibility must always be kept in mind and any temptation to romanticism banished: **armed action must be resolute, effective, applied without wavering and conducted with the greatest possible realism.**

This obvious point restated, the central question of the level of force, and how to apply it in order to implement the mission, is crucial for pre-

---

1. General commanding the armoured and cavalry school of instruction in 1981.

sent and future conflicts, one of the main characteristics of which is that they impinge heavily on the civilian population. General Desportes elaborates on this topic.

In comparison with have learned previously, we can to all intents and purposes see a reversal in the process of constructing military effectiveness. Yesterday, the fundamental principle for western forces was to destroy the enemy force, in order to break political will; whereas the principle is now, through our own use of measured force, to influence the will of the opposing entity, so that it renounces force.

This observation rightly leads Sir Rupert Smith to consider that armed confrontations will be much more 'a clash of wills' than 'a trial of strength' [1].

This clash of wills implies perfectly judged application of the use of force in the field. The principle of destruction, as a political tool, has been progressively devalued to the point of being delegitimised. With the information revolution, every destructive act – and its inevitable collateral damage – is now immediately brought before the court of local, national, and international public opinion. Thus the legitimate intervention force, through its exemplary behaviour, can be presented as being endowed with a degree of truth based on law and international will.

Finally, there could be no question of bringing this reflection to a close without raising the subject of the adoption in France of the new General Statute of Military Personnel [*statut general des militaires*], which marks a major advance in legal responsibility when on operations. The new statute – article 17.2 [2] – dealing with the legal protection granted during interventions outside metropolitan France, specifies that:

The serviceman or woman who, respecting the rules of international law and within the framework of a military operation taking place outside French territory, exercises coercive measures or uses armed force, or gives the order so do, when that is necessary for the completion of his mission, is not penally responsible.

This derogation from national law should be seen as a real revolution and a mark of the confidence that national representatives and political authorities have in the armed forces. In practice, until this article was adopted, only legitimate self-defence could be used to legally justify the use of armed force on operations, except in time of war. Today, the content of rules of engagement may expressly authorise the use of deadly

---

1. *La guerre probable, Penser Autrement* [The probable War, Thinking Differently], Economica, Paris, 2007.
2. Article 17.2 of the Statut Général Militaire, codified at article L. 4123-12.II of the Defence Code.

force, as soon as the needs of the mission demand it, subject to the immutable condition of respecting international law.

Through this new statute, the actions of the operational commander and the person carrying out the order are therefore legally covered, as long as the orders given are consistent with the authorised rules of engagement and are faithfully executed in accordance with the above-mentioned principles of action. This revolution has been possible only because genuine transparency and a relationship of trust have been established between political leaders and the military, thanks to the rigour and the self-control that French troops have exercised in recent conflicts. Such trust is just recognition of the maturity of the services; it imposes obligations on those in whom it is placed.

Now more than ever, the citizen of the world affirms what Blaise Pascal proclaimed several centuries ago, namely that *force without justice renders truth abject*. Drawing lessons from their history, from their failures as well as their successes, the armed forces of certain long-established nations today have standards based on the principles of moral rectitude, the preservation of life and respect for law, of which all the soldiers serving under their national flag are the inheritors. To borrow an expression from the Danish philosopher Soren Kierkegaard [1], the soldiers of these armies, thus recognised as bearers of a particular truth, can legitimately be considered as *ethicists*. Coined in 1842, the term was applied to men who had reached the highest degree of freedom through the imposition of rules of obligation. Acting in accordance with his duty, the ethicist is not the embodiment of some sort of submission to the rules of ethics, but on the contrary testifies to his freedom, because his commitment is the outcome of his free will. Unlike the slave (in a moral sense), who is dependent on his needs, the free man considers himself to be independent. But to be free of passion and temptation, he must have strong, just and impartial principles. He draws his freedom of action from thought and an attachment to moral behaviour. This brings us back to the Socratic notion of 'know yourself': the better one knows oneself, the more one can create harmonious behaviour.

By thus providing reference points for behaviour in an increasingly complex environment, the combatant's ethical principles must not be understood as burdens, but, on the contrary, as guarantees of freedom of military action. In a tightly defined legal context, they allow the commander to base his decisions on principles of action that respect man and his dignity, while keeping in mind the inescapable prospect of the aim of the operation and the so-called 'normalisation' phase. As Marshals Callieni

---

1. Either... Or... Originally published in Danish in 1843.

and Lyautey have pointed out, one does not take control of a village in the same way when opening up a strategic route in an area of intense combat, as when the aim is to progressively build up the conditions for a return to peace in a country in crisis. The final success of the intervention is in large part conditioned by how local people feel when faced with the presence – and the behaviour – of foreign forces in their country. The nobility of the operation lies in the fact that *the members of the force in the field are fully conscious of their actions* and that they *freely accept responsibility for the consequences of these actions.*

On the one hand, there are convictions that are the wellspring of humanity; on the other hand, a mission may seem at odds with such convictions, and it is responsibility of the commander to make them compatible. That this is possible, has been shown by the examples provided in this work. Nonetheless it is not easy, as the errors still being committed attest.

Yet questions remain. In the field of ethics, nothing is ever certain, nothing is ever settled. In reality, no-one can command an operation of reasonable size with the certainty of controlling all the consequences of his choices. Because of this uncertainty, will the operation therefore be reprehensible? Our reply to this question has been that the morality of a decision cannot be judged solely on the basis of its purpose or its consequences: it must be judged on the basis of its intention and the values inspiring it. If sufficient grounds exist to justify the act and if its purpose was just, the commander cannot normally be held responsible for any unacceptable consequences resulting from it.

Likewise, without becoming dogmatic, ethics must absolutely remain a question in man's conscience. But questioning is not the same as hesitation. Hesitation can be as dangerous as dogmatism. Therein lies the difficulty. Ethics must be a state of permanent questioning, an internal challenging of oneself, but, at the same time, it must also be *crystal clear.*

The greatest possible preservation of humanity is the only value capable of uniting adversaries, and goes beyond the reasons why they went to war with each other. This assertion gains greater legitimacy in that it is based on the suffering experienced throughout human history: if war can be seen as legitimate, not only is there a just way of circumscribing it – through strict respect for international law – but it is essential to add a further level of morality in respect of violent confrontations. Only the serviceman can be the agent of this, and French servicemen, along with those of some other countries, are the pioneers in putting it into practice in the field. These men include great humanists, who know that successfully carrying out their mission depends not on destruction, but on building up a new political framework with local elites.

In most modern crises, it is necessary to draw on the progress made in the control of force, in order to show that there is more to be gained by being exemplary than by being violent. This behavioural strategy must remain immutable, even in the face of random terrorism. It is true that counter revolutionary warfare demands superhuman qualities of those who undertake it. But even if the adversary's methods are rooted in the tactics and strategy of terror, outside all morality, it is not acceptable to allow our concepts, our ideals and our values to be contaminated by the temptation of tactical effectiveness – which is in any event still debatable – to the exclusion of all human morality. That would be to lose tomorrow what we are trying to save today. War, whether it be classic, nuclear, or counter-revolutionary, will never escape the audit of the law – and, it must be added – of conscience and morality.

It is to be hoped that the present book has provided the consciences of current and future commanders, as well as to their subordinates, with some of these *convictions of humanity*. And that is has also helped show the citizens of France that those who have the power to use force act, through their thoughts and their deeds, in accordance with their concerns and are more than ever worthy of their trust.

Finally, it is because those in the military take responsibility in the first instance for the human and moral consequences of war, that they have a duty to accept the burden of defending what we have learned about behaviour in combat. May these testimonies and these few thoughts convince them of the need always to involve themselves more deeply, in order to become, through implementing a *strategy of example,* new agents in the evolution of the ethics of conducting war.

> *The nobility of the profession of soldier, notably of the LEADER, who is responsible for making decisions in complex situations of extreme peril, in which there is no right solution, is shaped by the problem of the legitimate use of force, subject to conflicting principles of effectiveness on the one hand, and control on the other.*
>
> *There is no right solution, but a decision must be made. Very often, the answer is not to be found in the orders received, or in the rules of engagement, or in the law of armed conflict, but, for each person, in his innermost being, in the fullness of his freedom as a man, at the risk of losing his way* [1].

Engaged in a dialogue of blood, suffering and death, the soldier runs the risk of no longer being a man, of no longer being human. He needs to be ceaselessly on guard against this ever-present temptation. The army

---

1. General Bachelet, taken from a speech given to the officer training schools at Cöetquidan in 2004.

could not serve the nation without creating for itself an idea of the nation, which step by step, involves a doctrine of history, of the world, and of man.

Ethics is not a gift that we receive passively. We construct it, like a bridge over troubled waters, like a work of art or like a child developing from gestation to maturity. This also means that ethics is a living thing, that it belongs to a culture of life. Ethics is a question to which the answer is a particular kind of internal peace.

EPILOGUE

During the various lectures I gave after the publication of the first edition of *L'éthique du soldat français*, I was often asked what had provoked my interest in the ethics of combat, and made me write this book. The answer can be found in an event during my time as a unit commander. On that particular evening, I had gathered together my section commanders, both officers and NCOs, in an isolated location away from the regiment, for an annual seminar I used to organise. A few weeks earlier, the army had learned of the 'Mahé affair', in which an Ivorian bandit by the name of Mahé had been wounded then captured by French military personnel and subsequently executed by suffocation during his transport to hospital. It was known that this 'highwayman' was terrorising the local population. An acknowledged murderer and rapist, he had been captured some weeks previously, handed over to the local police, then freed with no action taken.

The military personnel who had confessed to the criminal act claimed to have received the explicit order from their superior that *this time* the wounded man should not arrive at hospital alive. The army Chief of Staff opened the case to legal scrutiny, and the affair had been a major topic of conversation in recent weeks.

I had therefore decided to have my section commanders reflect that evening on this real-world case. Without beating about the bush, I asked them, "If you had been in the position of that section commander, in that vehicle, and you had received the order to execute the prisoner from your superior, what would you have done?"

Long moments passed without anyone responding. So I caught the eye of a young lieutenant who had been with the regiment for a year and I asked him directly. He replied with considerable spirit, "I think I would have done the same, that guy got no more than he deserved."

I refrained from reacting and, looking at them, continued to appeal to the others present. Then a warrant officer turned to the lieutenant and said,

"You don't have the right to say that, sir, it is not up to us to settle the account of these bastards. That is not our job. As far as I am concerned, I would not have carried out that order."

I then waited for any further reactions. But no-one spoke. I had a real feeling that my question had thrown them. What's more, it seemed to have thrown them because they had never asked it of themselves.

I therefore asked another lieutenant, who seemed to be staring into infinity. He replied, "Colonel, I confess I don't know what I would have done. I would have been really stuck."

The rest of the evening allowed me to perform my role of educator of consciences and to pass on to my subordinates the messages I had prepared. For all that, the exchange left me perplexed, because I had not expected that there might be such a lack of ethical thinking among my young commanders. So I decided to take advantage of every possible opportunity to gather together testimonies and examples, on the basis of which I set myself the target of producing for my regiment a compendium of real-world cases. One thing led to another and, from a starting point of experiences retold, the compendium became more substantial and ended up becoming this book.

It is my hope that, in reading these testimonies, commanders likely to be called on to command in Kabul, Naqura, Pristina, N'djamena or Bouaké will learn the importance of having morally armed themselves in advance, so as to react with discernment and to correctly resolve unexpected crises, for which it is essential to be perfectly trained in the ethics of the soldier's profession.

APPENDICES

FRENCH ARMY HONOUR CODES

There are three honour codes in the French army: the Soldier's Code, which applies to all enlisted men and women, and the Legionnaire's and Paris Fire-fighter's Codes, which refer to other quite specific military populations. (Paris Fire-fighters are part of the military, but their Code is not included here).

THE SOLDIER'S CODE

Distributed and explained to all soldiers during their initial training, the Soldier's Code is composed of eleven precepts. It takes as its source "The exercise of the profession of arms: fundamentals and principles", a founding text of the all-professional army. The Soldier's Code is therefore a summary enabling the implementation of the four following principles, down to the very lowest rank:

– to cultivate and practise rules of conduct and the resolute implementation of controlled force, founded on firm and strong consciences and professional excellence;

– to bring to life military communities united in discipline and the brotherhood of arms;

– to serve France and the universal values on which it is founded;

– to cultivate strong links with the national community.

Article 1 – The soldier, at all times and in all places, is entirely devoted to the service of France.

Article 2 – He fulfils his mission with the will to win and to overcome, if necessary at the risk of his life.

Article 3 – Keeping his strength in check, he respects the adversary and takes care to spare civilians.

Article 4 – He obeys orders which are in accordance with the law, the customs of war and international conventions.

Article 5 – He demonstrates initiative and is adaptable in all circumstances.

Article 6 – As a professional soldier, he maintains his intellectual and physical capabilities and develops his competence and moral strength.

Article 7 – As a member of a community characterized by solidarity and brotherhood, he acts with honour, frankness and loyalty.

Article 8 – He is attentive to others, has the determination to overcome difficulties, and works for the cohesion and dynamism of his unit.

Article 9 – He is open to the world and society and respects diversity.

Article 10 – He expresses himself with restraint so as not to undermine the philosophical, political and religious neutrality of the armed forces.

Article 11 – He is proud of his commitment, and is at all times and in all places an ambassador of his regiment, the Army and France.

THE LEGIONNAIRE'S CODE

In response to the observation that young legionnaires were sometimes lacking in moral references, the Legionnaire's Code of Honour was written in the early 1980s, before the Soldier's Code. A veritable guide to the legionnaire's behaviour, it was partially modified (Article 6) after the Soldier's Code appeared, to ensure that the two documents were mutually consistent. Every legionnaire is given a copy of the Legionnaire's Code in his native language when he enlists.

Article 1 – Legionnaire: you are a volunteer serving France faithfully and with honour.

Article 2 – Every Legionnaire is your brother-at-arms, irrespective of his nationality, race or creed. You will demonstrate this by unwavering and straightforward solidarity which must always bind together members of the same family.

Article 3 – Respectful of the Legion's traditions and honouring your superiors, discipline and comradeship are your strength, courage and loyalty your virtues.

Article 4 – Proud of your status as a legionnaire, you will display this pride, by your always impeccable turn-out, your always worthy though modest behaviour and your always tidy living quarters.

Article 5 – You are an elite soldier: you will train vigorously, you will maintain your weapons as if they were your most precious possessions, you will keep your body fit and in the peak of condition.

Article 6 – Once you are given a mission, it becomes sacred to you, and you will accomplish it to the end and at all costs.

Article 7 – In combat, you will act without relishing your tasks and without hatred; you will respect a vanquished enemy; and you will never abandon either your wounded or your dead, nor will you under any circumstances surrender your arms.

APPENDIX 2

THE UNCOUPLING OF MORAL SENSIBILITY AT ABU GHRAIB

By Patrick Clervoy [1]

This is a partial reproduction of the article which appeared in issue 7 of the journal *Inflexions:* 'Le moral et la dynamique de l'action, Partie II' [Morality and the dynamic of action, Part II], La Documentation française, 2007.

WHAT HAPPENED AT ABU GHRAIB?

Geopolitical and strategic context

In September 2003 the American military completed the conquest phase in Iraq. Their technological superiority brought them rapid success. They had take advantage of their victory as soon as possible. At that time, they believed that weapons of mass destruction were secretly stockpiled in Iraq. Their mission was to find them as quickly as possible and to dismantle the presumed support networks for international terrorism.

It was a very auspicious period for gathering intelligence. The American army was arresting large numbers of civilians every day, not only armed militia but anyone who refused to collaborate with them. They were referred to as 'insurgents' and placed in detention in Iraqi prisons.

The prison and its population

The Abu Ghraib complex is a vast prison site situated on the fringes of Baghdad. The prison already had a sinister reputation. Saddam Hussein used to have his political opponents locked up, tortured and sometimes made to disappear there.

At the end of 2003, the complex housed two types of detainee.

– Common law prisoners, for the most part incarcerated for theft, rape or murder. These people were serving sentences handed down by the Baathist regime's normal courts, and were already in prison before the Ame-

―――――――
1. Senior Professor of Philosophy and Medical Psychology and Head of the Department of Psychiatry at the Armed Forces Teaching Hospital at Toulon.

ricans arrived. They had adapted to the violence of their environment. They could make a weapon from a scrap of iron, a stone or a stick. They were particularly dangerous.

– The insurgents were male adults of all ages and all social origins, in certain cases arbitrarily snatched from their homes and their families simply on suspicion that they might possess intelligence useful in the war against terror. The inquiries that followed the media scandal found that only 10% of these prisoners were legitimately detained.

The military personnel responsible for the camp

A battalion of military police was responsible for guarding the detention sites. At their head was a female general officer, the first woman general to hold an operational command. These military personnel were reservists. Most of them had no experience of managing a prison, nor were they familiar with the Geneva Conventions. In any event, in accordance with the State Department's wish expressed to Defense, the category 'insurgents' allowed those detained to be denied the protection of international law. From the moment the rules stipulating the status and rights of these detainees became vague, the standing instructions given to the military personnel taking over responsibility for them became equally vague. They were supposed to be securing the buildings and people against dangers from the outside – militia attacks – and from inside – revolts and escape attempts.

The military police were not trained to gather intelligence and it was not their responsibility to do so. That task was handled by other specialised military personnel and CIA civilians, who visited the prison specifically to interrogate the detainees. The military police assisted them only insofar as they brought the prisoners to the interrogation rooms and later took them back to their cells. However, the military police received instructions from the intelligence personnel to 'soften up' the detainees, in other words to prepare them for interrogation sessions by reducing their will to resist. A note from the Department of Defense specified what this preparation might be: a special diet, sleep deprivation, permanent exposure to light, and exposure to loud noise. In this way a typology was defined, but not in any sense a yardstick. It was up to each person to judge what he or she felt to be appropriate. The mistake was to imagine that they would refer to their ethical judgement.

Constraints of day-to-day life in the prison

The military police at the prison were soon in difficulty. Every day, the number of detainees increased, obliging them to sleep in makeshift encampments inside the complex. They could remain there for weeks on end with no idea why there were being held. There was absolutely no legal system in place. The military personnel were ill-equipped for taking them in; there was a lack of hygiene, bad food, and vermin, especially rats. The medical aid system was derisory. All consultations and treatment took place at a set time, through a metal grille, via an interpreter and protected by a guard, without exception.

A large number of detainees died for want of appropriate care. But they did not die solely from illness. Almost every evening, the camp came under mortar fire, causing deaths and injuries amongst the detainees and the American military personnel. To these external attacks was added the internal threat of violence by the detainees: stone throwing, rioting, insubordination, shouting, spitting, insults and so forth. There was no respite or refuge from all this. The military personnel were permanently stressed.

'Pressure towards cruelty'

The intelligence services were in a hurry to get results: the politicians were asking that proof of the existence of weapons of mass destruction be provided as soon as possible. Inspired by the camp at Guantanamo, they decided to apply the same interrogation techniques used on the detainees from the Afghan battlefield. The intelligence personnel ordered the military police to 'Gitmo-ize [1]' Abu Ghraib, urging them to adopt more effective methods for wearing down the insurgents' will to resist, especially those that injured their pride – nudity, filth, sexual humiliation – or produced prolonged stress – solitary confinement in the dark with heads hooded, being left for hours suspended by handcuffs, the deployment of attack dogs, threats of rape, and so on.

The first floor of the interrogation site became a veritable hell-hole. For forty nights, from 4 pm to 4 am, the detainees were handed over to the warped imagination of Sergeant Graner. When the military intelligence personnel had finished for the day and left the detainees in the hands of their gaolers, the sergeant's cruelty spiralled out of control and dragged those around him along with him. He staged scenes of piled-up naked men, being crushed, in positions imitating anything from sodomy to fellatio. He took dozens of photographs. He got other military personnel to pose, including Private England, his mistress. She had herself photographed, cigarette between her lips, holding a naked man on a leash.

The small group of military personnel clung to Graner, who in just a few days had become their de facto leader. The acts committed testified to their retrogression. The humiliations involved sex, urination and defecation. Sergeant Graner would photograph the blood-soaked detainees, covered in their excrement. He also physically assaulted them on a regular basis, with punches, kicks and blows from batons.

---

1. Gitmo is the nickname of Guantanamo, from the acronym GTMO.

All this had reached such a state that none of the protagonists was able to put an end to the escalation of violence and humiliation. Certainly not the detainees who, the more they begged for their torturers to kill them, the more they gave them the satisfaction of thinking they were doing their job well. Nor indeed the military personnel, caught up as they were in mutually imitative behaviour patterns and taking pleasure from watching each other invent or repeat their sadistic acts. They were blind to their own monstrosity.

The game is up

It was finally through the intervention of an outsider that this vicious behaviour was brought to an end. A soldier newly posted to Abu Ghraib had just joined the group of military police personnel. He was horrified, but did not dare react immediately, for fear of having his violent colleagues turn against him. He secretly made a copy of Graner's photo CDs, put them in a plain envelope and one night slipped them under the door of the officer responsible for criminal investigations.

An internal inquiry was quickly launched. Some weeks later, the media published the photographs and the scandal erupted. The army and the American people were equally ashamed, and both reacted with a display of speed and efficiency in the inquiry and the penalties imposed. Within a year, everything was wrapped up. Over twenty military personnel were given sentences, the severity of which reflected their crimes and responsibility. Graner was condemned to ten years imprisonment, the most severe sentence. The highest ranking officer, the woman general commanding the military police battalion, was demoted to the rank of colonel and discharged.

But over and beyond the trial determining the guilty and handing down punishments, people wanted to understand. How was this possible? How were these young Americans, brought up in accordance with the educational standards of their nation, built around the values of respect for freedom and the dignity of others, able to behave in this way?

[…]

The uncoupling of moral sensibility

With hindsight, anyone can say that the excesses of Abu Ghraib were foreseeable. But no-one was able to say so beforehand. This fact is worrying: we cannot be sure that this sort of thing will never happen again, in a different way, somewhere else. The right question is: will we be able to spot it quickly enough?

[…]

Enabling conditions

There are many environmental factors favouring the uncoupling of moral sensibility. There is no finite inventory in this area. Every human drama brings new factors to light. Those following derive from an analysis of the situation at Abu Ghraib.

Loss of identity markers

In prison, there are no longer any named and identified individuals. Their names and roles have been erased. For the guards, the detainees are nameless and simply designated by numbers. They must respond when their number is called and identify themselves in this way. Their role within their family and their social group has been abolished. They are detainees, prisoners, doomed to waiting, inaction and interrogation. For some of the prisoners, this loss of identity was compounded by the use of comic and degrading nicknames.

For the detainees, the guards did not have names either. Their name tags were masked with black tape, in order to be unidentifiable and so avoid the risk of reprisals. Their social role had also been temporarily erased. Whatever their profession or job may have previously been in civilian life, during their year as reservists their identity vanished behind the standardised function of a military policeman or woman, and identical uniforms.

When people believe they will not be identified, their tendency to transgress increases. Who among those military police could have thought that one day pictures of what they were and what they were doing there would be seen by those close to them? If they could have imagined at some point or another that someone from outside could see them, they would have behaved differently. It is rather like the principle of the carnival, when wearing a mask allows any liberty to be taken. A person who for a while does not have to answer to his identity, loses contact with his moral markers. There is a close relationship between a person's identity and his moral behaviour. Everyone behaves as he recognises himself in relation to others: if his name is masked, his urges are unleashed.

Dehumanisation of the victim

The Abu Ghraib prisoner lost more than his identity. He also lost his humanity. He was demeaned, he was naked like an animal doomed to obedience or punishment. His raison d'être was to produce intelligence as others produce milk or wool. His daily routine was degraded. He lived in deplorable conditions of hygiene.

There is a common psychological impulse called 'identification with the victim'. Generally speaking, this means that someone who learns of another person's misfortune tries to imagine himself in the same situation. At Abu Ghraib, the military police probably had an initial impulse to identify with the victim, but that then became intolerable because it generated strong unconscious feelings of guilt, threat and anguish. Faced with this psychological stress, the only solution was no longer to consider the detainees as people, but as things. Stripped of their humanity, the prisoners were reduced to the level of objects. They could be treated and counted as such, since what they were living through was not felt by their guards. They could be treated in a degrading manner without it impacting on moral sensibilities.

It should be added that the logistical constraints obliged the military police to mistreat their prisoners in terms of health and safety, specifically to make them live in overcrowded conditions with no hygiene, exposed to all weathers, without protection from external dangers, consuming an unhealthy diet, and so forth. From that point onwards, confronted every day by their own ethical questions and faced with these basic types of mistreatment and the spectacle of detainees dying for lack of treatment, the military police had to eradicate the moral questions raised by this situation.

[...]

Falsification of reporting

There were repeated shams. One example widely reproduced and commented on in the media was that of the death of an Iraqi detainee. American military intelligence personnel beat the detainee to death, then asked a medical auxiliary to attach the corpse to a drip, to make it seem that his death occurred as a result of a medical condition, despite attempts at resuscitation.

The falsification of reporting in relation to the truth is a factor which greatly favours the uncoupling of moral sensibility. False evidence for the existence of weapons of mass destruction, the false Jessica Lynch case, false medical care, false certificates, false briefings… These falsifications inevitably lead to a loss of normality, an erasing of the moral bearings which give human behaviour an ethical framework.

Even words were distorted. There was systematic use of euphemisms. For example, saying that a detainee had been 'prepared' meant that he had been subjected to various acts of cruelty before the interrogation session. In 2002, in a memo prepared for the US President by US Legal Counsel, the conceptual limit of torture was defined as "Physical pain amounting to torture must be equivalent in intensity to the pain accompanying serious physical injury, such as organ failure, impairment of bodily function, or even death [1]." The word 'torture' was never used during the trial of the Abu Ghraib military police, only the word 'abuse'. In regard to the breakdown of ethical behaviour, the use of euphemisms may be the first sign of the uncoupling of moral sensibility.

Anomie and impunity

According to Chambers Twentieth Century Dictionary, anomie is, "in a society or in an individual, a condition of hopelessness caused by breakdown of rules of conduct, a loss of belief, and sense of purpose". At the time when the events took place, none of the military police could have imagined having one day they would have to give an account of their behaviour. They were in another world, outside standards, outside frameworks, without law. Among the factors contributing to this state of anomie, we can note their lack of knowledge of the Geneva Conventions, the lack of any preparation for the tasks which they were given to complete in the prison, and the absence of regular supervision and local control.

Behind closed doors and under pressure

Being behind closed doors and under stress also played a part in this affair. The threat was external as well as internal. In a sense the military police were also locked up in the Abu Ghraib prison system, without having any opportunity for mental escape.

In all probability, had they been able to get out, meet other people, have mundane conversations with those on the outside about themselves and their life, as one normally does, they would have realised the horror of the situation into which they had slid.

Group anarchy

The group of military police at Abu Ghraib was no longer governed by the rules of conventional military operations: order, discipline, frugality and devotion. In the absence of supervision by a commander, the functioning of the group had regressed to the level of a pack. They were under the influence of a gang leader. Two of the women present at the camp were his mistresses – a good indicator of the degradation of the organisation of the group, fallen under the sole influence of a dominant male personality. It is also known that in this type of degraded social organisation, the dominant male is compelled to regularly demonstrate his strength, in order to maintain his power and hold over the other members of the community.

---

1. Gonzales Alberto R., *Standards of Conduct for Interrogation* under 18 U.S.C. §§ 2340-2340A. U.S. Department of Justice Office of Legal Counsel Memorandum, 1 August 2002.

Taken together, these factors produced, at that time and in that place, a very particular social configuration that one might term 'pressure towards cruelty'. This process can transform an ordinary person into an instrument of evil which nothing can control.

[…]

GENERAL DE MAUD'HUI'S TESTAMENT

General de Maud'hui (1857-1921) was one of the heroes of the French light infantry, heavily involved in the First World War. In the twilight of his life he bequeathed his 'testament on the subject of command' to the officers and NCOs of his regiment. The text, which retained much its pertinence, is taken from a former tactical course on the 'Moral Component' published in 1922. It describes the principles of command, drawn from Maud'hui's experience. They are present here because they have lost none of their relevance and because such rules of behaviour in the exercise of command are intimately linked to those concerning deontology and ethics.

The superior must respect the personality of his subordinates. Obviously, they never come up to his absolute ideal. But we must make use of our subordinates as they are, using their qualities and seeking to correct their faults, which are sometimes no more than exaggerated qualities.

Let us try hard to obey and command with good grace. The man who is in a bad mood and the man who is angry are ill, and therefore beings of a temporarily inferior quality.

Let us always be polite with our subordinates: when one is polite one elevates those whom one addresses, when one is rude one demeans oneself.

Towards a superior, impoliteness is an offence against discipline. Towards a subordinate, it is an act of cowardice.

Only politeness renders a reprimand bearable.

Let us speak quietly, which does nor prevent speaking with firmness, when giving orders: by making comments in a raised voice, one annoys subordinates and drives them into shouting themselves, and one makes duty frenetic.

Let us not reprimand a ranking officer or NCO in front of his men. By diminishing him in their eyes, we diminish the principle of authority.

Let us never doubt without reason the word of one of our subordinates – that would be a gratuitous insult. If we find that he has lied to us, we shall be duty bound to punish him even more severely, having demonstrated greater trust in him.

Let us not try to inspire terror in our subordinates, but trust, so that they do not fear the presence of the commander but welcome it.

Let us not seek popularity amongst our subordinates. If we love our men, they will love us of their own volition. Let us try to earn their esteem.

Let us always back them up when they have carried out, or believed they were carrying out, our orders.

Do not make pointless demands. The Frenchman does not like being perpetually bothered with trivia. But what we do demand, let us demand it absolutely and continuously. Let the why of our demands be felt, let us make everyone understand that discipline is necessary for the Service and the good of all, that it is intelligence and devotion at the same time as obedience, that it is the whole man working for the greatness of his homeland.

While being benevolent, let us never be weak. Above all, no sentimentality; the Army must be school of energy. Let us remember that discipline must be respected, everywhere and by everyone whatever it costs.

CONTENTS

The "Stratégies & Doctrines" Series

ARDANT DU PICQ Charles, *Études sur le combat*.

ARMÉE DE TERRE, *Les forces terrestres*.

ARMÉE DE TERRE, *Tactique générale*.

AUDROING Jean-François, *La décision stratégique*.

BECKER Cyrille, *Relire* Principes de la guerre de montagnes *du lieutenant général Pierre-Joseph de Bourcet*.

CAILLETEAU François, *Guerres inutiles ? – Contre-insurrection. Une analyse historique et critique*.

CARRIAS Eugène, *La pensée militaire allemande*.

COURRÈGES Hervé (de), GERMAIN Emmanuel et LE NEN Nicolas, *Principes de contre-insurrection*.

COURRÈGES Hervé (de), GIVRE Pierre-Joseph et LE NEN Nicolas, *Guerre en montagne*, 2ᵉ éd.

DESPORTES Vincent, *La guerre probable – Penser autrement*, 2ᵉ éd.

DESPORTES Vincent, *Comprendre la guerre*, 2ᵉ éd.

DESPORTES Vincent, *Décider dans l'incertitude*, 2ᵉ éd.

DESPORTES Vincent, *Le piège américain – Pourquoi les États-Unis peuvent perdre les guerres d'aujourd'hui*.

DESPORTES Vincent et PHÉLIZON Jean-François, *Introduction à la stratégie*.

DURIEUX Benoît, *Relire* De la guerre *de Clausewitz*.

FLICHY Thomas, *Stratégies chinoises – Le regard jésuite (1582-1773)*.

FOCH Ferdinand (maréchal), *Les Principes de la guerre*.

FORGET Michel, *Puissance aérienne et stratégies*, 2ᵉ éd.

FRANCART Loup, *La guerre du sens – Pourquoi et comment agir dans les champs psychologiques*.

FRANCART Loup, *Livre gris sur la sécurité et la défense*.

FRANCART Loup et PIROTH Christian, *Émeutes, terrorisme, guérilla... – Violence et contre-violence en zone urbaine*.

FRANÇOIS Philippe, *Tactiques de l'Armée rouge en Afghanistan*.

FRÉMEAUX Jacques, *Intervention et humanisme – Le style des armées françaises en Afrique au XIXᵉ siècle*.

GALULA David, *Contre-insurrection – Théorie et pratique*.

GILLET Maxime, *Principes de pacification du Maréchal Lyautey*.

GOYA Michel, *Irak – Les armées du chaos*, 2ᵉ éd.

GOYA Michel, *Res Militaris – L'emploi des forces armées au XXIᵉ siècle*, 2ᵉ éd.

GRAY Colin S., *La guerre au XXIᵉ siècle – Encore du feu et du sang*.

GUIBERT Jacques (de), *Essai général de tactique*, 1772.

GUIBERT Jacques (de), *De la force publique.*

HAÉRI Paul, *De la guerre à la paix – Pacification et stabilisation post-conflit.*

HENROTIN Joseph, *La technologie militaire en question – Le cas américain.*

KARPOV Anatoly et PHÉLIZON Jean-François (propos recueillis par Bachar Kouatly), *Psychologie de la bataille.*

KERDELLANT Christine, *Relire* Le Prince *de Machiavel.*

LA MAISONNEUVE Éric (de), *Stratégie, crise et chaos.*

LE ROY Frédéric, *Stratégie militaire et management stratégique des entreprises.*

MAISONNEUVE Charles, *Les combats de la cavalerie blindée.*

MALIS Christian (sous la direction de), *Guerre et manœuvre – Héritages et renouveau.*

MARILLER Roseline, *Quelle stratégie pour l'Europe de la défense ?*

MARTEL André, *Relire Foch au XXIᵉ siècle.*

MONTROUSSIER Laurence, *Éthique et commandement.*

MOUNIER-KUHN Alain, *Chirurgie de guerre – Le cas du Moyen Âge en Occident.*

Général PALAT, *La philosophie de la guerre, d'après Clausewitz.*

PHÉLIZON Jean-François, *L'action stratégique.*

PHÉLIZON Jean-François, *Relire l'*Art de la guerre *de Sun Tzu*, nouvelle édition entièrement revue et corrigée.

PHÉLIZON Jean-François, *Trente-six stratagèmes.*

POAST Paul, *Economie de la guerre.*

RAFFRAY Mériadec, *Afghanistan – Les victoires oubliées de l'Armée rouge.*

RAMEL Frédéric et HOLEINDRE Jean-Vincent (sous la direction de), *La fin des guerres majeures ?*

ROYAL Benoît, *L'éthique du soldat français – La conviction d'humanité,* 2ᵉ éd.

SCIALOM Michel, *La France – Nation maritime ?*

SMITH Rupert, *L'utilité de la force – L'art de la guerre aujourd'hui.*

TISSERON Antonin, *Guerres urbaines – Nouveaux métiers, nouveaux soldats.*

TRINQUIER Roger, *La guerre moderne.*

VENDRYÈS Pierre, *De la probabilité en histoire.*

VILBOUX Nicole, *Prévention ou préemption ? – Un débat d'aujourd'hui.*

YAMANAKA Keiko, *Relire le* Traité des cinq anneaux *de Miyamoto Musashi.*

YAMANAKA Keiko, *Relire* Bushidô – L'Âme du Japon *d'Inazô Nitobe.*

YAKOVLEFF Michel, *Tactique théorique,* 2ᵉ éd.

YCHÉ André, *Quelle défense pour la France ?*

Achevé d'imprimer en France en mai 2012
sur les presses de Normandie Roto Impression s.a.s.
61250 Lonrai
N° d'imprimeur : 121881
dépôt légal : juin 2012